Afterall
Spring/Summer 2020
A Journal of Art, Context and Enquiry

Foreword
– Charles Stankievech

It has been almost five years since the first Afterall editorial meeting was conducted in
Toronto, Canada, which in turn instigated a roundtable and subsequent symposium on
the question of the 'Global Indigenous?'. Since that time, the art world's discourse has been
supercharged with two concerns: a cyclical resurgence of identity politics and an acute
assessment of the environmental crisis. To list the global events and movements that have
pierced any sense of normalcy in the last five years would feel both banal, given the ubiquity
of such lists, and dislocating, given the speed of these developments. We exist in a state of
permanent urgency that risks giving way to burnout. At the time of writing (early March
2020), a novel virus is disrupting – on a truly global and unprecedented scale – political
orders, economic growth and public life. In the emerging emergency, perhaps there arises
a space for an unlikely solidarity where we pause and assess the most basic issues – not as
abstract issues, but existentially touching ones – as biennials are postponed, exhibitions
emptied, travel plans suspended and lectures cancelled. These disruptions are merely the
beginning for a reality that will affect everyone, much like the ecological crisis but with a
speed that propels a different politics. A contemporary world predicated on hyper-exchange
is facing a quick reality check. The precarity of our global logistical chains asks us to consider
what in our exchanges is really necessary, what is 'healthy'? What freedoms are we willing
to surrender for the greater good? All of this, instigated by a microscopic cross-over from
non-human to human via the act of eating, has subsequently exploded into speculative
behaviour of fear. How will we weather the test to our values in such states of exemption,
and will we realise how deeply inconsistent and superficial our beliefs are on such issues,
say, as migration – in all its forms?

While the nebulous theme for this issue revolves around exchange, say in the
intersubjective performances of Sonia Boyce and siren eun young jung, the most continuous
thread winding through it follows the clash between different communities' use of territory –
clashes over the sanctity of forests, the flow of rivers or the surrounding sea. The issue opens
with a conversation between Amar Kanwar and *Afterall* editor Ute Meta Bauer with Anca
Rujoiu, reflecting on Kanwar's decade-long project *The Sovereign Forest* (2012–ongoing), a
collaborative project in India with Sudhir Pattnaik/Samadrusti and Sherna Dastur that has
sustained a creative look at the intersection of 'crime, politics, human rights and ecology'.
Similar concerns are continued in Macarena Gómez-Barris's text on the installation *Forest
Law* (2014) by Ursula Biemann and Paulo Tavares, which contextualises the work alongside
other South American works confronting 'frontier capitalism', while referencing Michel
Serres's seminal *The Natural Contract* (1990), a text that proposes 'the emergence of nature
as a social, legal and ethical agent, challenging and complementing Rousseau's idea of the
social contract'. Flowing through these forests, great tributaries connect the most remote
communities to the rest of the world. The question of who owns and has the right to land is
already thorny enough, but the flow of water presents even more complicated conflicts. In
writing about Carolina Caycedo's ongoing project *Be Dammed*, Lisa Blackmore points out
the fact that two thirds of the earth's rivers are hydro-engineered, and that our constructed
dams are such megaprojects they have tilted the rotation of the planet. Blackmore continues
by drawing on the philosophy of food sovereigntist Vandana Shiva, who has argued for
'"ecological democracy", where all life, not just human life, has its rightful share in the
planet's water'. Echoing *Forest Law*'s argument for a forest to have inherent rights based
on cosmological foundations, New Zealand has relatively recently (after 140 years of
litigation) given a river the legal status of personhood, arguing the waterway is ancestral
kin to a local Māori tribe. Providing a detailed historical account, Mercedes Vicente writes
about Darcy Lange's *Māori Land Project* filmed in the 1970s, tracking it as an early case
study of an artist's well-intentioned engagement with indigenous resistance – albeit with
methodological failures and limitations, as the project remained beholden to a colonial
artworld infrastructure. The story is nothing new; art and activism since the 1960s have

often found themselves to be bedfellows for better or for worse, depending on one's priorities. Danielle Child's essay on 'artistic economies' considers three contemporary art projects, activist in intention, that attempt to engage a public outside of the artworld infrastructure while commandeering the resources of the art world. In doing so, she insightfully cautions us that since the 1990s the persona of the artist has been co-opted by neoliberal management as a paragon of the 'unalienated' precarious labourer. She points out the importance of understanding the intentions and processes behind this co-optation, as much as the career opportunities it has brought for artists. Continuing our more recent practice of commissioning an artist to create an intervention for the journal, this issue includes a recipe by the collective Cooking Sections. Growing out of their project *The Empire Remains Shop* (2016-ongoing), which highlights the colonial legacy of our eating habits, their more recent project *Climavore* (2015-ongoing), proposes a dietary practice of eating that actually helps climate problems - an important echo impossible to separate from colonial violence. In reflecting on their pop-up restaurant among the tidal pools of the Isle of Skye, May Rosenthal Sloan points out: 'It is no coincidence that the people suffering most today from the effects of climate change are the same people who suffered most from colonial projects - individuals with little financial means, people of colour and indigenous communities are disproportionately affected'. The two concerns mentioned at the beginning of this text, colonialism and environmentalism, are more and more being acknowledged as inseparable.

In closing, I acknowledge that the issues addressed individually in these pages remain just as present in the place from which I draft this foreword, the next place where the editorial team returns once again to craft a new issue. The rather young, modern nation state of Canada -forged out of the extraction of natural resources and the construction of epic infrastructure - is an apt site for the linked themes of the issue: extractivism and modes of exchange. A pause has been placed on the construction of oil and gas pipelines due to indigenous protests manifesting as blockades, their actions reducing construction, petrochemical flow, commodity exchange and investment across the country. Politicians and spokesperson on both sides are carefully trying to find a solution among the heated agendas from all angles - even beyond their own constituents. A solution is far from easy to see when attempting to account for a host of factors: traditional indigenous claims and their heterogenous positions within their communities, tyranny of the majority, constitutional rights, rule of law, economic survival, shareholder interests, international ecological agencies, and of course the most basic, the community vis-à-vis the individual. Hopefully, the artworks and texts in this volume contribute to a greater understanding of, and inspiration to engage with, these issues faced both at home and globally, for if anything has been illustrated in the last few months of a pandemic outbreak, it is that such concerns cannot be considered only at a distance, nor can they in isolation.

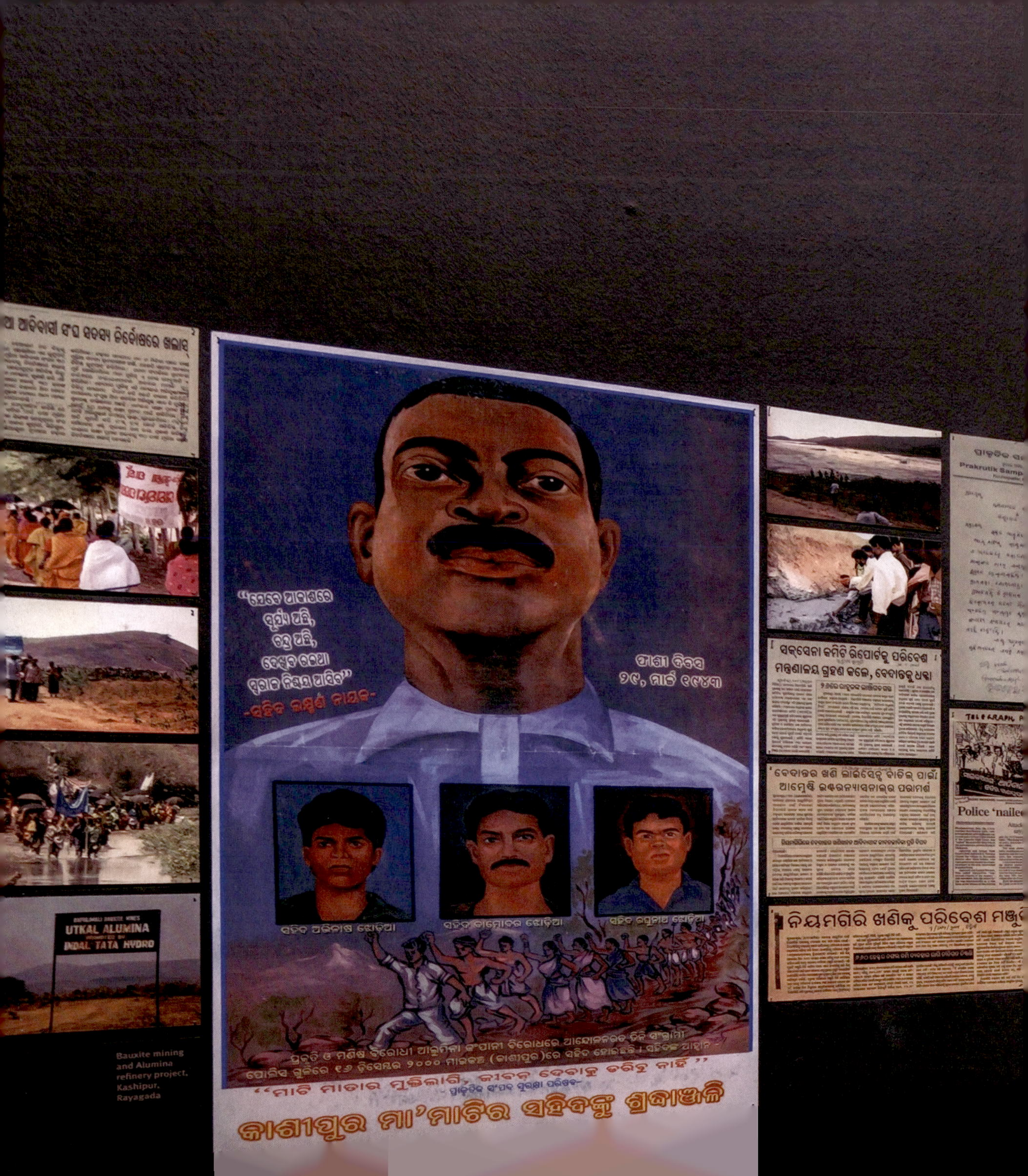

Bauxite mining and Alumina refinery project, Kashipur, Rayagada

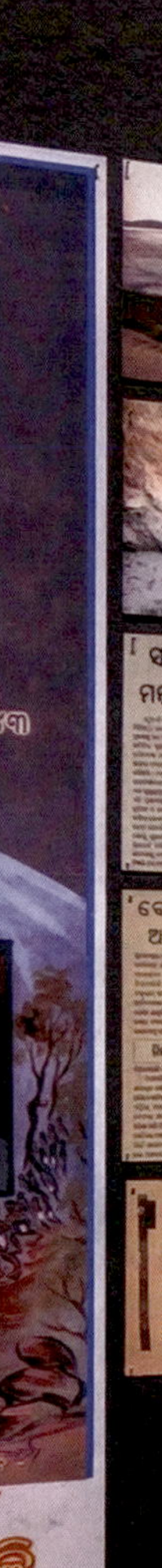

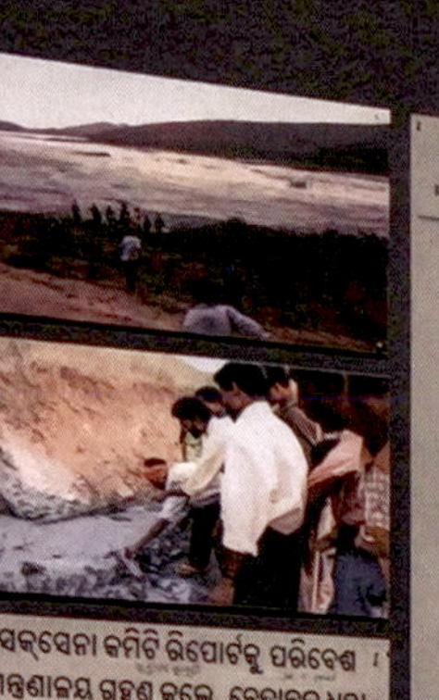

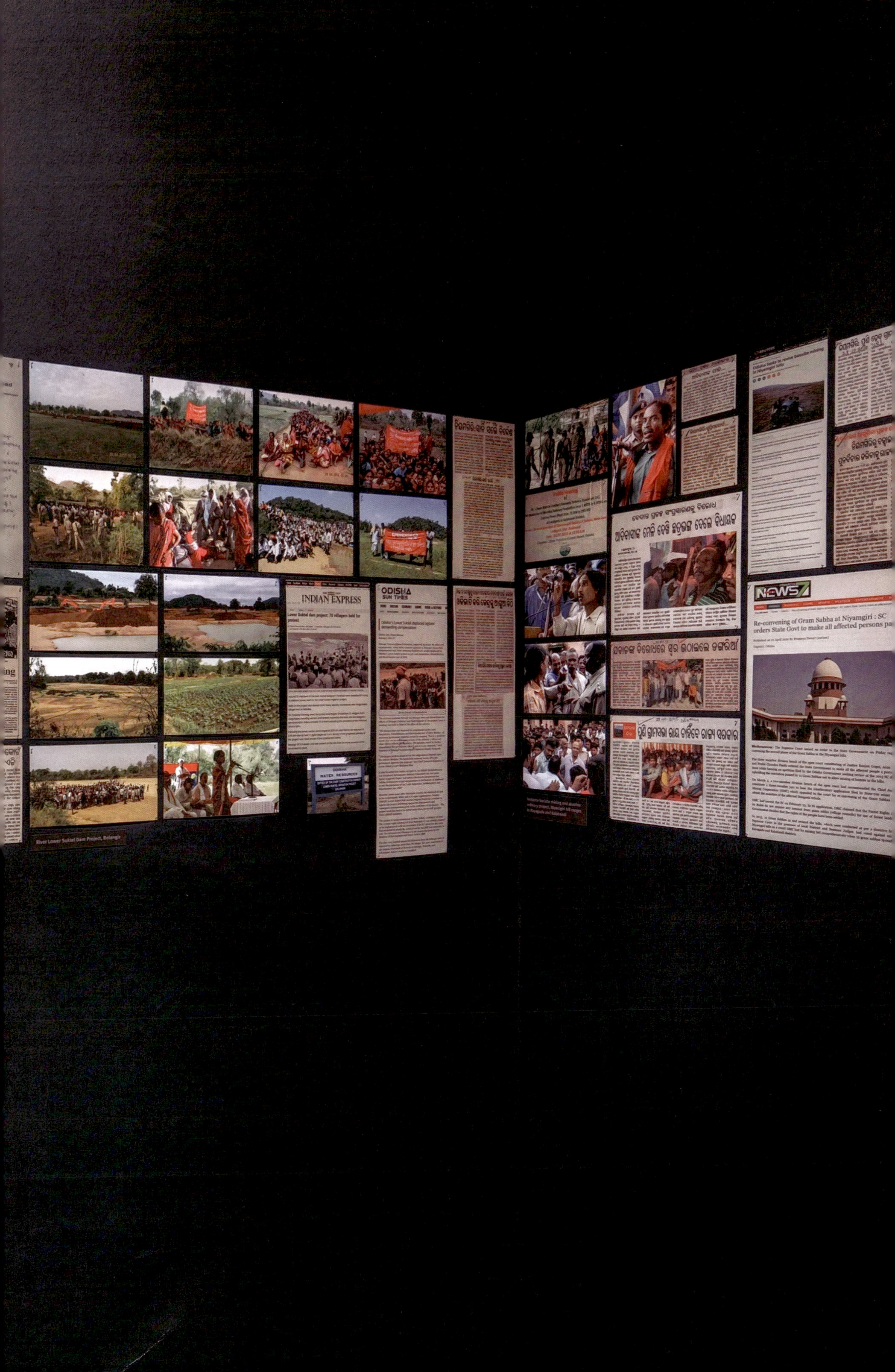

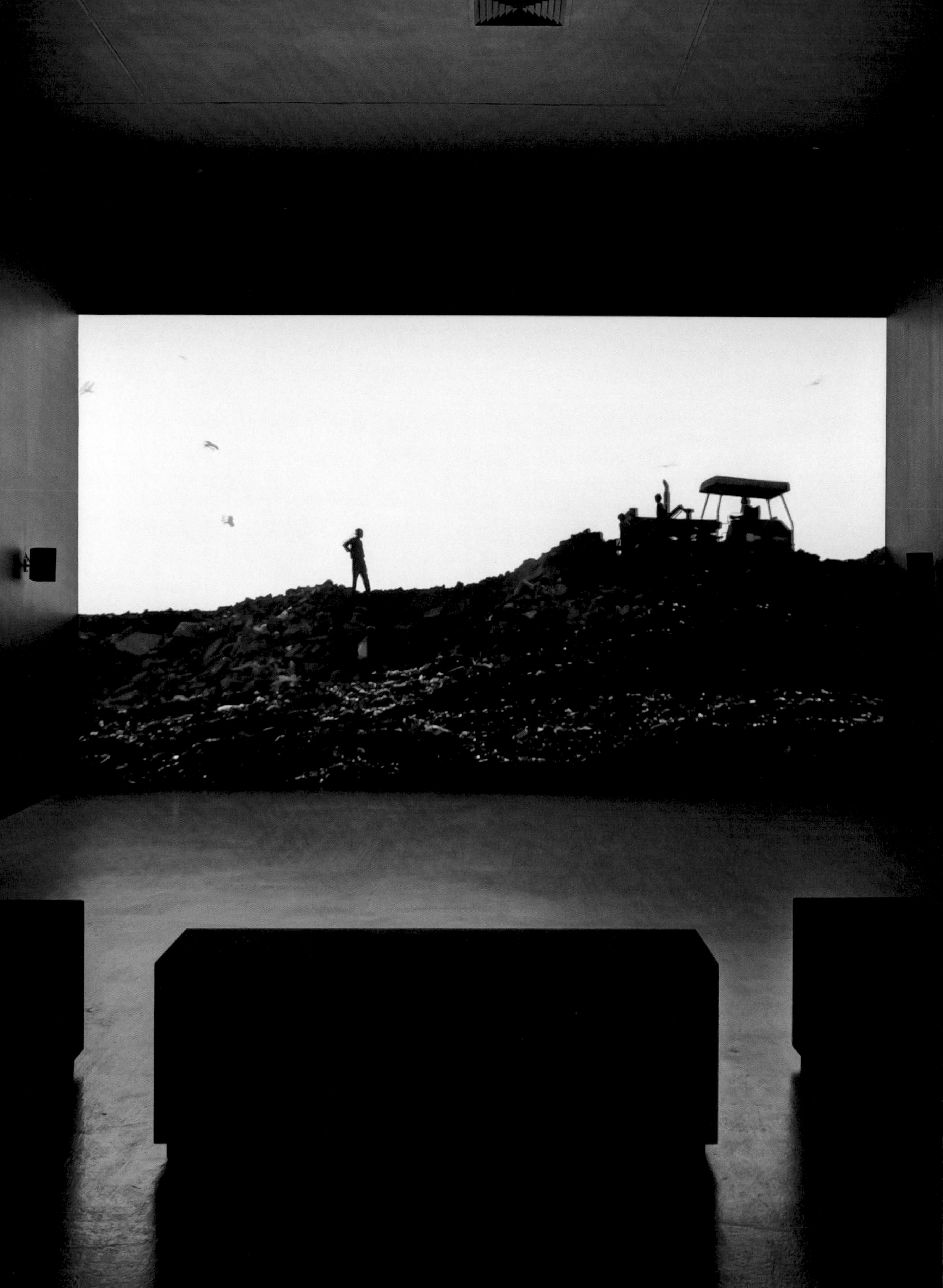

On *The Sovereign Forest*: In conversation with Amar Kanwar

— Ute Meta Bauer and Anca Rujoiu

The Sovereign Forest (2012-ongoing), a multilayered project, focusses on struggles over the resource-rich land of Odisha (formerly Orissa), in East India – a land marked since the 1990s by conflicts between local communities, the Indian government and international corporations. The Sovereign Forest, a long-term collaboration between artist Amar Kanwar, Sudhir Pattnaik/Samadrusti and Sherna Dastur, initiates a creative revision of our understanding of crime, politics, human rights and ecology. A constellation of films, texts, photographs and seeds are brought together in the project's investigation of the validity of poetry as evidence in a trial, discourses on vision, compassion and justice, and the determination of the self.

Ute Meta Bauer and Anca Rujoiu discuss with Amar Kanwar the various social and environmental struggles addressed in the artist's installation project.

Ute Meta Bauer and Anca Rujoiu: *The Sovereign Forest* is a long-term commitment to the resistance of indigenous communities and farmers in Odisha against industrial corporations, local organised crime and the government since 1999.

What brought you there first?

Amar Kanwar: In the mid-1990s, during the first wave of the so-called New Economic Policy, it was difficult for any ordinary person to get a sense of the scale of the operations. At that time, I decided to collect newspaper reports of the previous two years – of visits, transactions, Memoranda of Understanding and statements by various government and industrial leaders. Most of these news reports were brief and did not have much detail. It was a simplistic way to do research but I didn't want to ask anyone and I wanted information that was factual and had no spin.

Plotting this research and the areas of interest on a map of India became an obvious course of action. Corporations and cartels that were well known internationally had several reasons to come here. They were all targeting the coastal zones, especially Gujarat but also other states, the alpine regions of the lower and middle Himalayas, and all along the mineral seams of the Eastern Ghats, which is where Odisha is located. I then travelled extensively for a couple of years in these three regions, researching, meeting various people – villagers, activists, ecological groups, journalists, scientists, bureaucrats and others – trying to understand what was happening. I also filmed in all these areas. I made many friends and learnt a lot from these travels. In Odisha, I met Sudhir Pattnaik and worked with him. I worked in different ways with other groups and NGOs, taught film-making informally and filmed in many areas more or less at the same time. I saw several remarkable small villages and hamlets resisting against very powerful multinational industrial cartels, local politicians and mafias. These resistances were inspiring. There was also a history and experience that I came across there. I had no plans of an exhibition at that time; I was interested in multiple ways of responding to these experiences and was trying to find alternative ways of making, showing and relating.

UMB and AR: For industrial corporations, land is a money-making resource; for central and local government, land is a commodity. For the people, it's their home, their livelihood. On this disputed territory, the interests of corporations intersect with the corrupt apparatus of state while violently hitting the lives and landrights of farmers and indigenous communities. However, in your work, land is not reduced to a single image or definition. Is *The Sovereign Forest* a way to look at land again and again?

AK: For some, land is water. Water is a part of these people, and they can talk only when it flows. For some land is memory without which you cannot think. For some land is food without which there is no taste. For some it is miles underground, a site of labouring in the dark. For many it offers an embrace that calms them from deep inside. Just as I keep trying to understand life, I keep trying to understand land. At one point land, for me, had become words – words about information, anger, protest, the cycle of brutality and the response to it. Over time I felt the need to find a way to look again, not only at the land but at life, its meaning. Not just at the life of others but mine too. So I tried many things to shift the way I look – to slow down and think, to increase the awareness of every breath, to see every imperceptible movement: the shift of a blade of grass, the sound of a fishing net hitting water, light moving. I even tried to empty the image of emotion, distance the human form and then look and look again at the land, so as to be able to sense and see its inner narratives. I wanted to find the fluidity and interchangeability of these narratives so that any story of any being in any language from any memory could seep seamlessly inside any form or object, living or non-living, in any landscape. Finally, it became necessary to step back and look at the scene of the crime in order to prepare oneself, rather than researching the land. To prepare to enable, to increase capacity, to see the signs of what was no longer there, or of what was about to be erased. To see the enormous sorrow that perhaps had seeped into the soil and was now out of sight.

UMB and AR: What we see in Odisha resonates with other struggles against land grab. In Papua New Guinea, indigenous peoples are fighting against multinational corporations that often illegally try to get access to their land – that is protected under customary rights law – for logging, mining, land and sea exploitation. In Australia, sovereignty over land is yet to be ceded to Aboriginal peoples. This clash between property-savvy corporations and customary landowners has roots in colonial times. 'Who owns the land?' is an essential question in *The Sovereign Forest*. Do you see the conflict in Odisha as part of a larger history of community resistance against privatisation of land ownership?

AK: Everyone articulates their struggle differently. But yes the Māori resistance in Parihaka in New Zealand for the protection of Māori lands against the British army in the mid-1880–90s; the Chipko (tree-hugging) anti-deforestation movement of 1974 in Uttarakhand, North India; the 2002 occupation of the ChevronTexaco oil terminal in Nigeria by women from the Ugborodo and Arutan communities; and the 2011 'Lying Down Protest' by the villagers of Jagatsinghpur District in Odisha, against the forcible grab of their lands by the local government and the South Korean steel company POSCO – all have their roots intertwined with each other somewhere deep below the earth.

However, each of these communities is also hierarchised, and they all experience constant aggression, transgression and conflict. There are also systems and traditions of regulation, negotiation and dialogue, most of which have been destroyed in the last several decades. Further, corporations and governments seem to have lost all capability for ecological sustainability, security, self-preservation, justice or respect. From the perspective of the Earth, the human species has become fascist. From the perspective of *The Sovereign Forest*, perhaps no one owns the land. The land is sovereign. The land owns itself.

UMB and AR: Similar projects that you conceived as complex – and long term – investigations into violence and crime, such as *The Torn First Pages* (2004–08) are defined by a multiplicity of materials and voices. Yet each work pays tribute to individuals who fell victims to repressive regimes. In *The Torn First Pages*, there is Ko Than Htay, the bookseller in Myanmar who was imprisoned for tearing out the first page of each book containing the mandatory junta slogans. There is the high-school student Ma Win Maw Oo, who was killed during the 1988 pro-democracy student demonstrations in Myanmar. One of the components of *The Sovereign Forest* is a handmade book with projection dedicated to Shankar Guha Niyogi, the late workers' leader. Another book, *Memory Of* (2012–14), remembers and names each of the farmers in Odisha who lost their lives fighting against the dispossession of their land. You situate their individual experiences and memory in a wider narrative of collective struggle. You also highlight how these communities denounce crimes and express knowledge of their rights in order to demand justice. You bring to the fore the creativity of these communities' resistance and resilience,

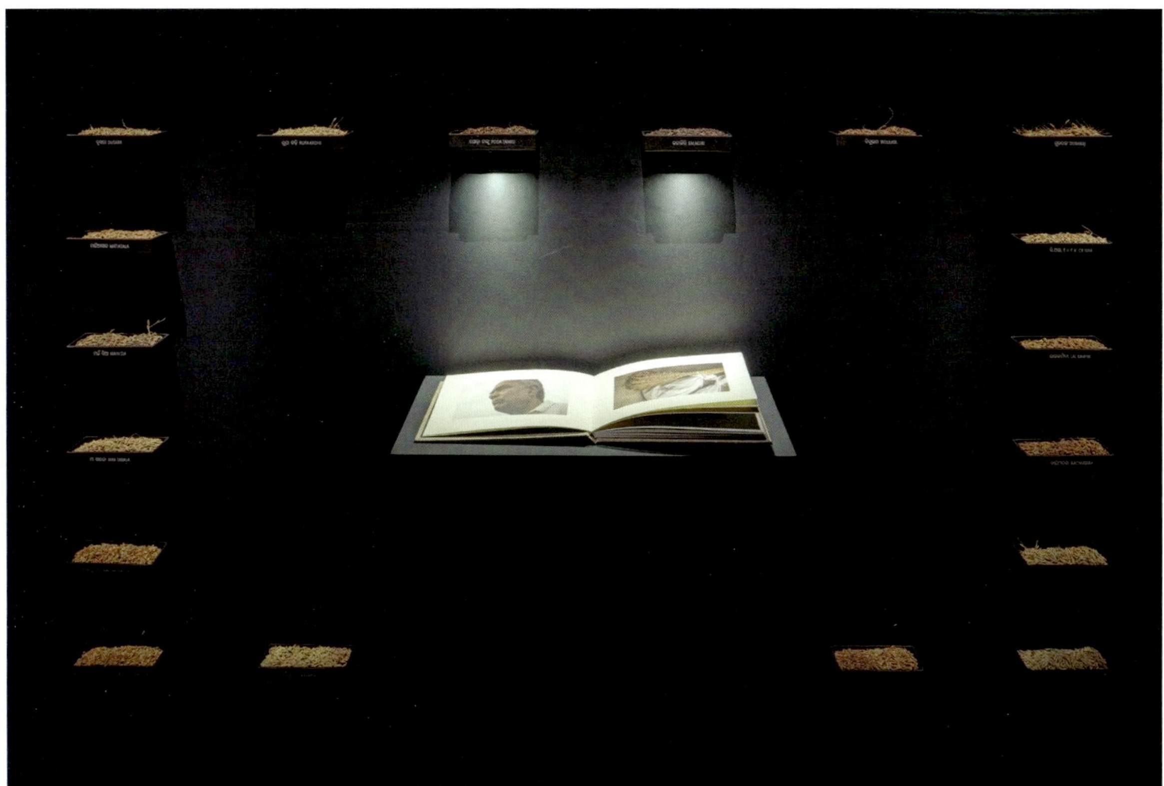

expressed through songs, poetry, craft and theatre, and, last but not least, through your own work as a film-maker and an artist.

AK: The Burmese dictatorship has been one of the most brutal regimes in recent times. Not much is really understood about the scale of its violence or the incredible sacrifice made by several generations of students and citizens. Many have been killed or imprisoned for years because they defied the military. The resilience of the resistance has often felt almost impossible to understand.

Ko Than Htay's act of defiance came at great risk to himself and his family. If discovered, any punishment was possible. And yet he continued to tear out the first page before selling his books. It was a personal act of defiance against the junta, if no real serious threat to the regime. When I heard about him I was quite struck by what he had done and also by the fact that it was a completely private act, almost anonymous, between him and himself. Later he was discovered and arrested. I felt that I – or maybe anyone who makes, writes, or films – owed something to this quiet and principled act of courage.

8 August 1988 was an important day of student resistance in Burma. Parents had hope and told their children to go out and demonstrate against the military. Many students were in the crowd as part of the 8888 Uprising when the military opened fire, including 13-year-old Ma Win Maw Oo. One photograph was taken of her being carried away, seconds after she was shot; this shocking image was published worldwide as news of unrest in a faraway country. It then suddenly disappeared, as often happens. I wanted to remember the moment when she was being carried away, bring back that image, make the image breathe and come alive again. Pixel by pixel, if need be. In many ways the significance of the student movement in Burma, its duration, scale and strength hasn't really been acknowledged or understood, when we should see it perhaps on a similar level to 1968, Vietnam, South Africa or Tiananmen.

To fully account for the story of Niyogi's life and that of the Chhattisgarh Mukti Morcha ('Chhattisgarh Liberation Front'), in the state of Chhattisgarh (earlier Madhya Pradesh) in East India, an organisation of workers, farmers and indigenous communities in the Indian state of Chhattisgarh, will perhaps take several books and oral narratives. In the context of this discussion I am reminded of a perspective that Niyogi himself put forward, not just as a slogan or stated vision but as a prerequisite for any form of social-political action. His call was to 'Create and Struggle

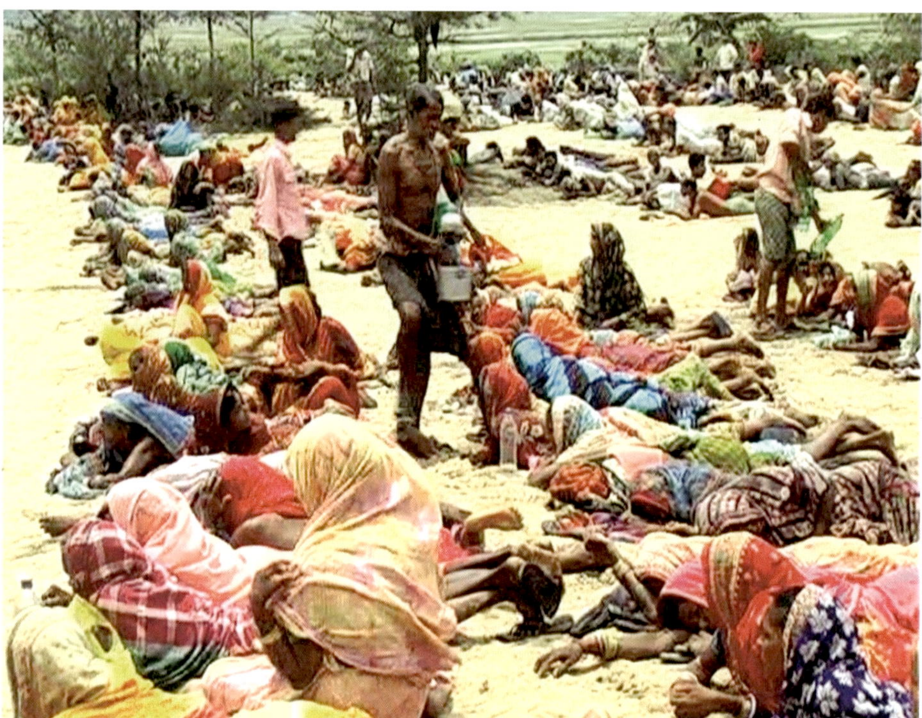

or Create as You Struggle'. Whenever I lose track or am overwhelmed by the negativity around, I recall this vision. Regardless of how small or insignificant a work I may be doing. It is the act of making, of creating something for one's self or for others, of contributing to a collective, of generosity alongside or even entwined with resistance that makes life more meaningful.

In *The Prediction* (1991–2012), a part of *The Sovereign Forest*, the story of a murder trial that took place over two decades is presented. Those who conspired to kill were first convicted, but all were finally acquitted. Justice was supposedly delivered. And so *The Prediction* presents a counterpoint from the past, to the present unfolding of crimes in Odisha.

UMB and AR: When anticipating his assassination, Shankar Guha Niyogi didn't ask for protection. Instead, you write: 'he had asked [...] for a film-maker.'[1] What were the hopes underlying this appeal, but also the responsibilities projected on film-makers? And how did you cope with your own emotion, being more or less aware of the potential dangers?

AK: Niyogi predicted his assassination, but didn't tell anyone about his apprehension. He knew that for the companies to get full access to the land, and the mineral seams, his organisation would need to be destroyed first. He anticipated a severe attack on the local populations, on all kinds of people's organisations and on the land and forests of the region after his death. All of which has come true unfortunately. But at that time no one knew why he was asking for a film-maker to be around. In hindsight we can see his logic. He wanted the events to be filmed, for a witness to be there, to record the onslaught on the lands and the experience of the people. He was killed in 1991. I was a young film-maker. It was a very disturbing experience but also one that opened up, for me, a world of solidarity and resistance that I hadn't seen before.

UMB and AR: Can poetry be a form of evidence of a crime? *The Sovereign Forest* engages a variety of forms of expression and documentation that are yet to be accepted in legal cases. While it redefines the concept of evidence, the project also challenges our understanding of crime. Is crime only a one-off event? Can the series of suicides committed by farmers be understood as a systematic assassination of those who were deprived of means of existence, but also of dignity? Does this systemic violence call for a revision of our legal systems and rules of law?

AK: If every moment contains both the possibility of being alive and of being dead, then could an acute awareness of every moment also create an acute consciousness of living and dying? Central to the notion of crime is the question of evidence. When you look at any crime, it is investigated by an agency, the police or the criminal justice system of any society. The process of justice is based on an investigation that is in turn based on the collection of evidence. Only evidence defined as permissible by the law is presented in court – all other evidence is dismissed as invalid. The carefully crafted texts of the law tell us what is permissible and what is not. They analyse the 'permissible' evidence; they then come to an understanding and make a conclusion that all must finally accept.

But what happens if a crime continues to occur regardless of the enormous evidence available? Then is the crime invisible or the evidence invisible or are both visible but not seen? And what constitutes the scene of crime, what is its footprint? Is the crime always a single cataclysmic event, or can it also be something that expands and is an accumulating process? And which is the

> *Central to the notion of crime is the question of evidence. When you look at any crime, it is investigated by an agency, the police or the criminal justice system of any society. The process of justice is based on an investigation that is in turn based on the collection of evidence. Only evidence defined as permissible by the law is presented in court – all other evidence is dismissed as invalid.*

vocabulary most capable of understanding the scale and extent of a crime? If I do not understand the meaning of loss, its scale, its extent, its multiple dimensions, how can I even know what it is that is lost?

And who defines evidence? What if the given definition of what is 'permissible' and 'impermissible' evidence is incorrect? Is legally valid evidence adequate to understand the meaning and extent of a crime? What vocabulary is needed to talk about a

series of simultaneous disappearances occurring across multiple dimensions of our lives?

What happens if I ask for permission to 'officially' present poetry as evidence in a specific criminal or political trial? If I present poetry not metaphorically or esoterically but formally as evidence in one of its multiple forms? And if I request that you see, consider, evaluate, and compare the nature of the insights and forms of comprehension that you may then acquire about the scale, meaning, and implications of the crime. That is what *The Sovereign Forest* is about. In other words, it could be an attempt to understand life. Mine, yours, ours.

UMB and AR: You often bring into discussion a state of inadequacy that emerges when art addresses experiences of violence and inequality. You describe inadequacy as a form of incompleteness. *The Sovereign Forest* is an open-ended project unfolding over more than a decade – it keeps growing and accumulating materials. Is it this form of incompleteness that keeps you going in the process of art-making?

AK: I think my work has continuously been about doubt, about inadequacy, about blind spots and unknown attenuations, and about momentary comprehensions. Almost every film is grappling with obvious and hidden ethical crises and the repeated experience of losing voice and finding it again.

What we perhaps have to relate to and embrace is the inadequacy of the archive or of *The Sovereign Forest* itself. Presence activates absence. The collection activates the unknown. It is not the archive itself that we cling to but the uncertainty at the core of the archive. Testimonies and memories are fluid and constantly changing. It is this temporary fragility that is mobile, potent, and revealing.

If the attempt to remember is presented along with what is remembered, if what seems definitive is presented along with what is uncertain, if the part and the whole are both simultaneously visible in the same moment, even if only momentarily, then perhaps it may, possibly, create a kind of comprehension that seems new. Maybe we then get a brief glimpse into contemporary memory and what is unfolding. The experience of shifts, transitions, between different methods of comprehension is perhaps the key.

Everything is actually unfinished – an accumulation and disintegration that reveals something temporary. I am mostly concerned with doubt, disturbances and the hope for these temporary insights. I am concerned with intentions too – felt, stated, desired, hidden, unknown intentions. Each of these may spiral into a series of questions. The nature of the hypothesis or enquiry or dilemma inevitably shapes the methodology used to address it – the gaze, the way to be, sit, look and talk. Each answer is different, and even different from itself as the minutes pass. I am concerned with this fluid, repeating, crippling ethical crisis, and the attempts at resolution that accompany it. Each resolution is the search for a language, a way to speak. I am concerned with sharing these attempts. Repeated unsuccessful attempts at answering questions opens out form and helps create a way to talk. The consistent public sharing of these 'failures' is what is interesting.

UMB and AR: *The Sovereign Forest* has been presented in several institutions outside India, from dOCUMENTA (13) in Kassel, Thyssen-Bornemisza Art Contemporary (TBA21) in Vienna, Yorkshire Sculpture Park, to NTU Centre for Contemporary Art in Singapore, Bildmuseet in Umeå and most recently at NYU Abu Dhabi Art Gallery.[2] In parallel, a version of *The Sovereign Forest* was displayed at the Samadrusti campus in Bhubaneswar, Odisha, from 2012 until 2016. You have said that *The Sovereign Forest* is a collaborative work with Sudhir Pattnaik and the journal *Samadrusti,* and with film director Sherna Dastur. What role did each of you take in creating *The Sovereign Forest*? There are plans for a permanent location of *The Sovereign Forest* in Odisha. What type of institution do you envisage this to be? What does it mean for the work to be presented in the context from which it emerged? How do you and the community seek collective responsibility? Or is it fully up to the local community?

AK: It's very difficult to make a film. There was no initial plan. I wanted to make a certain kind of film and then assess it, see what emerged, how people responded, what kind of experience it created and so on. This film was *The Scene of Crime* (2011), where I looked at landscapes marked for industrial acquisition and erasure in Odisha. To make that film, I needed to go through the process of making of another, shorter film, *A Love Story* (2010) which, in many ways, helped me find a way to film *The Scene of Crime.* There were two other friends and long-term collaborators, who made this possible: the cinematographer Dilip Varma and the editor Sameera Jain.

Subsequently, the possibility arose of taking it further, finding different ways to comprehend the same terrain of crime. At different times I had several discussions with Sudhir Pattnaik and Sherna Dastur and we began to add elements to the film as and when the opportunity arose. Stories, more films, books, texts, seeds, different ways of reading, knowing and looking and exhibiting in and outside Odisha. *The Scene of Crime* became central to *The Sovereign Forest* and we grew around it a spectrum of evidence. Sudhir and Sherna have both co-created and nurtured *The Sovereign Forest* over a long time, in too many ways to list here. They usually also don't talk much about their work, so I interviewed both of them. These texts can be read in the book on *The Sovereign Forest* and will give a deeper idea of the range of this collaboration.

Two months after first presenting the exhibition at dOCUMENTA (13), we installed it in Bhubaneswar and it was then open to the public for four years, until we had to let go of the building. If it had no meaning it would not have lasted more than a month. If it has and is felt to be of some use, then it will reincarnate, improve and resurface. The next possible location in Odisha is still being worked on, most likely in a rural space, in collaboration with a rural trust/organisation. It will perhaps change quite a bit so as to relate more deeply with more issues around agriculture. Everything is always tentative. We move ahead a bit, discuss with as many people as we can, think more and then try again. We are under no illusions – about ourselves, about our impact or about the communities involved. We are in a terrain of conflict, of depravation, of ecological and livelihood destruction, and acting in this terrain is fraught with contradictions and dilemmas. We try to address these, and to do the best we can without harming anyone, supporting as many people as we can, and are always learning through the process.

UMB and AR: You started your practice with films destined for single projections, typical of cinema presentation. Gradually, your projects expanded in time, but also in

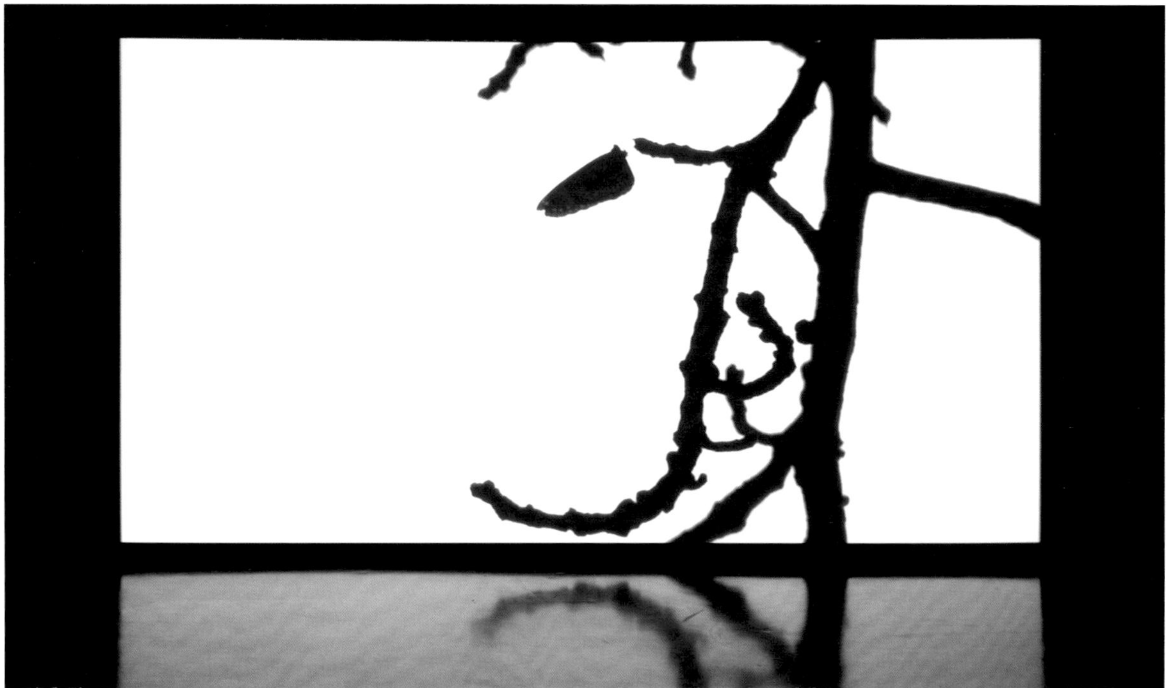

space. The complexity and intensity of the themes and stories you were addressing translated into multi-layered installations. In *The Sovereign Forest*, the acts of looking, reading, touching and listening intersect. What are the aesthetic and conceptual considerations that inform the presentation of this project in an exhibition space? How do the visual, sonic and tactile experiences of *The Sovereign Forest* become an integral aspect of this long-term inquiry into social injustice? Can an aesthetic and poetic language capture crime in a different way than corrupt systems of justice?

AK: The question of the 'document' in the documentary has long been up in the air. Is an illusion less real than a fact? Which vocabulary is most appropriate for a dream? How can a pamphlet be a poem, a poem the story of a murder, the murder then recalled as a ballad? How can the ballad become an argument, and the argument become a vulnerability, the expression of which might negate the argument or instead eventually shift all positions?

If you are in solitude for a few days it is likely that forgotten parts of yourself may slowly reveal themselves. If you are in a forest for a few days it is likely that your sense of hearing begins to improve. You may be able to distinguish between sounds of different kinds of leaves. If you are a dancer and you find the central line inside your body during a performance, the audience sitting several metres away may suddenly experience a moment of joy and revelation.

All revelations and comprehensions are important but all are temporary too. Momentary discoveries of new routes into a thing are exciting. These chance discoveries of new or forgotten senses, physical or bodily forms of comprehension, the loss and regaining of understandings – seem to be valuable terrains to explore. However, I am most interested in the methods that create the possibility of experiencing multiple such passages, allowing for continuous shifts between one and the other.

1   Amar Kanwar, 'The Little Museum', Ute Meta Bauer (ed.), *SITAC VI: What's left…What remains*, Mexico: SITAC/Patronato de Arte Contemporáneo, AC, 2009, p.183.
2   The project was produced with the support of: Samadrusti, Odisha; Thyssen-Bornemisza Art Contemporary, Vienna; Centre Pompidou, Paris; Yorkshire Sculpture Park; Public Press, New Delhi; and dOCUMENTA (13), Kassel.

Roj kishor mohapatra

Jnana Ranjan Samantaray

Sanjaya panda

Sailabala Barik.

Ranjay kumar Sahu

Bhramarabarba bell

Anupama Sahoo

Sovereign Forest

— Usha Ramanathan [1]

*Define me a forest, they commanded. Isn't it
a forest when there are trees, lizards, dung
beetles, elephants, deer?*

*Ahem! came the reply, dipped in the
dulcet tones of uncertainty, in shuffling
embarrassment. A forest is a forest when
the state says it is a forest.*

It doesn't need trees?

*N ... n ... no, it springs into being, and stays
a forest, by virtue of ... a notification.*

No wildlife?

*N ... n ... no. Bare and cultured, protected
and diverted, it is simply a forest when it
is said that it is. Such is the law.*

And the forest dwellers?

Usha Ramanathan discusses the politics and future of the forest beyond the violence of State rationality.

*Uh, we let them be, as was their will, or
moved them out, as is our wont, when the
forest gave way to factory, a dam, a mine,
oh and so much more.*

Till 2005.

2005?

*Aha, 75 years in the forest and the rights –
they shifted, to the dweller. That too became
the law.*

Ah, then the forest returns to common sense?

*Mmm, maybe, just maybe, ways will be
found not to regress into meaning, but to
progress ...*

There are reserved forests. And protected
forests. And village forests. And reserved
trees. Traditions of power and practice have
grown around these and have spun and
spiralled and twined and corded into many
tales, in many tellings.

It was in times long past, well *before*
1878, that trees had turned precious.
Trees had given shade and shelter, fruit
and flower; had knitted the soil together,
caught the rain, shed leaves and splintered
into firewood; had been logged to provide
lumber for boats and roofs; had harboured
the beast, nested the bird and clustered
together in pacts for mutual preservation.

Then it was 1878, and administrative
practice and regulation metamorphosed
into the force of law. The expansionist state
could now declare and appropriate what it
wanted for its purposes. The years rolled by,
and in 1927 a renewed and reinvigorated
version of the 1878 law 'consolidated the
law relating to forests'. This 1927 law was to
survive the ravages of time, the cataclysms
of history, the winds of change, the advent of
modernity and many clichés of like import.

It is interesting, the law. Manufactured
by using the authority of the state and
its genius, it can declare, deem, define,
prescribe, prohibit, provide, regulate, revise,
record. It can punish, reward, protect
against prosecution.

So it came to pass that – by notification,
proclamation, and inquiry, by the power
vested in the forest settlement officer – the
law enabled the 'extinction of rights'. So
too, it said, once the process for declaring a
forest to be a 'reserved forest' has been gone
through and 'from the date so fixed', such
forest shall be 'deemed' a reserved forest.
There was much that was prohibited in the
reserved forest. A person may face the force
of the law who

*makes any fresh clearing where the right to
the forest had been taken away, starts a fire,
sets fire to the forest, or leaves any fire
burning in a way that may endanger the
forest*
*kindles, keeps or carries any fire except at
such seasons as the forest officer may think
it can be permitted*
*trespasses or pastures cattle or permits
cattle to trespass*
causes damage by negligence in felling a

tree or cutting or dragging timber
fells, girdles, lops, taps or burns any tree;
strips off the bark or leaves; or otherwise
damages the tree
quarries stone, burns lime or charcoal,
or collects, subjects to any manufacturing
process, or removes any forest produce
clears or breaks up any land for cultivation
or any other purpose
contravenes any rules in hunting, shooting,
fishing, poisoning water, or setting traps
or snares.

That's a host of things-not-to-do. That's a
lot of rule making and prohibiting-by-the-
authority-of-the-law. Breach the directives,
and it would be a 'forest offence'. The
threatened consequences for committing a
forest offence: imprisonment, fine.

There is more where that came from,
conjuring many realities. The state may
assign a village community 'the rights of
government' over a reserved forest, or it
may decide not to, or it 'may cancel such
assignment'. 'Forestland' or 'wasteland'
that is the 'property of the government' or
over which 'the government has proprietary
rights', or 'the whole or any part of the forest
to which the government is entitled' – this
may be declared a 'protected forest'. The

**Amid this building of a
nation lay, hardly noticed,
the victims of develop-
ment – the displaced and
deprived. The nation
needed the sacrifice.**

government may, in the protected forest,
'declare any trees or class of trees … to be
reserved from a date fixed by notification'.
It may declare that 'the rights of private
persons' over portions of the forest 'be
closed for such term, not exceeding 30
years'. It may prohibit too 'the removal of
any forest produce in any … forest, and the
breaking up or clearing for cultivation, for
building, for herding cattle or for any other
purpose,' any land in the forest. If the state
were to consider control over the forest not
quite enough, and that it might be an idea
to 'acquire (it) for public purpose', it may
proceed to expropriate the forest or the land.

Control, ownership, proprietary
rights, expropriation, assumption of
management, the authority to impose
restrictions on alienation in any way – by

sale, grant, lease, mortgage 'or otherwise'
– the power to license otherwise prohibited
activity and use: with these, sovereignty and
territory were acquiring a significance that
was to profoundly influence the contours of
'eminent domain'.

Eminent domain was, after all, about
land and territory and about the authority
vested in the state. As a doctrine it was
really about

the power of the state
to take private land
for a public purpose
on payment of compensation.

The idea of the forest and forestland changed
all this, and a legal fiction emerged to alter,
unrecognisably, the relationship between the
state and land. The state as owner? As master
of territories and resources on and under
land? As agent with the power to permit,
license, authorize, prohibit or punish?

The law does not merely state. It also
deems. The deeming provision is a deceptive
device. It can make a bear of a wolf, a tree
of a plant, a herd of a loner. It just needs
to deem it so. It can make the state almost
anything it may imagine itself as being. In
the forest it may be a modest aspiration: for
'all timber found adrift, beached, stranded
or sunk'; 'all wood or timber bearing marks
which have not been registered … or on
which the marks have been obliterated,
altered or defaced'; and 'in such areas the
state government directs, all unmarked
wood and timber' – all these 'shall be deemed
to be the property of the government'. That's
all there is to it: the wood may belong to
anyone, but the state declares by law that
it shall be deemed to be the property of the
state. Anyone who picks up sticks could be
committing a forest offense.

Well, not quite anyone. Forest officers
are indemnified for their 'acts done in good
faith', which, in keeping with the nature of
the state, is presumed.

Interesting that when the trees and the
grass and the brush vanish from the forest it is
still deemed to be a forest. It is a reserved forest, and so it shall be until it loses its reserve.

The law's achievements are varied.
There is the annexation of territory by the
state through appropriation and exclusion.
There is the capturing of resources to be
deployed in projects of expansion and development. There is the valuable commercial
resource captured by law and controlled
by the state.

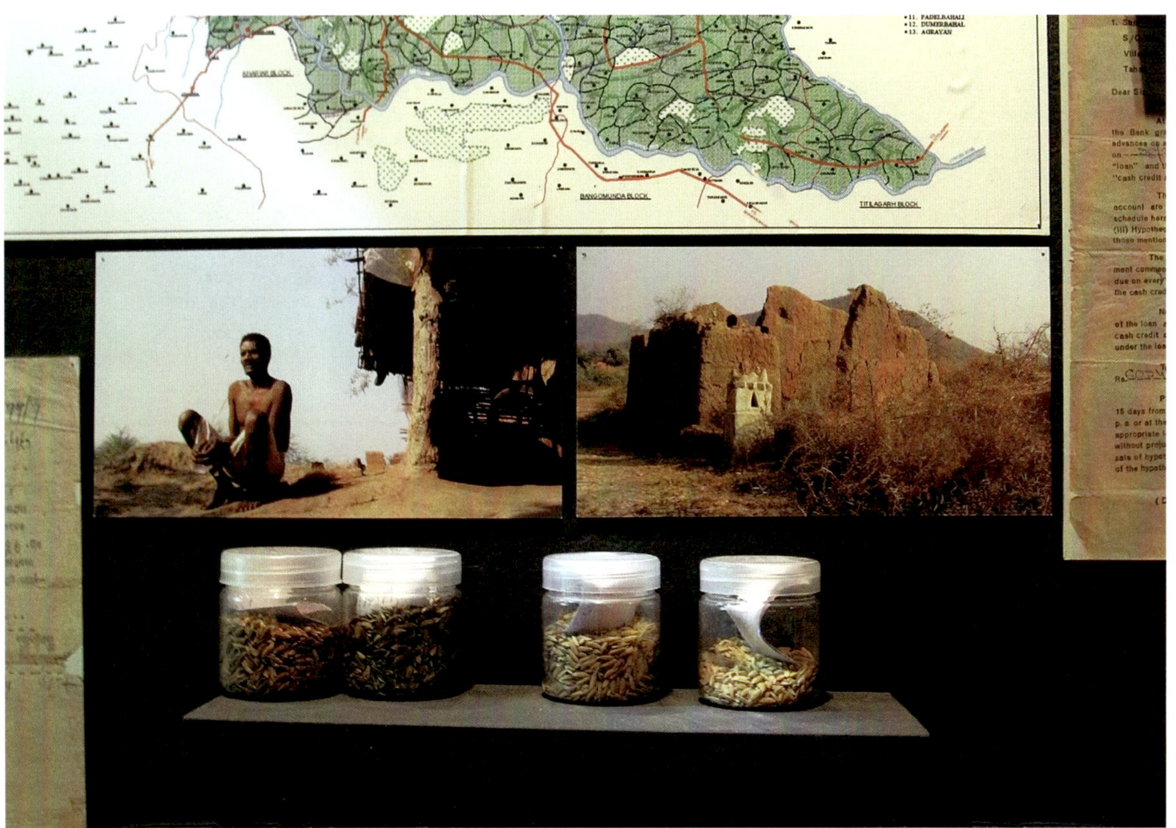

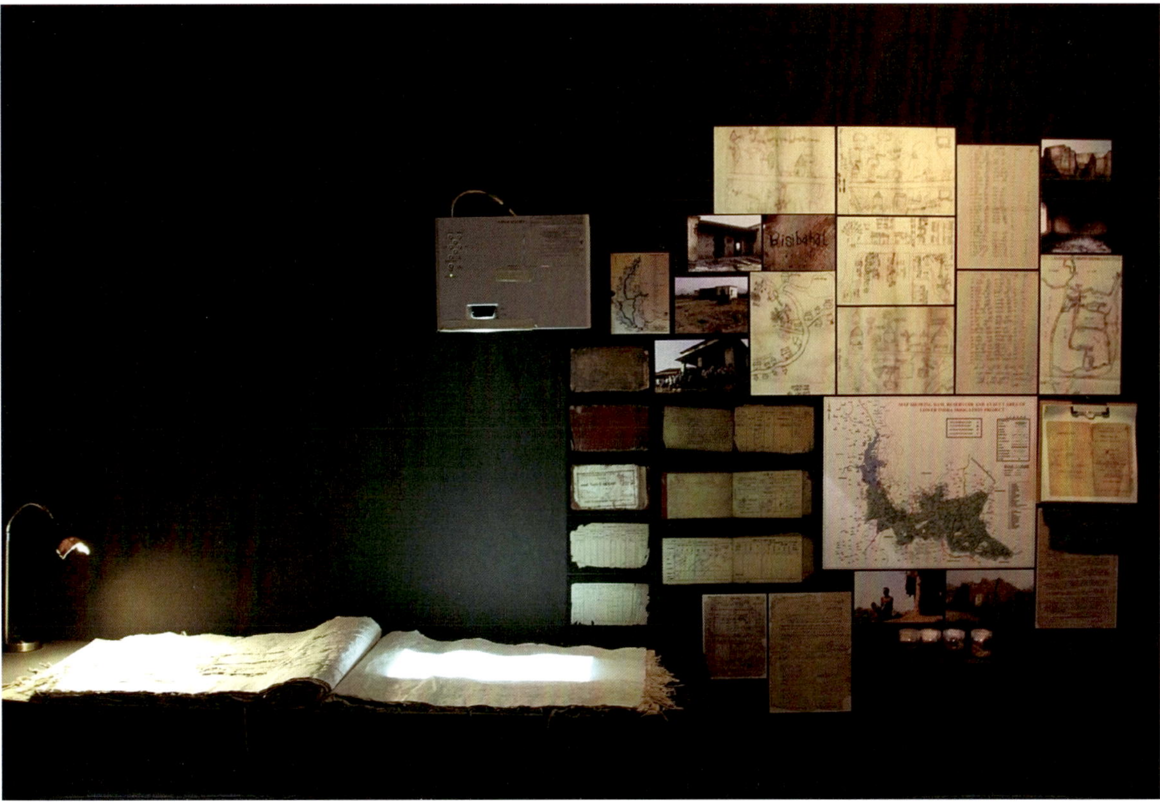

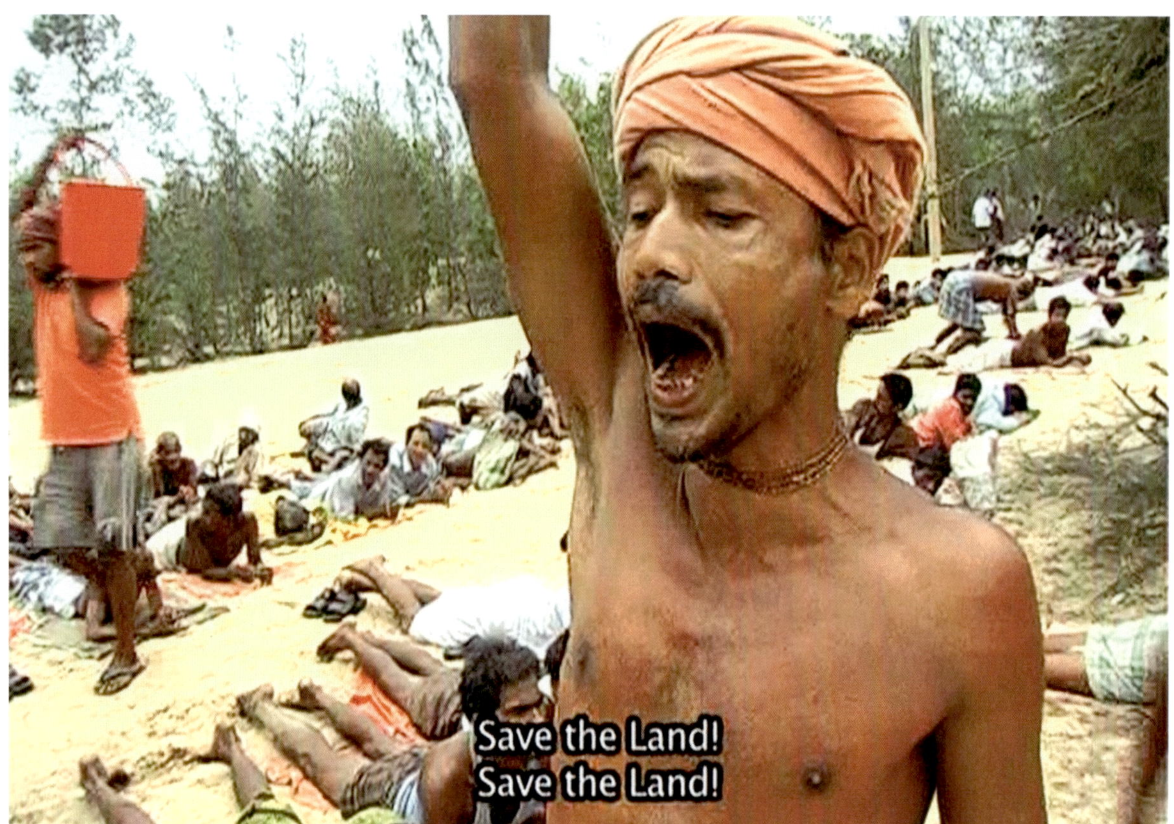

The years went by, and the disintegration of colonial government came
to pass. As the country moved through
independence into constitutionalism, a
break with the past was held back, severely,
by pragmatic continuity. The defiant
exhortation of some years past, 'leave us to
god or anarchy', held in it an impatience
with colonial rule. When the time arrived,
though, anarchy seemed no option. 'All
the laws in force in the territory of India',
said the constitution makers, 'immediately
before the commencement of this constitution shall continue in force therein
until altered or repealed or amended'. So it
was that the 1927 assertion of territorial
sovereignty by the state survived the tectonic
shifts in borders and boundaries and
political geographies.

The national project of development
dwelled on themes of self-sufficiency, infrastructure and self-reliance, for everything
from pins to battleships. The state placed
itself at the epicentre, planning and
executing, encouraging and facilitating
diverse projects of development. Dams
were the temples of modern India.
Factories were symbols of progress. The
underground wealth of iron ore, coal,
bauxite, and uranium emerged as a corner-
stone of the new economy. Amid this

building of a nation lay, hardly noticed, the
victims of development – the displaced and
deprived. The nation needed the sacrifice.

In time, the experience with displacement was to evoke images of impoverishment. This was not poverty. Poverty is a
state, a condition in which the poor are
found. Impoverishment is goaded along
and made to occur. Displacement produces
states of poverty through processes of
impoverishment.

Impoverishing people is not an
offense. Impoverishing forest dwellers or
forest-dependent communities is not a
forest offense.

Skipping a few decades, we reached
a time when primitive became pejorative
and not a synonym for being a part of
nature. Primitive Tribal Groups, or PTGs,
were renamed Particularly Vulnerable
Tribal groups (PVTGs). Vulnerability was
to become the defining characteristic.
Was it a state of being? Or was it induced?
What stands between vulnerability and the
forest dweller?

*karonda, gooseberry, bel, banana,
bullock's heart or ramphal, jamun, lemon,
melon, mosambi, mulberry, papaya,
pomegranate, custard apple, chikoo,
water chestnut, peepri*

Above and pages
19, 20, 22: 'Lying
Down Protest'
by villagers of
Dhinkia, Gadkujang,
Govindpur and
Nuagaon, Odisha, 11
June 2011. Various
Photographers.
Courtesy the artist

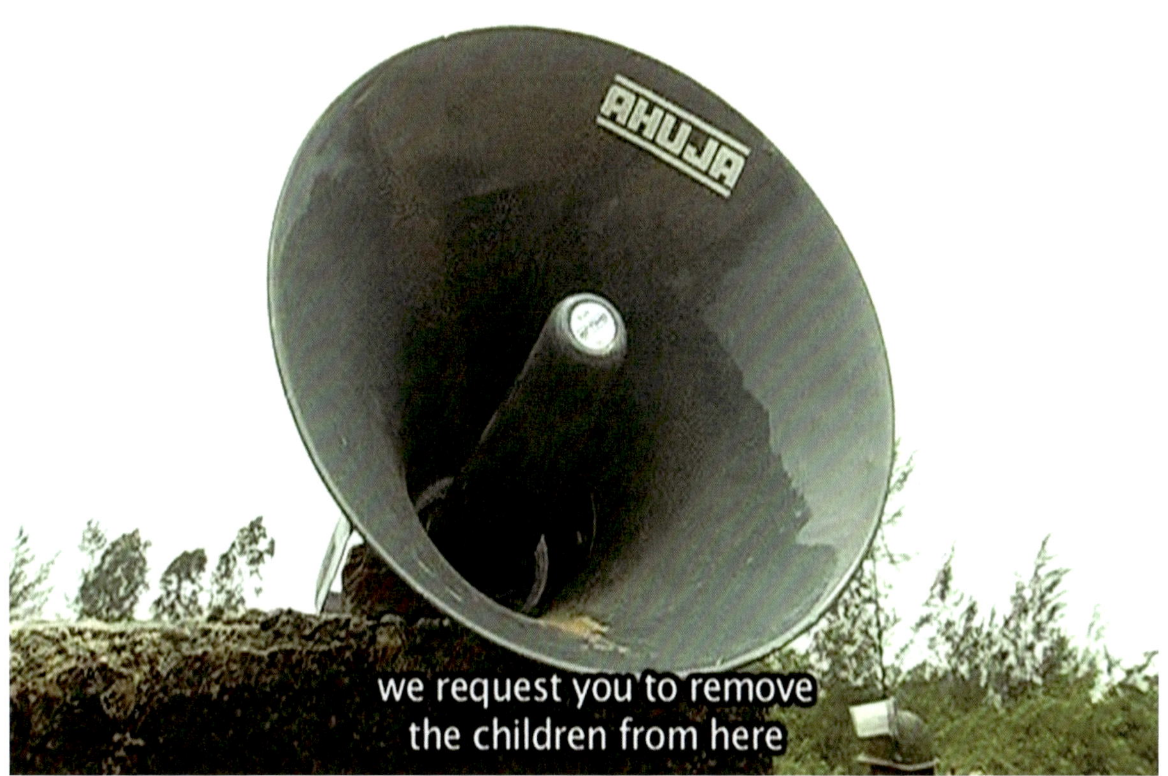

karela, brinjal, cauliflower, cluster beans, cucumber, okra, big chilli, lotus root, banana flower, ridge gourd, tomato

finger millet, pearl millet, little millet, kodo millet, italian millet, sorghum, maize, amaranth seed, barley, paddy, samai

hirva, tivra, black gram, field bean, red gram, bengal gram, masoor lentil, matar, cowpea, green gram, soybean, rough green lentil

coconut, sesame, groundnut, flat seed, mustard, niger seed, ceylon oak carrot, colacassia, onion, potato, radish, sweet potato, golden eye grass, jhimi kanda

The barriers to vulnerability have many names. Fence the resource in, keep the PTGs out, and there is a prescription for induced vulnerability. Induced vulnerability is no forest offense. But let the forest-dependent cross the fence to reach their tree: that, have no doubt, is a forest offence.

It was the 1970s, and the environment had begun to be articulated as a global concern. In India the irreplaceably rich diversity of the Silent Valley was threatened with destruction, saved by a significant act of statesmanship in the arena of conservation and respect for nature. With the country teetering on the brink of unendurable loss and waking up to the depleting forest cover in 'reserved forests', the 1927 act was layered with another law in 1980. The Forest Conservation Act. Decentralised diversion of forestland for that which could generically be called 'nonforest purposes' was revisited. Decisions about diversion would now converge at the centre; state governments would petition the government in Delhi when they had plans for forest areas.

The tide was turning, or so it appeared to the undiscerning. The forest had not been for the dweller or the proximate-dependent for a long time. Use had changed to exploitation. The proprietorial state had been sharing the trees with pulp and rayon makers for years running into decades.

An inset in memory: the roof of a dwelling with a recent repair using two logs that had been carefully cut, leaving behind a regenerative stump. A slip of paper that recorded this as a forest offence. Looking up from the slip, one can see the tail lights of a truck carrying an overload of logs to be pulped for profit. It seemed that there was a chasm between a wrong and an offense.

Trees needed to cover at least a third of the land mass, but the forestation stood at something close to 11 per cent. Reserved forests were deemed to be forests, a fiction that perpetuated control over land even where the forest had gone missing. Tree planting became the new celebration. Monoculture – the answer that pragmatism, ignorance and callousness offered management of forests – was an expression representing cynical optimism.

Yet diversion was at the heart of the development project as envisioned. Thus was engendered the idea of compensatory afforestation. Cut a tree; plant two. There is little to say about this idea, except that it was doomed to fail, which it did.

It was 10 July, 2009. A case had made its way to the Supreme Court and had been up and running for close to fourteen years. The court was monitoring activity in the forest. The hopelessness of expecting project proponents to find land and plant trees that would survive was staring everyone in the face. Yet there had to be a price that the project should pay even as the forest gave way to nonforest activity.

Some while ago an acronym had been born. CAMPA. In small type, a fizzy cola. In capital letters, it was an impressive array of severe words. Compensatory Afforestation Fund Management and Planning Authority. CAMPA, it was portentously announced, was 'meant to promote afforestation and regeneration activities as a way of compensating for forest land diverted to non-forest uses'. An ad hoc CAMPA had already been set up to collect monies intended to be used for compensating the loss of trees. It was time to find ways of deploying the funds for afforestation. The sums were large, indicating the vastness of the diversion and the extent of the depletion of the forest, and the court considered 'sudden release and utilisation of this large sum all at one time may not be appropriate'. So the monies were to be released, for the time being, at Rs. 1,000 crores each year for 5 years. There is a tragic futility in the court's pronouncement. [2]

All this is about the forest and forestland and territorial sovereignty asserted by the state. Where are the forest dwellers? Where are the forest-dependent communities?

It was September 1949. The Constituent Assembly was discussing how constitutional protection was to be extended to tribal communities. Ways of life, practices, cultures and continuities made up tribal life – as, poignantly, did land.

It had to do with territory. Lands where tribals led their lives were to be marked out and 'scheduled'. Alienation was anathema. Tribal land was not to be alienated. The transfer of land from a tribal to a nontribal could happen, if it were to be allowed to happen at all, only after the government had its representative verify why and wherefore this transaction was proposed. And what it would do to the tribal community and to tribal identity.

The state was the protector, except when the state needed land in the public interest. So it was that in the 1950s a steel plant was set up in Rourkela, in Orissa (now Odisha), and tribals in villages spread over twenty thousand acres found their land handed over to a public-sector company, vested in the state. And a pattern emerged.

The year was 1992. Tribal lands were being leased by the state to mining industries, which eagerly extracted mica and limestone from the ground. This may have been more difficult to contest where the state had extensive eminent domain powers, but in a scheduled tribal area, there were fetters. The state's presence had to mean protection of tribal interest, and yet here was the state acting in ways that reduced tribals to wage labour! This was not an impropriety; it was a constitutional wrong.

The court was asked to step in, which it did, in 1997. The verdict: a nontribal person is both a natural person and a juristic person. Private corporations are juristic persons. Ergo, the state cannot hand over tribal land to corporations that are not run by the state. When the state transfers land to itself, it is an 'entrustment of public property'. The aim of public corporations is the public interest, and that cannot be equated with handing over tribal land to private corporations.

This was a brake on territorial ambitions.

This was the era when the state was reinventing itself as a friend and collaborator in the transfer of resources. Ecological explorations and extrapolations had proven that the earth hid a plenitude of minerals. Forest, tribals, a multitude of species, tradition, and culture were wasting the

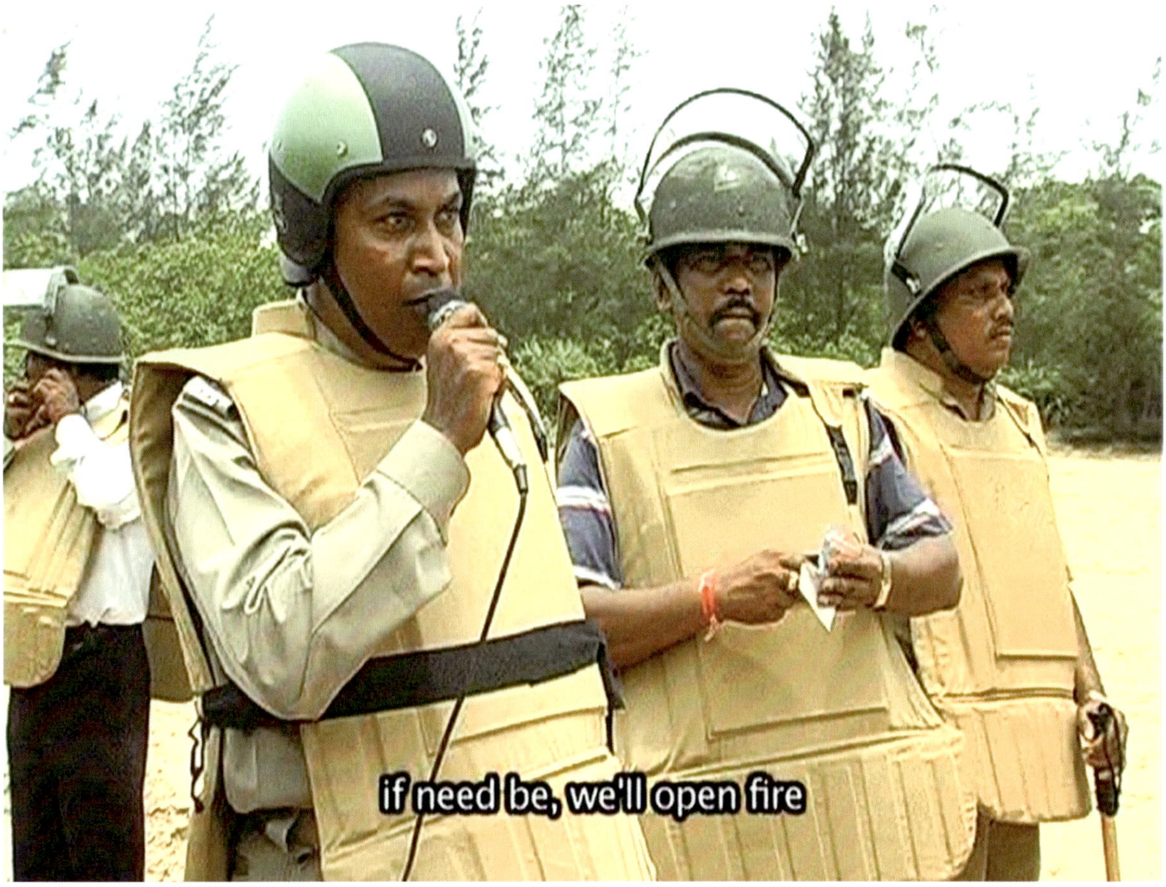

if need be, we'll open fire

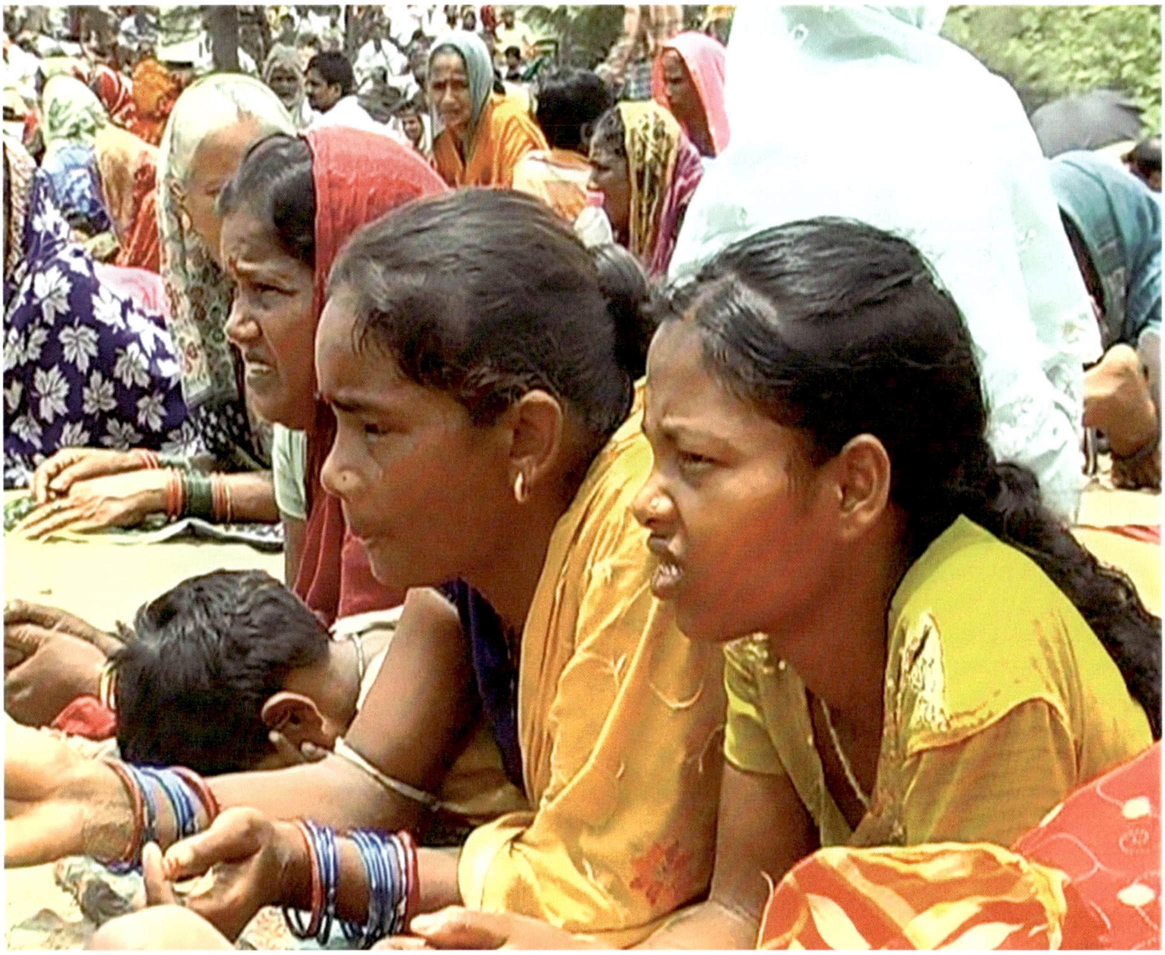

opportunities that were so tantalisingly close and yet so hard to reach.

There are ways. There are always ways.

On 10 December 2001, its 1997 decision became unpopular with the Supreme Court. If land 'predominantly inhabited by aboriginal tribals' cannot be sold, transferred, or otherwise transacted, there was still a law that excluded a lease from the proscription. Lease a land for mining operations and it will never be the same again, and disrupt life it inevitably will. Yet the law helps opportunity along. So the state takes tribal land because it has the authority to do so, and leases it to private corporations because the law said that it could. No offence meant.

Where the law does little to support, deliberate misinformation may work as well. It was 23 November 2001. The Supreme Court had been dealing with 'forest matters', cast in the role of the preserver of the forests. The language of 'encroachments' had taken over the discourse. Encroachment sounds like it has to be a wrong, but oftentimes it is merely illegal. There are encroachments, and then there are encroachments. There are the tribals and their activities, over which the law passes control to the state. They have been there a long, long time, but the law makes them precarious. There are forest-reliant industries, sometimes legal, oftentimes not, but fostered by the agencies of the state. The court moved to restrain the state from 'regularising encroachments' without getting its 'permission' – a strange instruction to one who is not conversant with the instrumental use of the law. This opens up possibilities for misreading and misdirecting.

The letter is dated 3 May 2002. The Supreme Court has spoken, the letter-writing bureaucrat informs and, as though in a natural progression, goes on to instruct all governments in the states to 'frame a time bound programme for eviction of the encroachers from the forest lands' and a 'comprehensive list of encroachments' and 'current status of eviction processes' be reported. By August 2004 parliament was being informed that 1.3 million hectares were under encroachment and that 1.52 lakh hectares of forest area had already been evicted. Arbitrary evictions of tribal and rural populations were hidden in these figures.

The reaction was intense and wide-spread. And it forced a turn in the law to recognise the rights of forest dwellers and forest-dependent communities as individuals, as communities, as belonging to a habitat. That was in 2006, and that was the law that validated the rights of forest dwellers and forest-dependent communities. The nature of the offense was altered even as the synonymity between the forest dweller and the encroacher vaporised, but the right to recognise the rights remained where it had always been, with the state. Wrongful refusal to recognise rights is, of course, no legal wrong.

Control had begun to slip away. Yet there were ways. There always are ways. What could the state do to salvage its sovereignty over forestland?

Well, it could resurrect the crime of sedition – for 'exciting disaffection towards the government established by law'.

It could crowd its prisons with resisters, protesters and a host of unconnected others as part of a strategy to teach silent acceptance.

It could set the stage for a civil war, arm unformed youth to take on the political violence of a nonstate movement whose legitimacy was in direct proportion, even if not quite exactly, to the abdication by the state. This could empty out villages and leave land free for fresh opportunity.

It could seek to establish parks and sanctuaries. It could set up core areas for wildlife protection. And stretch the boundaries to buffer areas.

It could be elephant corridors.

It could be tiger reserves.

It could be ecologically sensitive zones.

It could be electrified fencing to keep the elephants in, which serves to keep the tribals out.

It could mesh a genuine concern with gaining ends that are both offensive and lacking legitimacy.

Of course, it could also take rights seriously, but sovereignty over territory would take a big hit.

The gods reside on the mountain. The community inhabits the sides. Every year, on a day of worship, they congregate on the mountaintop and offer ritual prayers. There are medicinal plants on the slopes and on the mountain. There is land to cultivate, and there are orchard trees and wild berries to provide sustenance, along with the grain from the government shops. But the mountain was not just the repository of the wisdom of the gods; in it lay a mineral valuable in the world beyond.

Are the gods really gods? Or do
they represent an idea whose time is past?
Are opportunity and profit and growth
and development more powerful than
a way of life? Must people be rescued
from primitivity and introduced to the
mainstream, where water flows from taps
and rivers are distant imaginings? Should
the mountain be excavated whether or not
the tribals are ready or willing to make the
ecological shift? Are there limits to the state's
territorial sovereignty? The people have
spoken. They want to be left to live with their
god. How are they to protect their word
from being forgotten or overridden?

There is, to begin with, the offence, and this
the law defines; then there is the wrong,
which is recognised and experienced. There
is the offender, and there is the wrongdoer.
There is consequence, and there is its
absence.

If impunity precludes prosecution, is
there still a crime?

1   This essay was originally commissioned for Daniela Zyman (ed.), *Amar Kanwar: The Sovereign Forest* (exh. cat), Berlin: Sternberg Press, 2014, pp.121-25, accompanying the eponymoous exhibition at TBA21 in Vienna, 23 November 2013-24 March 2014. Reprinted with the kind permission of TBA21 and the author with a new introduction.
2   A crore is a unit in the South Asian numbering system equal to ten million.

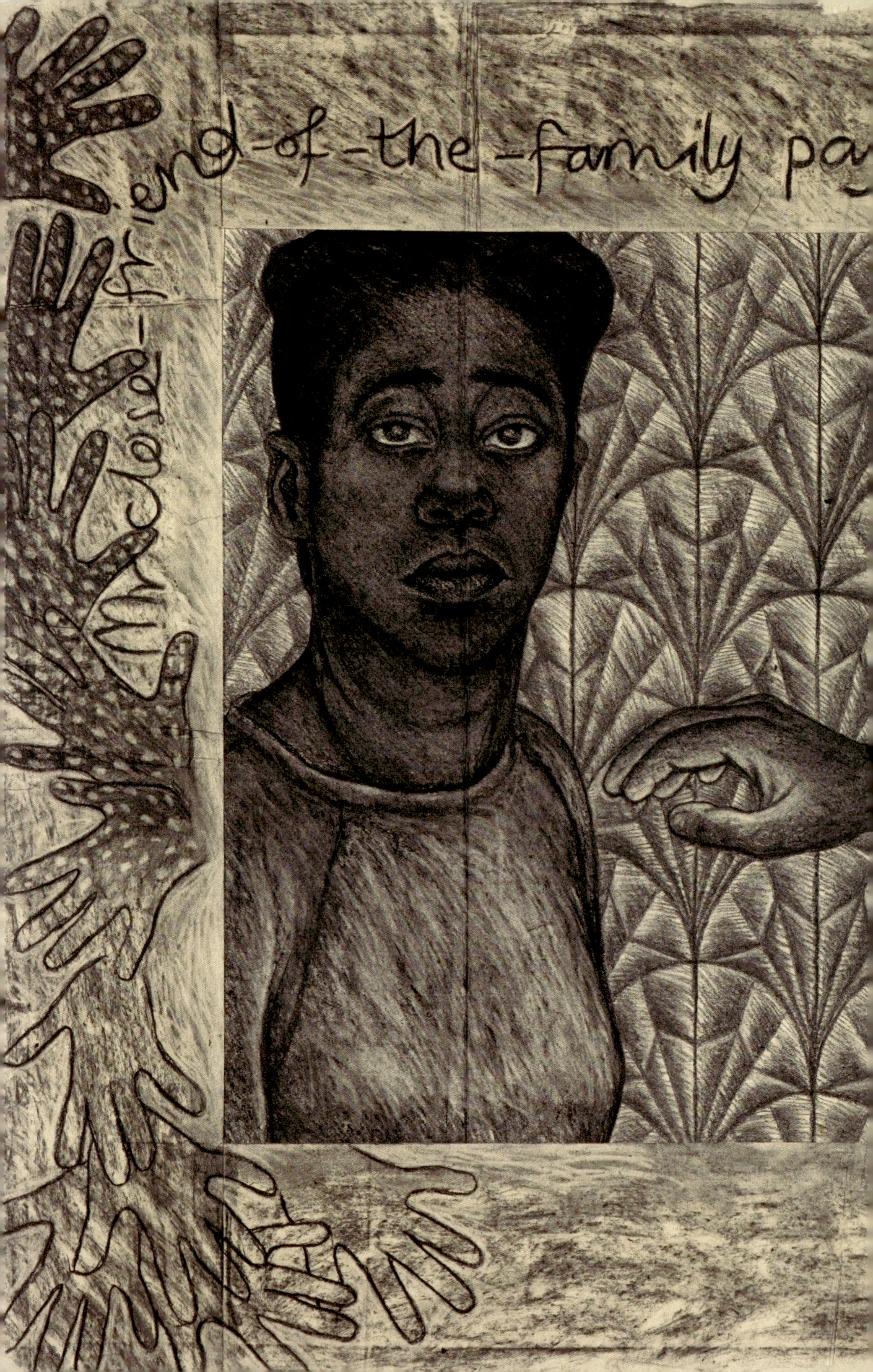

friend-of-the-family
iend-of-the-family pa

a visit whilst everyone else is out

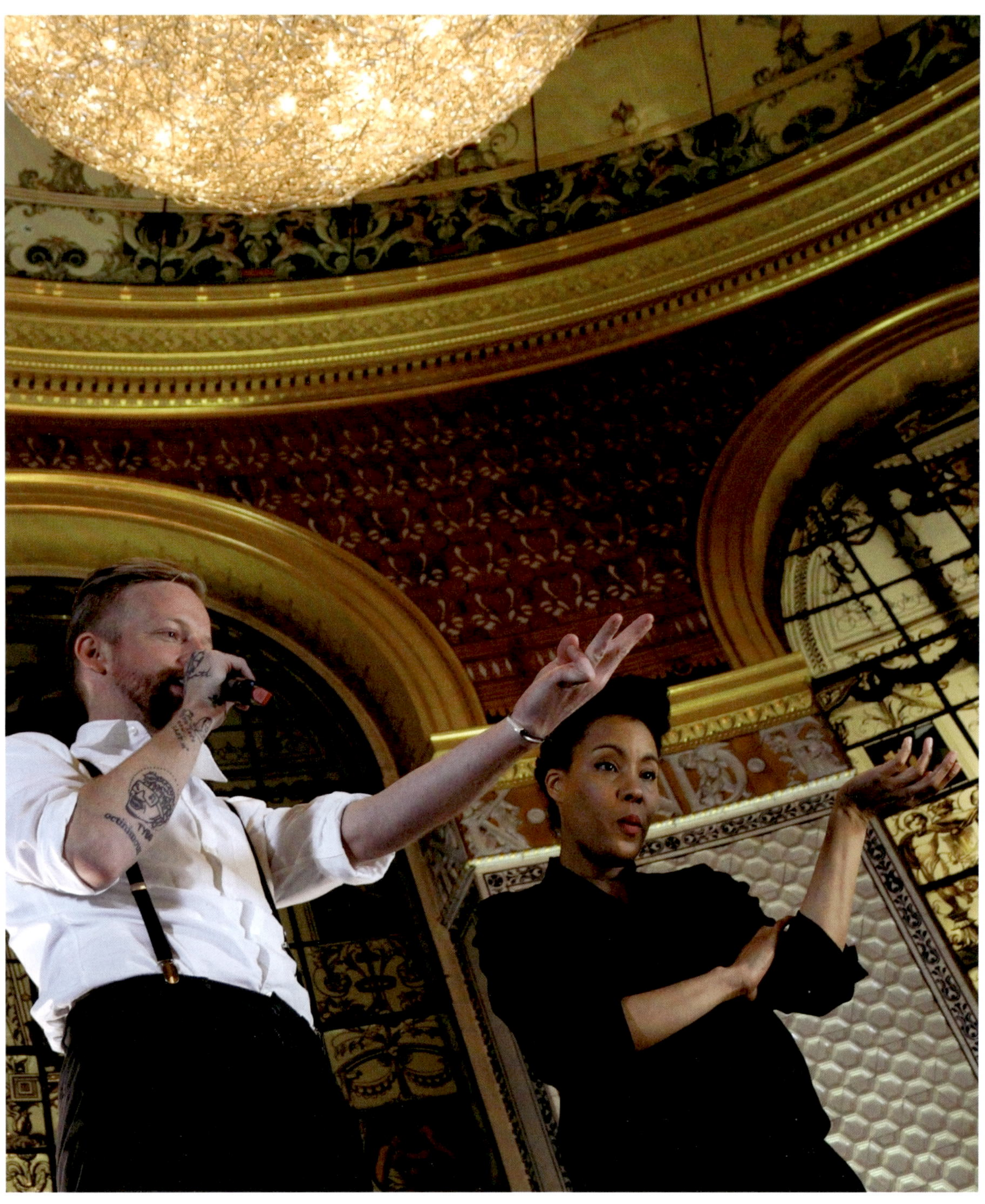

Sonia Boyce: Reclassifying Classification

— Nizan Shaked

Classification and comparison are fundamental tools within academic disciplines ranging from sciences such as geology and biology to virtually all the fields of the humanities. Problems of classification, which frequently occur, have also been at the heart of how scholars have revised and reinterpreted natural, economic, social, and cultural phenomena. As methods of taxonomy are assessed and re-assessed, and one type of measure or comparison replaced with another, new and different mistakes are made. 'Fail again. Fail better' goes Samuel Beckett's well-known quotation from *Worstward Ho* (1983). Art is no

Nizan Shaked traces the interventions of Sonia Boyce's work in received categories of artistic practice, considering how these interventions suggest means of classification beyond media, artistic intention and identity.

different. As we classify art practices according to the paradigms of the moment, and measure them against the recent or more distant past, we are always likely to miss certain aspects of artistic contribution. This is a given condition of reception for historically underrepresented artists like Sonia Boyce, who have entered into the field of art from a position at odds with the discipline's received parameters. Boyce's work has responded to these parameters and proceeded to debate them, charting a path previously unseen to contemporary critical analysis, constrained as this had been by paradigms blind to the kinds of interventions that Boyce's work makes. In hindsight it is clear that Boyce's specific points of entry, both artistic and discursive, have reshaped the field itself, expanding the parameters within which we understand the meaning of certain gestures.

Boyce became visible in the 1980s with lush, large-scale figurative pastel works on paper, at a time when drawing, painting and the figure were trapped within the poles of Conceptualism and post-conceptual

photographic practices on the one hand, and on the other an urgent need to tell stories not yet told and to address broad swathes of aesthetic oversight. While the former tendencies rejected pictorial or narrative representation and the hand-made, the latter revolted against the narrow prescriptions of a latter-day avant-garde. Feminist or other forms of identity-based critiques of the claims presented by conceptualist practices aimed to highlight the blind-spots of practices that developed in opposition to high modernism but still perpetuated some of its assumptions. For example, Mary Kelly introduced the material and discursive work of social reproduction into the philosophically abstract domain of Conceptual art's analytic propositions. Her *Post-Partum Document* (1973–79) pointed to the gendered division of labour that relegated childcare, and the domestic sphere in general, to women.[1] Kelly's emphasis on the parameters determining the construction of (gendered) subjectivity disputed Conceptual art's claim to neutrality, objectivity and other enlightenment-based presuppositions. Instead, the work posed a synthetic proposition, showing that it is not only white Western male subjectivity that can be the basis for totalising concepts, but that more politically-specific issues, in Kelly's case stemming from feminism, can also pose a model from which universalist underpinnings might be abstracted, so they can be then applied toward a broader conclusion (or political goal). Kelly's work demonstrated new modes of conceptualist abstraction. Juggling multiple swords, her work also aimed in another direction, using the Duchampian-born non-pictorial strategies of Conceptual art to critique the feminist strand of art practice that used representations of the female body in an attack on patriarchy's blind spots.

Boyce has positioned her early work as a response to key feminist debates of the 1970s and 1980s: 'some people align themselves with what could be called the Mary Kelly position, within feminist art discourses, or, there was another camp you could say that was very much about the performative body and claiming the body within visual

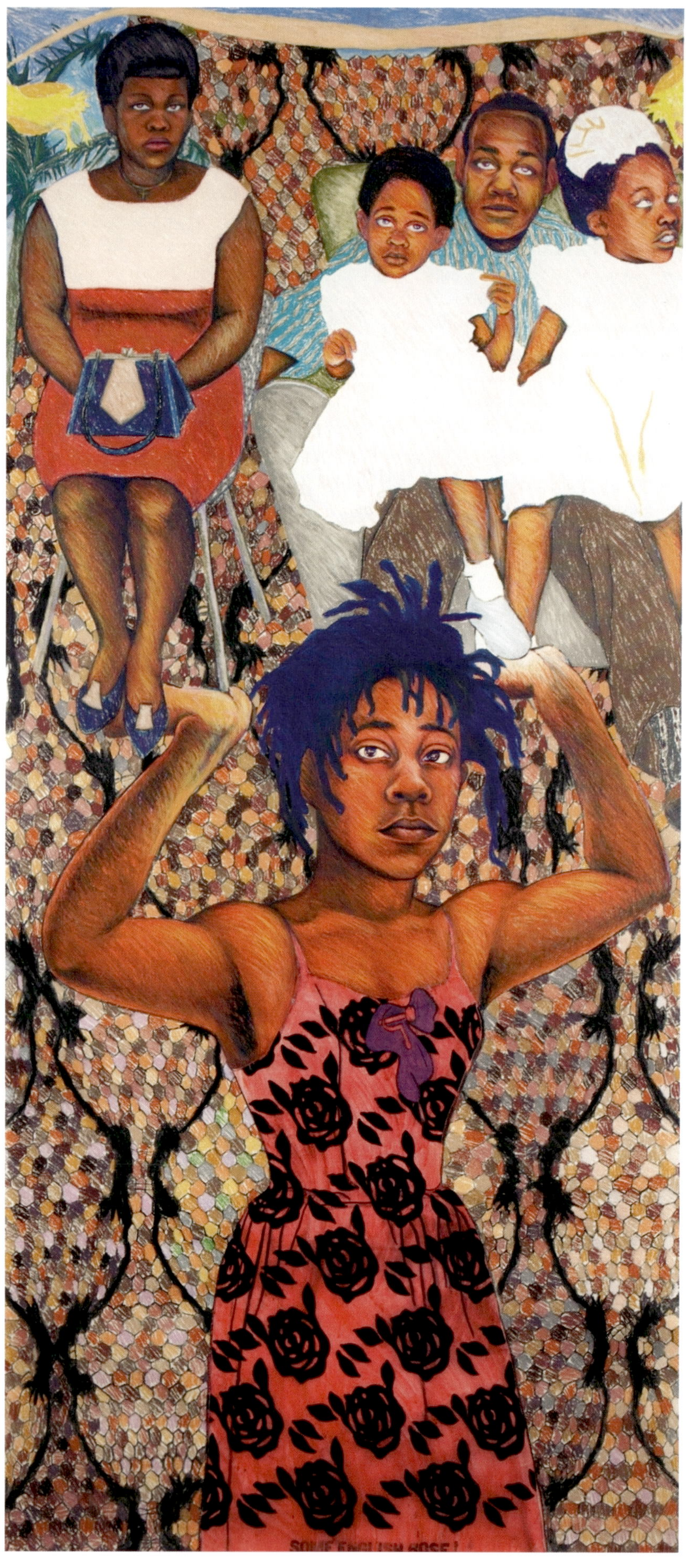

SOME ENGLISH ROSE !

arts.'[2] She recalls how 'painting was absolutely the troublesome ground to be working in … and at the same time there was also a huge debate about whether one should use the female form or not.' But there was such a lack of what Boyce calls 'rich images of the black female body', that she did not want to 'evacuate' that space. Synthesising these antimonies, Boyce's early works added the vector of race representation to the crossroads of identity political debates.

By viewing Boyce's early work in retrospect, in terms of how it has transformed and developed, we can see not only that the drawings sit within a complex matrix, but also how Boyce's imposition of this matrix has related to and informed broader tendencies in art. Boyce's development can be placed *en abyme* by asking about the sig-

Even when artists previously excluded from the long game of art were admitted onto the playing field, the establishment of art history and criticism was often unable to expand its outlook beyond a limited set of contemporaneous debates.

nificance of drawing as a medium, the use of materials themselves as critical tools and social signifiers, the question of imaging women, and the question of conceptualist anti-narrative and anti-subjective modes of art-making. In this way we can think about the reintroduction of narrative in art in the 1980s not as a return to iconographic referencing, but as an intervention into the cerebral forms of post-conceptualist practices. Thus, while in some respects Boyce develops her practice in contrast to the synthetic conceptualism of Mary Kelly by insisting on a direct representation of the body, her later work, which utilised found objects, the haptic semiotics of materials and orchestrated chance recitals, comes close enough to conceptualist paradigms to merit consideration in that vein. Boyce's work illustrates the development of conceptualism since its revision by feminism and other forms of synthetic propositions through critical, postcolonial and queer perspectives.

Another key area of contention in the 1980s was the concern to unify the parameters of Black arts. The anthology published for the conference 'Shades of Black' (2005) provides an excellent summary, pointing out the historical lack of Black Art's documentation, and highlighting the archives and exhibitions set up by artists themselves to remedy invisibility and erasure.[3] As these practices developed, critical reception stumbled at first but then slowly found its footing. Debates ensued over whether there was such a thing as a 'black-diaspora aesthetic', if and how 'Black Art' was an effective category, and what aspects of production the term referenced – the artist's ethnic or cultural origins, subject matter, media, methods, forms, style, etc. Initial misunderstandings and art historical dogma explain the marginalisation of the work by curators, and the insistence of mainstream critics to only read the work through the ethnicity of the artist, sidelining the broad scope of contributions performed by the work. The reduction of work to the identity of the artist, the demands on artists of colour to represent their community and the literalisation of complex gestures are just some of characteristic attitudes that framed the reception of underrepresented artists at the time, not only in the UK but also in the US. Funding and institutional constraints shaped the presentation of works, which were often relegated to secondary spaces (corridors rather than galleries, for example), while reception also affected the ways in which the work was understood. The attempt, for instance, to remedy oversight by funding a Black arts exhibition forced a classification that overshadowed nuances of practice and replaced marginalisation with essentialism, constraining the interpretation of the work to biography right at the time where a nuanced approach to biography was wielded as critique. As a result such critiques were misread. The American context was overlooked, as was the work's interaction with other disciplines in the arts such as theatre, music and popular culture. In fact, in cases where artists used portraiture or figuration, it was not only the subject matter but also the choice of media that were aspects of the intervention – the act of claiming an authorial space within the broader public discourse from which Black artists, especially women, had previously been barred. Because such practices were widely received within the conventional paradigms, in which narrative

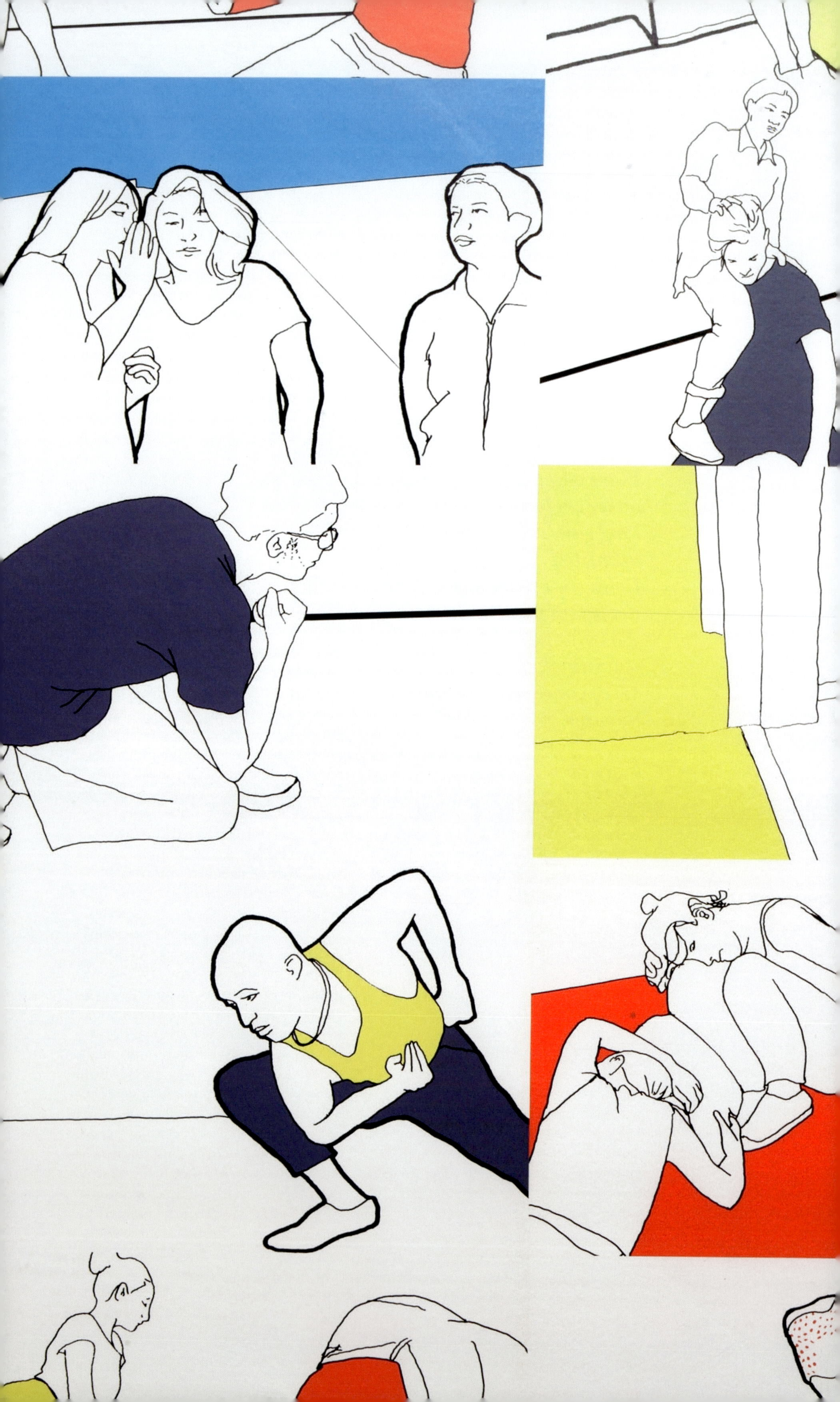

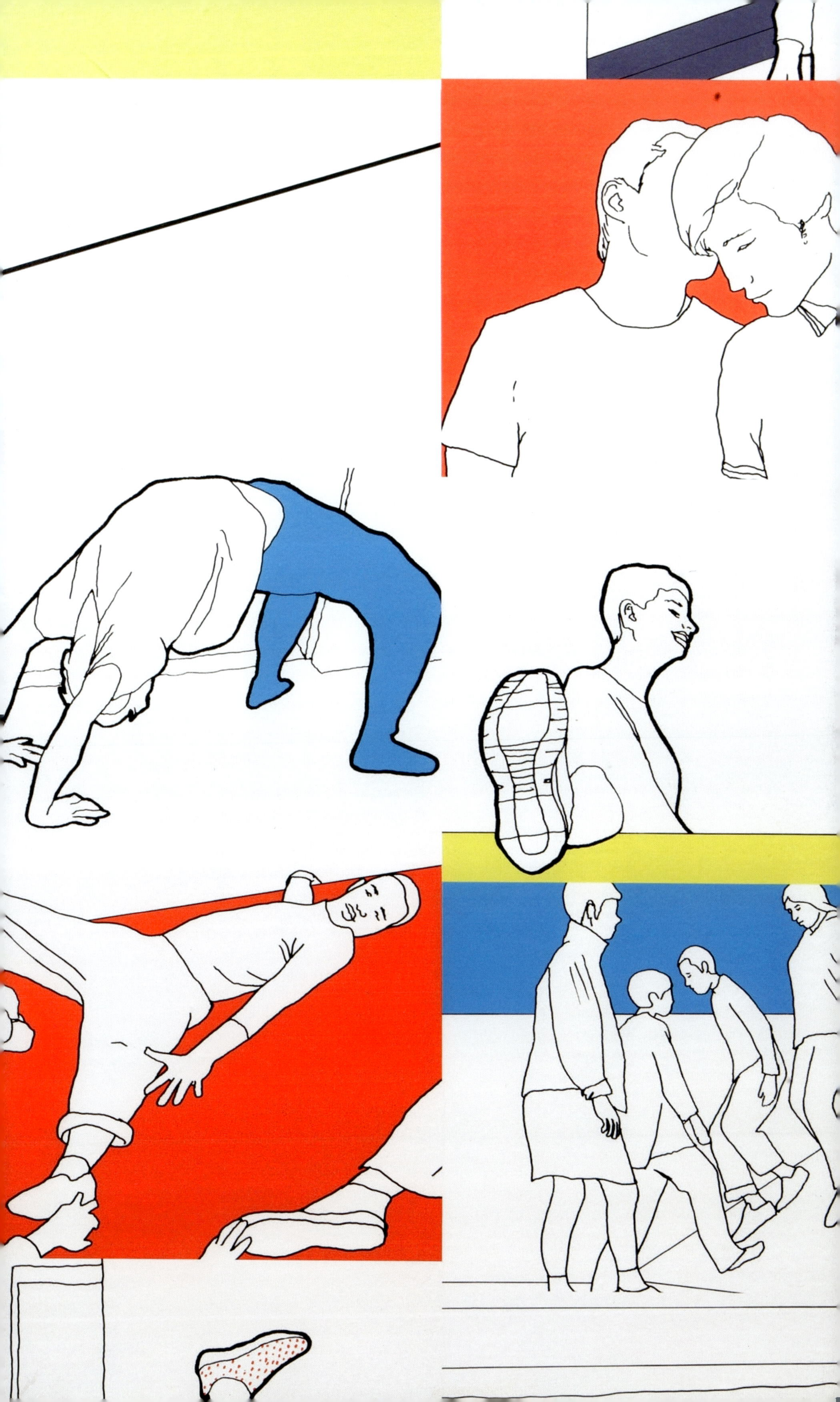

and the pictorial were considered outmoded, they were often cast as a return of strategies that had been surpassed by a more abstract approach to form or to content.[4] Of course, since black women had been prevented historically from creating images of themselves, the meanings of these representations, the right to which had been hard won, were necessarily new. Shouldn't we, all of us, then as now, want to see images that black women (or any other underrepresented identity) have made from their own point of view? Much like artists such as Claudette Johnson, Lubaina Himid and Sutapa Biswas, to name a few, Boyce, who picked up 'the worst possible media, at that particular moment', offered a template for future generations of artists, as well as works for viewers and critics of all backgrounds who remain hungry for such images.[5]

Rather than relying on the authority of oil on canvas, Boyce took on the more vulnerable medium of pastel on paper.[6] Nevertheless, many of these works command a life-sized or even larger scale, defying the traditional role of drawing, with its typically modest dimensions, as medium of draft or sketch. Works such as *She Ain't Holding Them Up, She's Holding on (Some English Rose)* (1986), *Missionary Position II* (1985) and *Big Womens' Talk* (1984) are some of the rich images upon which Boyce insisted, splendid in their boldly-coloured outlines, intense diagonal hatching and shading, use of complementary colours and proliferation of patterns where backgrounds merge with subjects' clothes. These works are also rich in content, with layered frames of reference to British-Caribbean diaspora cultures, family legacy, cultural and national identity and gender politics. Narratives of sexuality repressed and oppressed by norms and traditions are given consensual and nonconsensual manifestations. But even the solemn *Mr. close-friend-of-the-family pays a visit whilst everyone else is out* (1985, charcoal on paper), where the young woman is clearly being victimised, leaves the viewer with a sense of future overcoming. While her eyes emanate deep sadness and her face is expressionless and still, the figure of the teenager nevertheless stands tall and strong, even as the arm of the man, whose face is cropped, stretches out over the span of the decorative tiled background between them, his hand reaching to touch her. The title of the work is written around the top of the broad border framing the central event,

while the bottom is adorned by bouquets of human palms, blooming with threat. Of the vectors forming the drawing's grid, which appear stronger here and there, one strong vertical splits the length of the girl's head and torso – an armature reflecting how systematic gender and power dynamics undergird her existence. That the girl's intent gaze is aimed directly at the viewer turns the work from being a portrait of a specific woman to a calling for collective accountability, pushing what would otherwise be an atomised audience into their collective state as a society. Inevitable pleasure derives from the magic of the charcoal, where from one material so many different textures can be rendered. Nevertheless this pleasure positions the onlooker on the side of the perpetrator, since both stand to enjoy what the young woman has not consented to offer. We can read the relation of the text and image in several ways. If we are to understand the words literally, the image uncovers what the words hide. But we could also read 'Mr. close-friend-of-the-family' as an ironic statement, and watch the drawing declare in words what it depicts as an image. In any case it reminds us that Boyce's rendition of this specific story, which is also the story of many other bodies, is meant not solely for the enjoyment of the audience, but also as a political provocation. The choice of medium activates this productive clash.

Even when artists previously excluded from the long game of art were admitted onto the playing field, the establishment of art history and criticism was often unable to expand its outlook beyond a limited set of contemporaneous debates. As Kobena Mercer identifies, 'In the case of Jean-Michel Basquiat, his association with wildstyle graffiti (merely one of several iconographic sources) outpaced the understanding of the critical intelligence of his intertextual selection and combination of references that articulated his work as a subversion of modernist primitivism'.[7] The critical reception of a set of artists, including Basquiat and Lari Pittman specifically was, according to Mercer, 'sidelined' by the 'often doctrinaire positions in art criticism that were skeptical of the medium of painting.'[8] For Pittman – whom we can firmly classify as a painter – painting, together with all the specific drafting techniques he combines to form his tableaux, was in fact a strategic choice wielded in the larger field of art – as a political statement both through and about the grand historical

Above:
Sonia Boyce, *Plaited and Knotted*, 1995.
© Sonia Boyce.
Courtesy DACS/ Artimage

Below:
Sonia Boyce, *Big Womens' Talk*, 1984, pastel on paper, 122 × 122cm. © Sonia Boyce. Courtesy DACS/Artimage

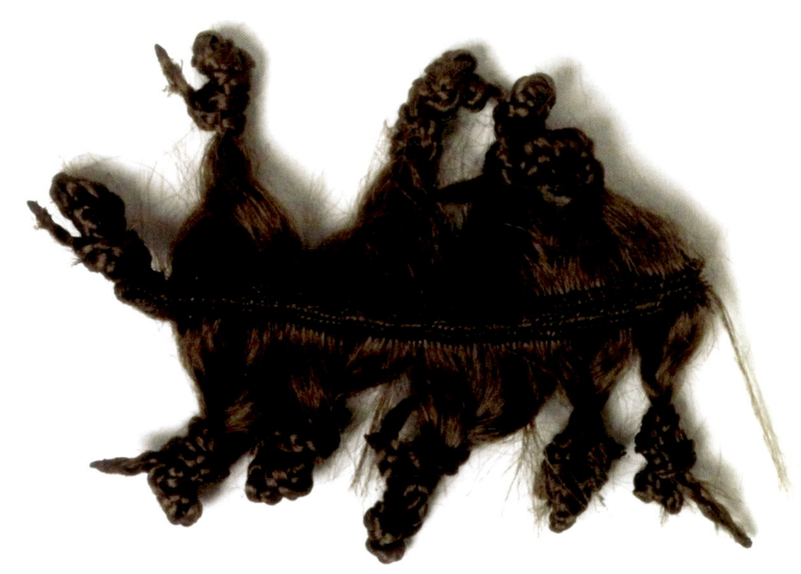

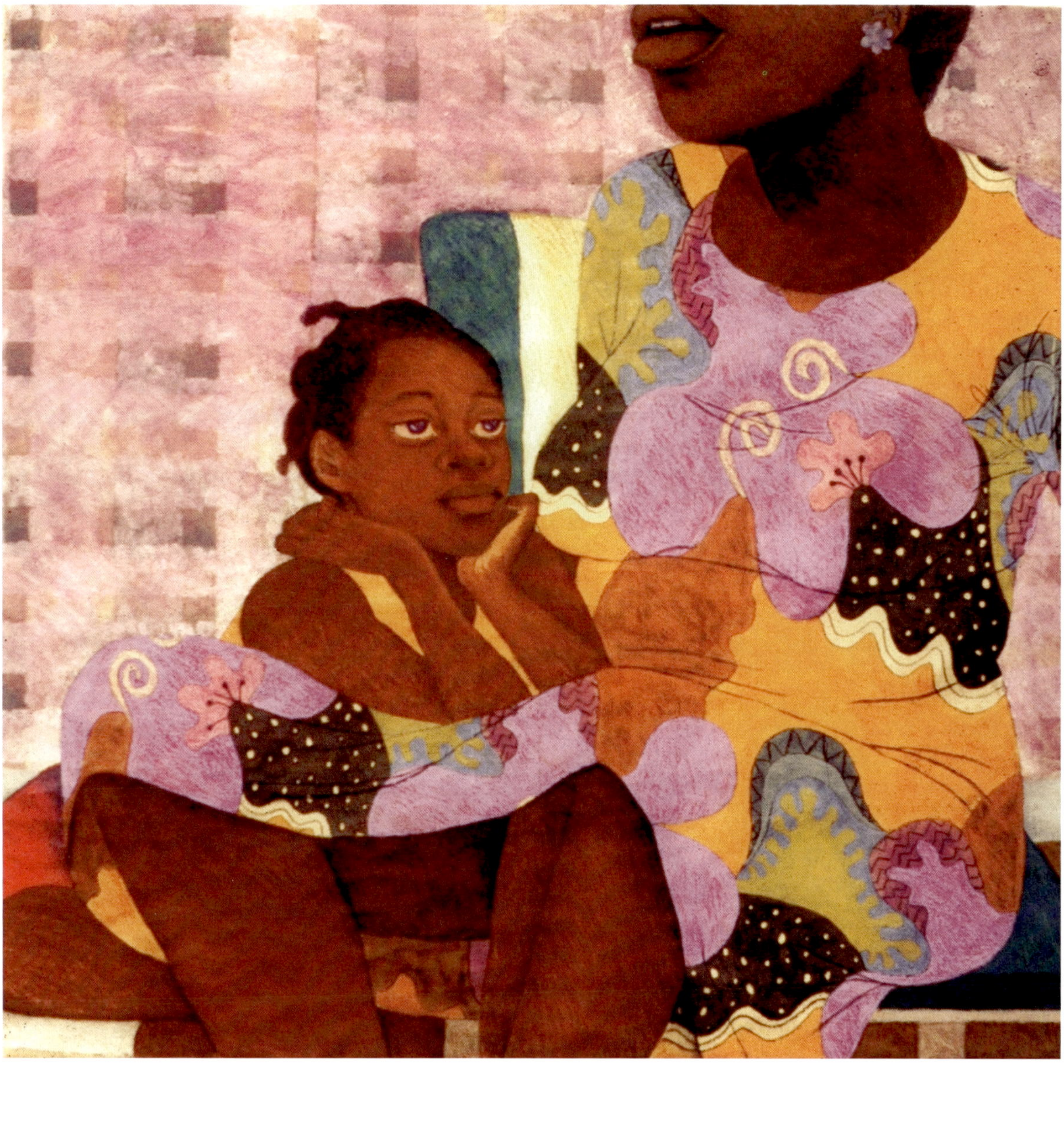

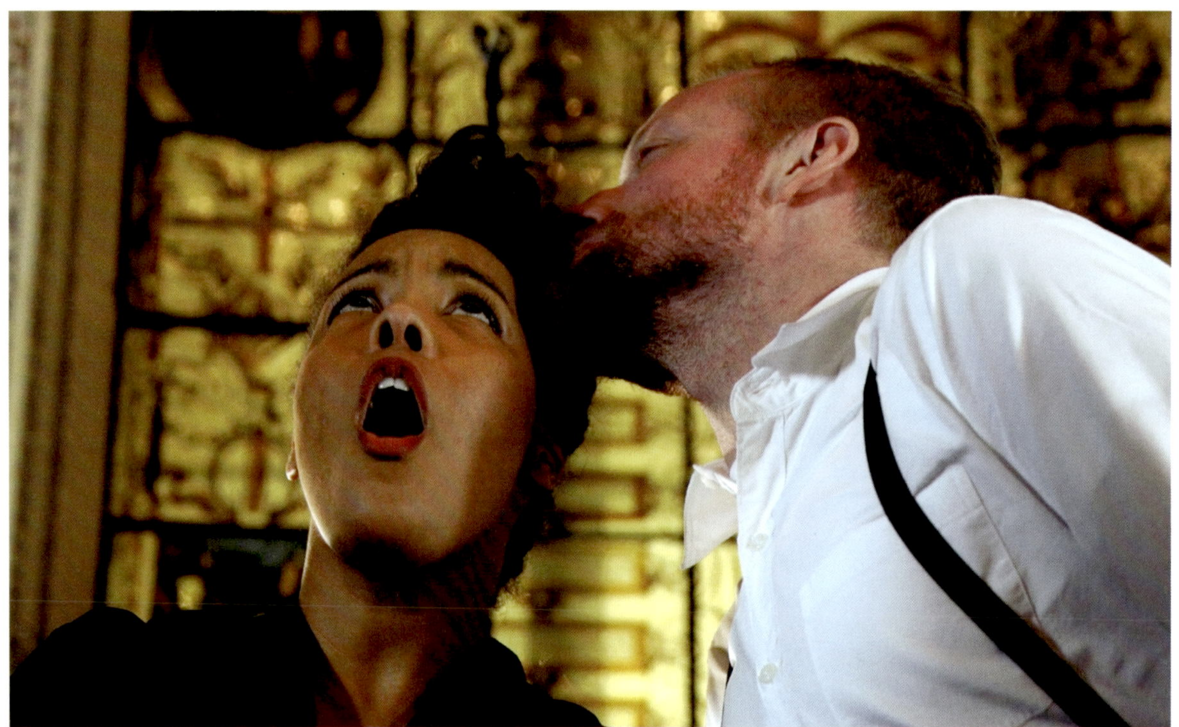

medium. 'Painting is queen', goes Pittman's motto, queering the medium's regal status and its inherited place as the primary mode of the fine arts, at least since Modernism. In this context, the introduction of the artist's identity within the work was not a return of the enlightenment-based notion of the creative genius. The reclaiming of painting, drawing and other traditional media in the 1980s followed the post-conceptual or 'pictures' practices that followed Conceptualism, both rejecting the notion of art as an expressive practice.[9] In this context, the insertion of one's identity perspective into the making of an artwork was not a means to express the self, but rather the use of identity as a model of a social position – an approach to art as a site for broader social discourse.

The bearing of the artist's identity on an artwork can be considered both in terms of the artist's status as the work's maker, and in terms of the content they bring to the work.[10] The introduction of psychoanalysis as a tool for critiquing Conceptual art's orthodoxies – an agenda declared in Mary Kelly's art – allowed for distinctions between the self, identity and subjectivity. The subject was no longer assumed to be the self-sovereign individual of rational choice. It was forged instead by the passage through the social structures of class relations, further stratified by race, gender, sexuality, ability, age and so forth. By the 1980s it was

clear that identity in art was constructed, strategic and discursive, not at all meant to represent an authentic state of being that the artist transmitted to their viewer. Rather, it was a re-presentation – there to be 'read' as a post-structuralist text. Like authorship, image, material, narrative and context, identity was an element in the work that was to be dissected for both its denotative and connotative aspects.

Do you want to touch? (1993–ongoing), a series of sculptures from the early 1990s made of hair or hair extensions and other materials, is a literal invitation, as the viewer is actually allowed to touch the work. The title references the disturbing license people take when touching, or asking to touch, other people's hair (or a pregnant women's belly, to name another example Boyce gives).[11] As Gilane Tawadros explains, these works 'develop some other familiar themes in Boyce's work: the relationship between private and public; the "spectacular" triangle between artist, viewer and object'.[12] In placing on a pedestal a combination of found materials and materials shorn from the human body, these twists on the 'assisted Readymade' underscore in retrospect the forgotten aspect of Duchamp's urinal. There, Duchamp not only displayed the artifice of art as a constructed value system, but also intimately related it to the human body and its need to dispose of the excesses of the

Sonia Boyce, *Exquisite Cacophony*, 2015, single-channel HD video, colour, sound, 35min. © Sonia Boyce. Courtesy DACS/Artimage

metabolic process. Several of Boyce's artistic strategies can be traced back to the cerebral core of the Duchampian legacy, which locates the meaning of the work not in the artist but rather in the viewer at the moment of reception.[13]

In rejecting what she identified as the Victor Burgin model of intention, where the artist presides over the artwork's meaning and anticipates viewer reception, Boyce later turned to facilitating situations between artists and makers from various fields, who are given general directions but no specific instructions.[14] In this larger body of collaborative performance works, Boyce establishes frameworks for live events, theater or video productions, setting up situations with unpredictable outcomes. In this respect her work is closer to the Adrian Piper model of Conceptualism, aimed as a catalyst for unprescribed viewer reaction. For the video installation *Exquisite Cacophony* (2015) Boyce paired the classically trained experimental vocalist Elaine Mitchener with the American rapper Astronautalis for an unrehearsed session, filmed at the Victoria and Albert Museum, where the two performers improvised to prompt-cards handed to them by the audience. The piece points to a split within the Conceptualist tradition between works that rely heavily for their interpretation on an outcome directed by artistic intention, and those that place emphasis on the plan, allowing the potential of meaning of the outcome to proliferate.[15]

Instead of classifying the work of Sonia Boyce through media, we have a gyrating constellation, where characteristic aspects of several genres or movements revolve around one another, although not in the combinations they did in their first iteration in history. In this way, Boyce's works break with prescribed perspectives on which ideological positions align with which artistic styles or practice typologies. In reorganising previously incompatible configurations of forms and content, Boyce opens the door for new configurations of politicised aesthetics.

1   This is clearly stated in the first page of Mary Kelly, *Post-Partum Document*, Berkeley: University of California Press, 1999. See also M. Kelly, *Imaging Desire*, Cambridge, MA: The MIT Press, 1996.
2   Sonia Boyce in conversation with Tim Marlow at Manchester Art Gallery, 'Sonia Boyce Objects of Obsession: Sonia Boyce in conversation with Tim Marlow', YouTube, 53min 56sec, available at https://www.youtube.com/watch?v=GJsXyZRP0MU (last accessed on 11 September 2019). An important contribution here is Amelia Jones, *Body Art/Performing the Subject*, Minneapolis: University of Minnesota Press, 1998.
3   David A. Bailey, Sonia Boyce and Ian Baucom (ed.), *Shades of Black: Assembling Black Arts in 1980s Britain*, Durham, NC: Duke University Press, 2005. See also Lubaina Himid, '"5 Black Women", "Black Woman Time Now" and "The Thin Black Line"', in Nick Aikens, Teresa Grandes, Nav Haq, Beatriz Herráez and Nataša Petrešin-Bachelez (ed.), *The Long 1980s: Constellations of Art, Politics and Identities: A Collection of Microhistories*, Antwerp: Valiz and L'internationale, 2018, pp.253-55.
4   Although this tendency was quite broad, often cited is: Hal Foster, Rosalind Krauss, Silvia Kolbowski, Miwon Kwon and Benjamin H.D. Buchloh, 'The Politics of the Signifier: A Conversation', *October*, vol. 66, Fall 1993, pp.3-27.
5   S. Boyce in conversation with T. Marlow, *op. cit.*
6   John Roberts, 'Sonia Boyce: In Conversation with John Roberts', *Third Text*, vol.1, no.1, 1987, pp.55-64.
7   Kobena Mercer, 'Where the Streets Have no Name: A Democracy of Multiple Public Spheres', in Helen Anne Molesworth (ed.). *This Will Have Been: Art, Love & Politics in the 1980s*, Chicago and New Haven: Museum of Contemporary Art Chicago and Yale University Press, 2012, p.137.
8   *Ibid.*, p.138.
9   See Douglas Crimp, 'Pictures', *October*, vol.8, Spring 1979, pp.75-88; Douglas Eklund, *The Pictures Generation, 1974-1984*, New York and New Haven: Metropolitan Museum of Art/Yale University Press, 2009.
10 See Michel Foucault, 'What is an Author?', *Language, Counter-Memory, Practice* (ed. Donald F. Bouchard and trans. D.F. Bouchard and Sherry Simon), Ithaca: Cornell University Press, 1977, pp.113-38.
11 Rebecca Fortnum, 'Sonia Boyce', *Contemporary British Women Artists: In Their Own Words*, London: I.B. Tauris, 2007, pp.112-19.
12 Gilane Tawadros, *Sonia Boyce: Speaking in Tongues*, London: Third Text Publications, 1997, p.8.
13 This has been identified by Rosalind Krauss in 'Sense and Sensibility: Reflection on Post '60s Sculpture', *Artforum*, vol. 12, no. 3, November 1973, pp.43-53.
14 R. Fortnum, *op. cit.* Also see Allison Thompson, 'Sonia Boyce and Crop Over', *Small Axe*, vol.13/2, no.29, June 2009, pp.148-63; Sophie Orlando (ed.), *Sonia Boyce: Thoughtful Disobedience*, Dijon: Les Presses du Réel, 2017.
15 For Boyce's collaborative work see: S. Orlando, *ibid.*

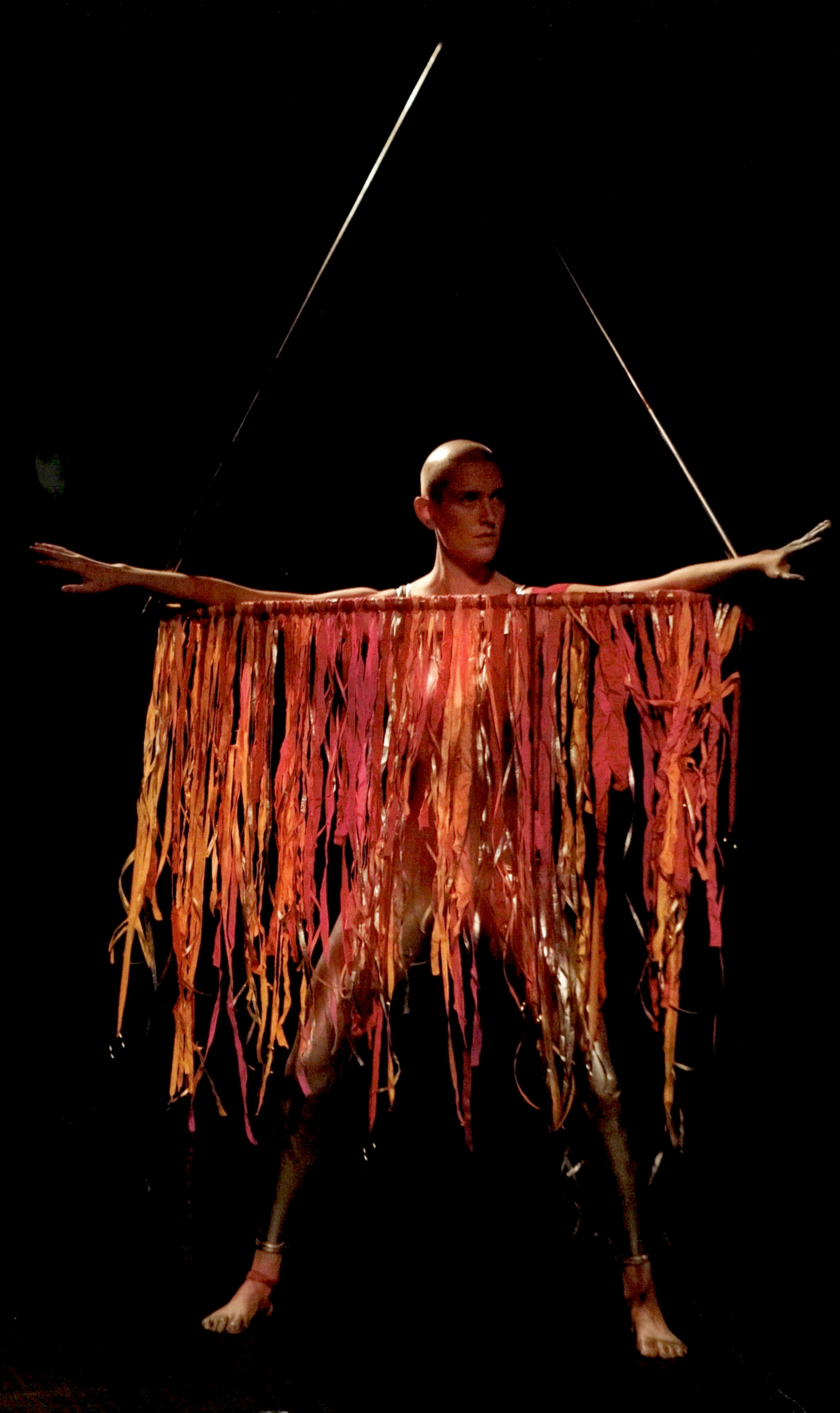

From Representation to Collaboration (and Vice Versa): Antagonisms in Sonia Boyce's Participatory Projects[1]

– Cayo Honorato

Cayo Honorato explores how questions of language, authorship, artistic autonomy and the performative are implicated in Sonia Boyce's turn towards participatory art.

From Representation to Collaboration

Different sources acknowledge a similar – conceptual and material – shift in the work of Sonia Boyce (b.1962) that has been taking place since the 1990s. Boyce's early figurative and semi-autobiographical works address issues of race and gender in the media and day-to-day life, notably through large pastel drawings and photographic collages. These critically intertwine the experience of black British women with the legacies of the British Empire. More recently, Boyce has focussed on collaborative and/or participatory inter-media projects. In these she brings people together to engage performatively through improvisation and exploratory gestures.[2] In this regard, her work has become less straightforwardly about identity politics and more (sometimes controversially) about notions of difference, intersectionality, appropriation and masquerading.

That shift, however, did not follow a linear path from determined position to open-ended practice, but instead involves two interwoven threads. The first concerns Boyce's move from conveying an explicitly political message – connected to civil rights struggles, particularly to do with black feminism – to experimenting with language. In *For You, Only You* (2007) and *Exquisite Cacophony* (2015), for example, she draws on the historical avant-garde, specifically Dada, and practices like scat singing. The second thread involves collaborative processes in which authorship and authority are negotiated through dialogue and interaction, a step away from earlier works in which Boyce confronted the viewer with predefined narratives. As an artist, she has become an 'anti-director', as is clear in *Paper Tiger Whisky Soap Theatre (Dada Nice)* (2016) and *We Move in Her Way* (2017).

Different politics are woven along these two threads. What the first loses in social engagement, it gains in assertion of artistic autonomy. What the second loses in 'authenticity', it gains in collective creativity among unrelated collaborators. Throughout this transition, however, Boyce's work has maintained a degree of continuity. For instance, as Boyce herself puts it, 'the performative element has always been there',[3] seen both in the early drawings, in which she staged herself as a central figure addressing the audience, and in the later works. The collaborative works maintain representational elements (wallpaper, film, installations – sometimes artworks themselves), which serve to further mediate the documentation of live performances, or the 'recouping [of] the remains of the situation', as Boyce has called it.[4] This element of continuity also applies to the role that 'collage' plays in the artist's work, from the flattened space of the early drawings to the editing and cutting of the recent films. 'I have always been collapsing a number of things together', says Boyce.[5]

Throughout Boyce's career, the question of 'blackness' has never disappeared. In relation to *For You, Only You*, a collaborative piece that probed the boundaries between sound art and classical music, Boyce comments that the composer and sound artist Mikhail Karikis, whom she invited to collaborate, 'was basically asking Alamire', the consort of singers under the direction of David Skinner, also invited, 'to be in the space of double consciousness'. The term 'double consciousness', coined by W.E.B. Du Bois, in this usage evokes Paul Gilroy's reference to individuals whose identity is divided, who can only see themselves 'through the eyes of others', as they strive to be 'both European and Black', 'inside and outside the West'.[6] Indeed, in a

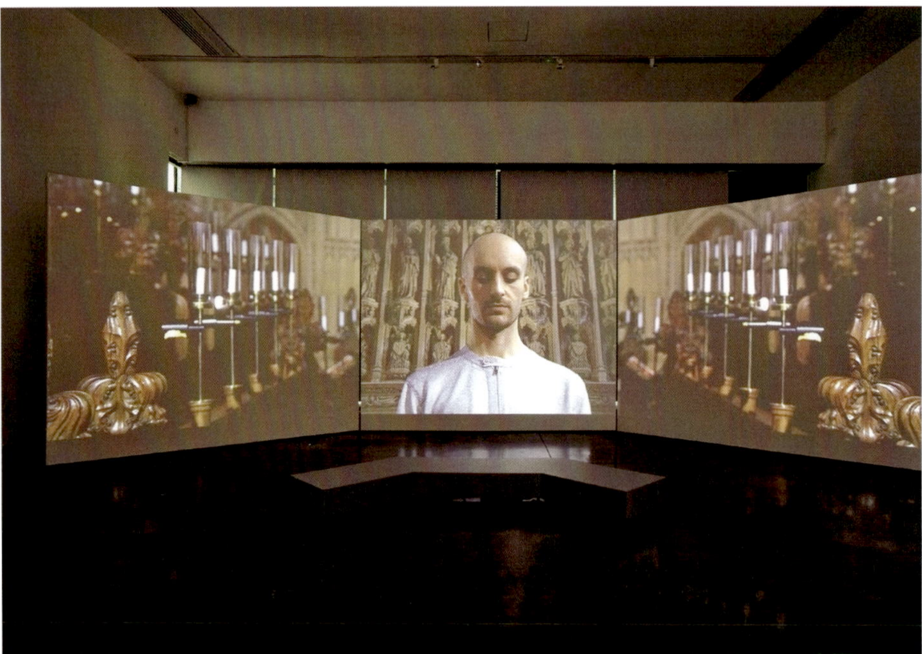

compelling text about some of the tropes in this work, Jean Fisher argued:

As 'meeting and conversation' between one (linguistically) incomplete self and others, antiphony in For You, Only You *speaks both to these hospitable forms of sociality and to the pathos of the diasporic subject, needing to negotiate a sense of belonging between displacement from the place of departure and cultural estrangement from the place of arrival, in which he or she must bear the mark of difference.*

Fisher further contends that the main trope of the work is 'chiasmus', which she defines as 'repetition and revision effected through the crossing of difference [...] a trope familiar to African and African diasporic hermeneutics and narrative convention [...] central to the practice of "signifying", which doesn't signify some *thing*, [...] but a manner of *doing*'.[7] In this sense the recent *Six Acts* (2018) is perhaps an eloquent summary of Boyce's entire trajectory hitherto. For instance, as performance artist Lasana Shabazz responds to a portrait of the renowned black Shakespearean actor Ira Aldridge, the piece juxtaposes collaborative de-individualisation (through the 'cross-dressing' of bodies and histories) with questions of representation and identity politics (particularly those of gender, race and sexuality).

There have, of course, been other shifts in Boyce's work, giving way to further,

different interpretations. Artist and art historian Eddie Chambers, for instance, recognises the 'shift' towards performance and installation as 'largely reflective of contemporary art practices of the 1990s'.[8] However, he mostly refers to Boyce as part and parcel of the 'Black Art' generation in the 1980s who, for the first time in Britain, decided to (positively) name their practices as 'Black'.[9] Art historian Sophie Orlando writes on the 'deep-seated changes' in Boyce's strategies post-1989 in favour of photography, installation and video. The author notes that these changes initially contested dominant artistic models in contemporary art, then governed by post-painterly Abstraction and Conceptual art,[10] followed by a 'change in' (or a questioning of) Boyce's own place of utterance and 'the constriction of her representations'.[11] This change took place just as identity politics was being deconstructed by postcolonial thinking and black cultural studies. Boyce begins to favour a collective body and memory, as well as a more intercultural and transnational subject.[12] To quote Orlando once again, the artist moved, 'From a criticism of representations within the canonical modernist history of art and of the postures of conceptual white feminists [...] to the constitution of critical tools capable of presenting and undoing the stereotype, from the place of utterance of the international mass culture of blackness'.[13]

This kind of change was elaborated by Stuart Hall in the late 1980s, in relation

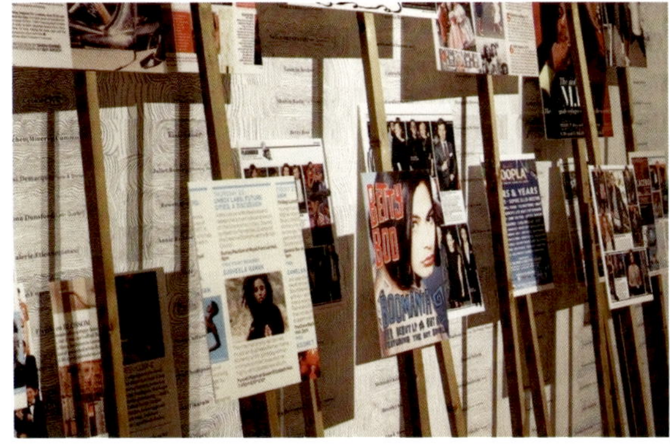

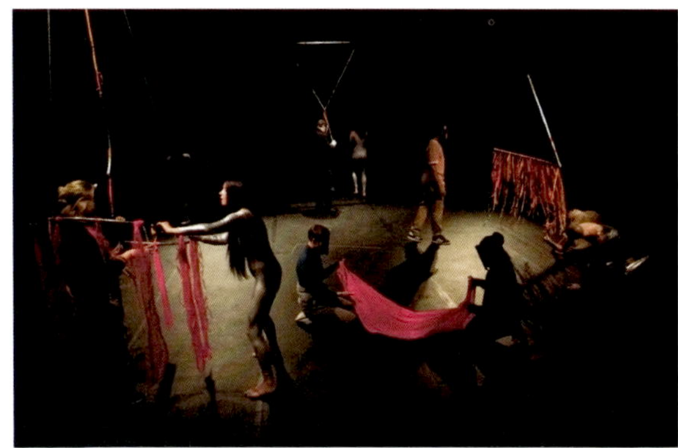

to a shift in black cultural politics: from 'black' as comprising a unifying identity to a 'new' phase in which the term refers to a non-essentialist 'ethnic' position. The latter, he writes, 'locates itself *inside* a continuous struggle and politics around black representation, but which then is able to open up a continuous critical discourse about themes, about the forms of representation, the subjects of representation, above all, the regimes of representation'.[14] This in turn effects a shift in the positionality of the spectator. In her discussion of *Three Legs Stuffed with Hair* (1995) – a triptych of photographs showing curly black hair emerging from stuffed tights – and its differences to Sarah

> ### Boyce appears to look for a combination between the aesthetic value of representation and the political value of collaboration.

Lucas' series *Bunny* (1997), Orlando reckons the 'Viewers are given the context in which identity-based racial and sexual representations are elaborated as well as the formal tools for deconstructing those representations'.[15] More specifically, the desire to constitute a collective place of utterance – from the handing over to the viewer in the *Clapping Wallpaper* (1994), through the openness to participation in *The Audition* (1997), to the constitution of a collective archive in the *Devotional Series* (1999–2004) – led Boyce to assume a non-essentialist 'black' *manner of doing* by which she progressively embraces collaborative projects. Additionally, considering the increasingly 'dynamic relation' that Boyce 'ushers in with the spectator', Orlando finally associates this

change with relational aesthetics in the 2000s.[16]

From Collaboration to Representation
With relation to works that mobilise people, I would like to briefly recall a broader debate, which includes and surpasses relational aesthetics, about 'dialogical aesthetics', socially engaged art and the 'educational turn'.[17] Grant Kester's self-described 'dialogical aesthetics' works depend on conversation in so far as they can only be developed in consultation with participants.[18] This idea is arguably antithetical to dominant beliefs in art criticism that typically praise individual authorship and traditionally respond to finished objects. These works claim a paradigm shift; a definition of aesthetic experience that is intersubjective and durational rather than self-determined and immediate. Kester contends that, in these works, the locus of judgment should reside in the condition and character of dialogical exchanges themselves, whose effects he tends to view positively. For him, the very act of participating in these exchanges makes us 'better able to engage in discursive encounters and decision-making processes in the future'.[19] This shift from physical objects to an intersubjective space has notably been objected to by Claire Bishop, for whom its correlative authorial renunciation would explain, to some degree, why socially engaged art has been largely exempt from art criticism, as far as throughout this process, 'disruptive *specificity*' gives way to 'a *generalized* set of moral precepts'.[20]

In any case, Boyce's work – which is neither disruptive nor ameliorative – explores a third way that stands outside of these controversies. While Bishop identifies a divide between the nonbelievers (aesthetes who reject social artworks as shallow and

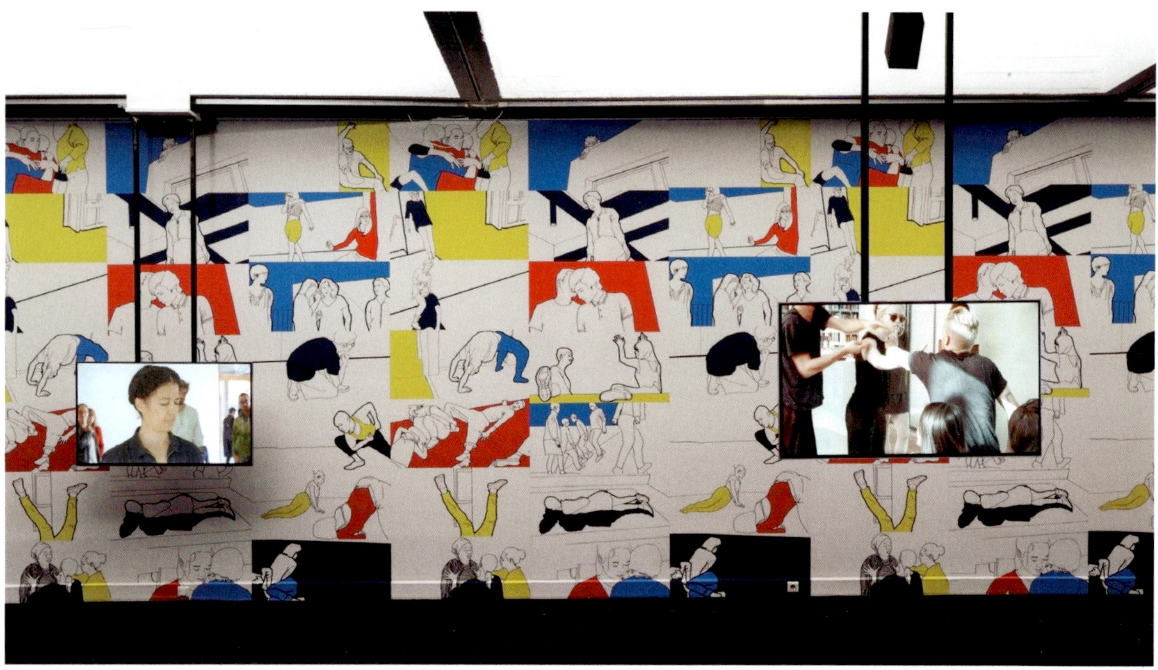

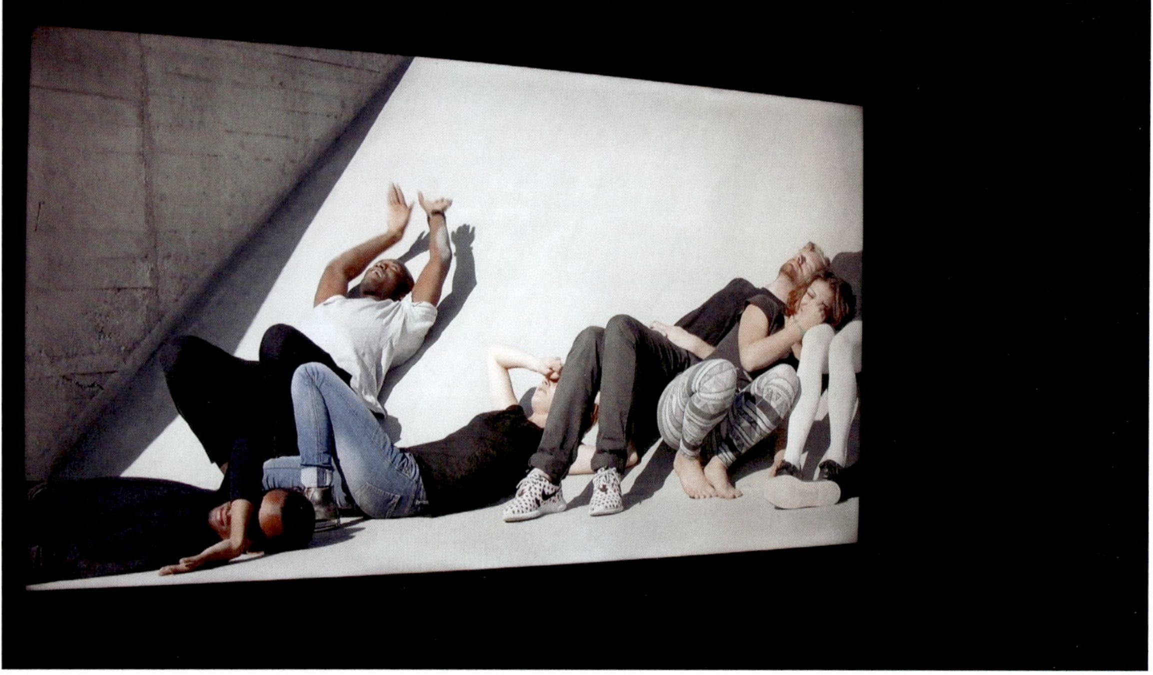

misguided) and the believers (activists who reject aesthetic questions as synonymous with the market and neoliberalism), Boyce appears to look for a combination between the aesthetic value of representation and the political value of collaboration. The artist says that she 'work[s] with people' and that she is 'fascinated by what people do when they come together'.[21] Yet, this cannot be taken as her final say.

Art historian and curator Allison Thompson comments on the artist's identification as *voyeur* who 'becomes excited by the prospect of observing how participants negotiate terrains, architecture, obstacles, relationships in the act of asserting their own agency and voice'.[22] In less appreciative terms, the catalogue for the 56th Venice Biennale asserts that 'Sonia Boyce's approach to making art is appropriative, [...] because she uses other people. She disguises herself through other people's efforts in what she likes to call "unrehearsed", "improvised", and "spontaneous" collaborations'.[23] Adopting a more balanced view, curator Marie-Anne McQuay argues: 'There is a pragmatic and also deeply respective dynamic of give

Above and below:
Sonia Boyce, *Paper Tiger Whisky Soap Theatre (Dada Nice)*, 2016, multi-channel, video, colour, sound, wallpaper. Installation view, Villa Arson, Nice, 2016. Photograph: Jean Brasille. Courtesy the artist

and take operating within Boyce's practice that also allows her to maintain a crucial sense of autonomy.'[24] The ambivalences of collaboration – in some Schillerian terms, between making people the end of an artwork, and using people as its material – are here made apparent.

At this point, one could ask how much of the artist's power (in deciding what is seen, under which regime of representation) is unquestioned in these collaborations. 'It's not an easy thing to do so [producing work with other people], because contrary to the discussions by critics like [Nicolas] Bourriaud, conviviality is not automatic when working in this way. [...] Antagonisms sit underneath most of my interactions in these participatory encounters',[25] notes Boyce. Indeed, in some of her works she appears to deliberately play power games with participants; in *We Move in Her Way* (2017) either 'she' dictates our movements, or we obstruct 'hers'.[26] On a project called *The Future is Social* (2011) developed with students at University of the Arts London, where Boyce has been a professor since 2014, she writes: 'we had constant battles amongst the contributors about a mistrust of being documented. Documenting the process was treated like it was an act of theft, as if participants' sense of agency and distinct identity would get lost.'[27] The artist doesn't seem committed to undertaking the 'burden of representation',[28] in the sense of standing up for their contributors. Referring to the production of *Like Love* (2009–10), curator Zoë Shearman pointed out that 'Boyce didn't attempt to speak for the others, but rather to interpret them'.[29] While loosely defined, 'interpretation' could here refer to a sense of autonomy – as the license to watch, use and take from others.

Similarly, Boyce doesn't seem committed to producing dematerialised projects that 'carry on the modernist call to blur art and life'.[30] It is curious that the antagonism mentioned above revolves around the ownership of representation, in the sense of re-presentation (*Darstellung*), which Boyce dismisses as 'a room full of competing egos'.[31] As I said before, representational elements will always re-mediate the material generated through collaborative performances, in a process she calls (perhaps euphemistically) 'recouping the remains of the situation'. Boyce certainly spends a lot of time beforehand, 'locating the participants and then setting out a basic framework that everyone can work towards'.[32] In relation to *Like Love*, Shearman understands that it is through this process 'that she construct[s] the framework of an intermediary visual language to which she, and they [her collaborators], could contribute'.[33] According to Boyce: 'The drawings [as that intermediary language in *Like Love*] are a mixture of the participants' marks, my marks, and the interviewees' statements.'[34] Such a framework can also be achieved through collaboration. In *For You, Only You*, scores by Josquin Desprez – introduced by Skinner and then rewritten by Karikis to include the thirteen beats per bar – became the 'structure' through which Alamire and Karikis were able to find a 'tune' in common – 'something they were familiar with, but in an unfamiliar way'.[35] In this regard, Boyce thinks her role is 'to translate and shape the documentation into a discernible art work'.[36] According to McQuay, the material generated by participants is subsequently 'absorbed into her visual vocabulary and distanced from context through various aestheticizing effects'. In other words, '[...] there is still very much a "Sonia Boyce aesthetic", a singular voice that can also comfortably accommodate many positions'.[37]

While making use of representation, i.e., while re-actualising documentation into another artwork, the artist regains control (and final authorship) over the open-endedness of collaboration, guiding what shape collaboration will take, even when other artists are involved. While the value of representation is vulnerable to questions – of whether it is in fact possible to re-present, portray or depict shared experience in collective work – representation of collaborative performance nevertheless challenges the importance of immediacy and addresses the work to a wider audience than those present at the live event. The gap between the original performance (collaboration) and the final installation (representation) is sometimes seen as a gap between initial participants and future viewers. In *We Move in Her Way*, for instance, journalist Katie McCabe complains that, 'Essentially, it's a film of a performance that's already happened. [...] We cannot feel the electricity and raw discomfort of audience participation. [...] the remains feel a little bare boned'.[38] Similarly, for writer and editor Liese Van der Watt, 'The audience [of the exhibition] remains mostly unmoved, passive, and excluded from the original context and what may

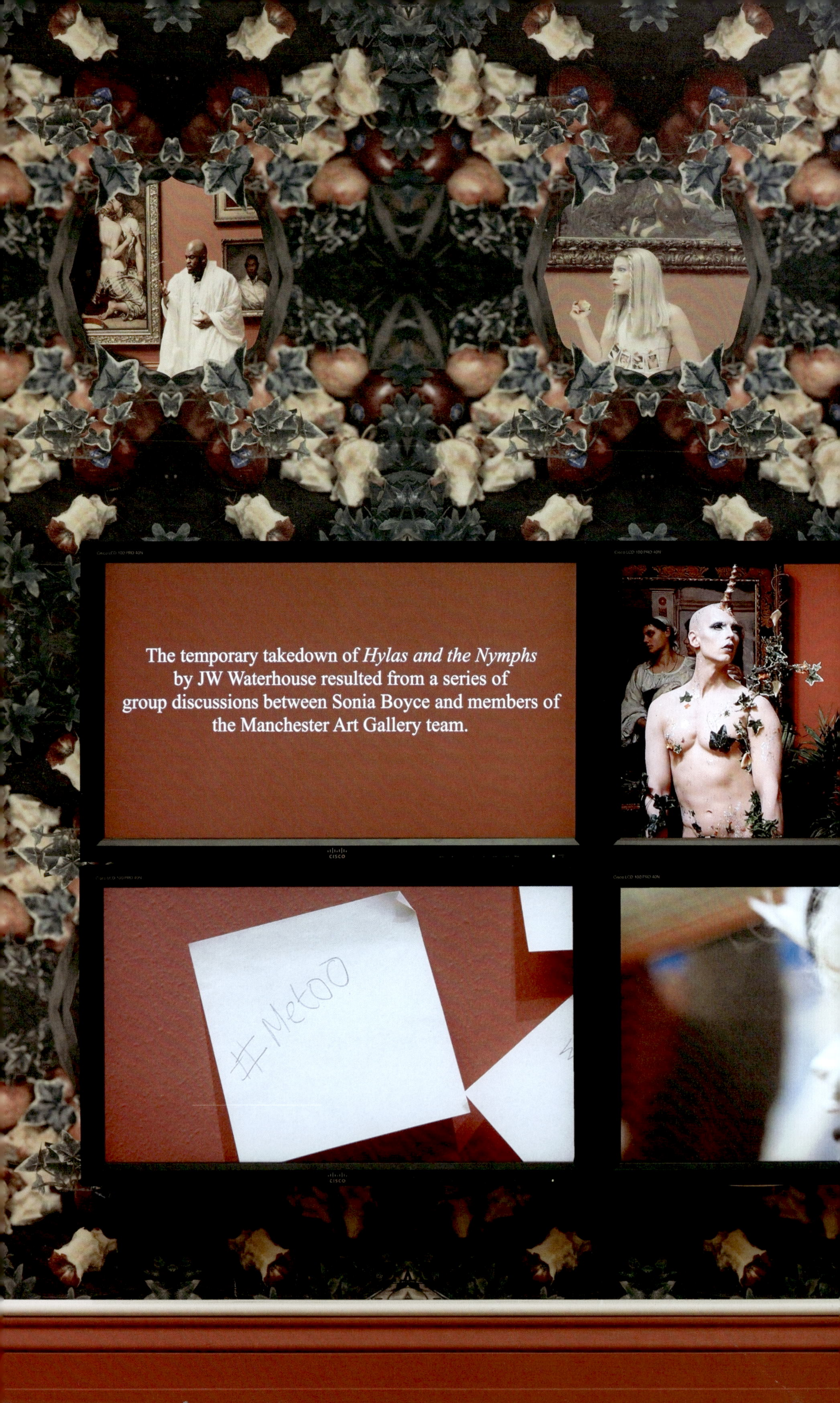

The temporary takedown of *Hylas and the Nymphs*
by JW Waterhouse resulted from a series of
group discussions between Sonia Boyce and members of
the Manchester Art Gallery team.
#MeToo

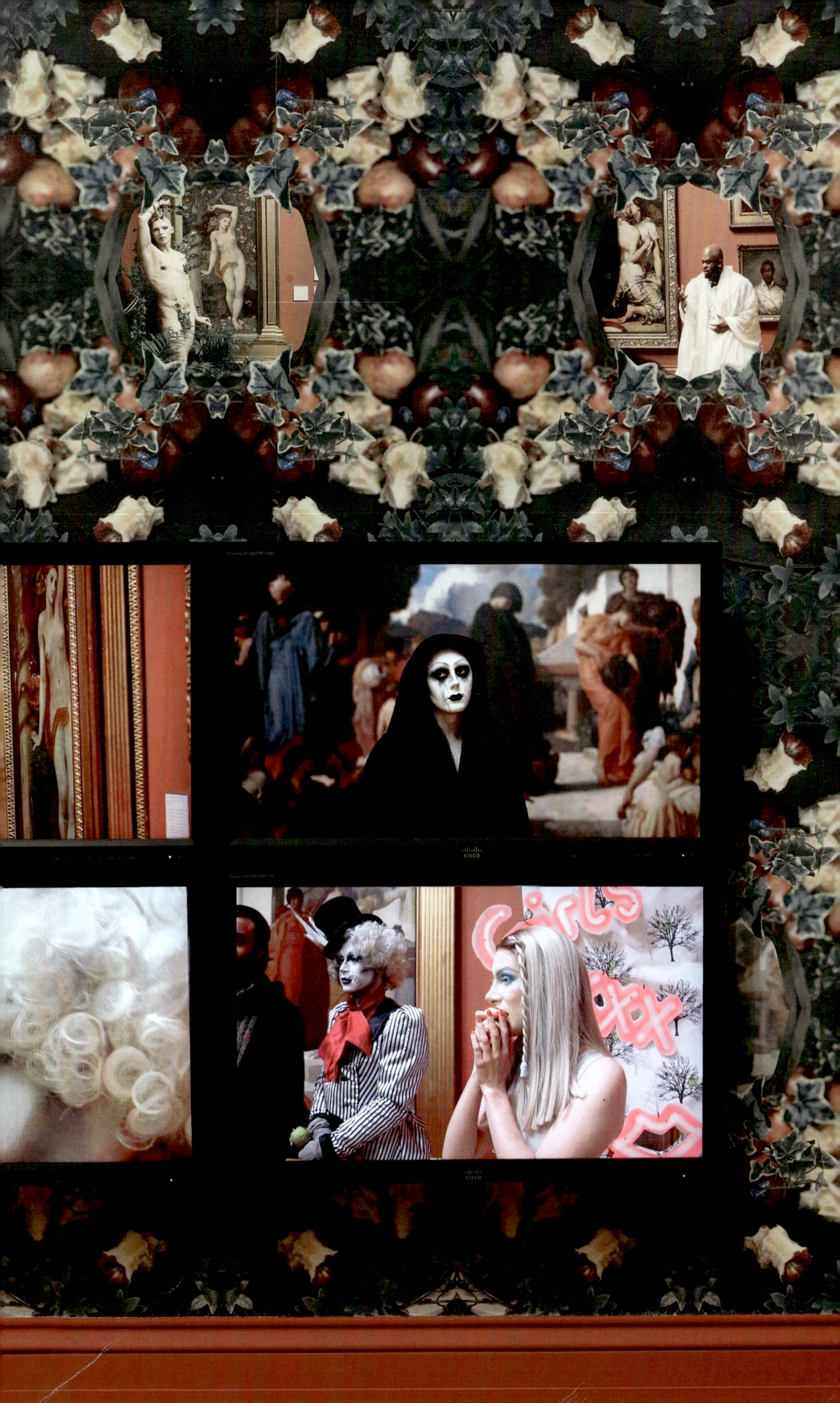

have been an energizing and boundary-pushing experience. [...] The remnants of the performance used in the final solo art work feel inaccessible, just too distant to be recouped in a meaningful way'.[39]

These quotes contrast with those of critics who consider representation in Boyce's work as *resulting from* collaboration or renegotiation, and *consisting of* inter-subjective exchanges. They raise the question of whether 're-couping the remains' – reflecting on collaboration, translating document-ation – is a collaborative, dialogical or relational process. They clearly state that three very different moments – collaboration, representation and reception – are often conflated. Indeed, it seems either that repre-sentation does not satisfy their demands for immediacy (in the sense of completeness or proximity), or that it fails to be of interest to those outside the immediate collaborative experience. Either way, it is seen as a poor surrogate.

The demand for immediacy, however, and the expectation that the final artwork should make the performance 'present' again are in fact mistaken. The gap McCabe and Van der Watt identify between performance and representation can prevent us from overlooking the fact that Boyce is the editor of the collaborative practice, not just its 'anti-director', as well as the fact that control over the shape of collaboration implies a control over the third, important moment: reception. If on the one hand, representation allows collaboration to be differently addressed to future viewers, on the other, it postulates the artist as a special viewer and, arguably, that reception can by extension be integrated into the artwork.

Take, for instance, the media storm around the temporary removal of J.W. Waterhouse's *Hylas and the Nymphs* (1896) – one of the *Six Acts* – from the walls of Manchester Art Gallery. As the exhibition leaflet has it: 'All the conversations, actions and responses which have come about could be described as part of the work'.[40] The viewer's position, then, can be seen as sublated by the artist's. Certainly Boyce's work, and the controversies around it, set out a kind of institutional self-learning process within the gallery, in conversation with its audiences. [41] It is also true, however, that the prevailing media response to this work involved misrepresentation.[42] This situation demonstrates not only that a representation is not a finished object, but also that (counter)publics can exert on an artwork unexpected sense of agency in ways that cannot be controlled – neither by the artwork itself nor by the museum that houses it.

1 I would like to thank Natasha Howes, Senior Curator at Manchester Art Gallery and Susan Skingle, Assistant Librarian at the Institute of International Visual Arts for their kindness in providing time and institutional resources. I also have to acknowledge the support I received from Brazil's Co-ordination for the Improvement of Higher Education Personnel (CAPES) during my stay in London through the Visiting Professors programme.

2 See, for example, Anna Coatman, 'Sonia Boyce: "If We Can Go to Mars, We Can Send More Kids to Art School", *RA Magazine*, 28 July 2017, available at https://www.royalacademy.org.uk/article/as-i-see-it-sonia-boyce (last accessed on 11 September 2019); Clare Gannaway, 'Interview: Sonia Boyce at Manchester Art Gallery, her first retrospective', *Artimage*, 5 March 2018, available at https://www.artimage.org.uk/news/2018/sonia-boyce-at-manchester-art-gallery-her-first-retrospective/ (last accessed on 11 September 2019); 'Sonia Boyce: We move in her way', press release, Institute for Contemporary Arts, London, 1 February–16 April 2017, available at https://archive.ica.art/whats-on/sonia-boyce-we-move-her-way (last accessed on 11 September 2019); Jennifer Higgie, 'Sonia Boyce: 30 Years of Art and Activism', *Frieze*, 29 May 2018, available at https://frieze.com/article/sonia-boyce-30-years-art-and-activism (last accessed on 11 September 2019); Natasha Stallard, 'The Female Artist Who Helped Define the British Black Arts Movement', *AnOther*, 6 April 2018, available at https://www.anothermag.com/art-photography/10704/the-female-artist-who-helped-define-the-british-black-arts-movement (last accessed on 11 September 2019).

3 Sonia Boyce quoted in A. Coatman, 'Sonia Boyce', *op cit*.

4 See Zoë Shearman, 'Desiring-Machines', in S. Boyce (ed.), *Like Love*, Berlin: The Green Box, 2010, p.70.

5 S. Boyce in conversation with Tim Marlow, 'Sonia Boyce RA: Objects of Obsession', Manchester Art Gallery, 8 March 2018, available at https://www.youtube.com/watch?v=GJsXyZRP0MU (last accessed on 11 September 2019).

6 *Ibid*. See W.E.B. Du Bois in his book *The Souls of Black Folk* (1903) and Paul Gilroy in his book *The Black Atlantic* (1993).

7 Jean Fisher, 'For You, Only You: The Return of the Troubadour', in Sonia Boyce, *For You, Only You: A Project by Sonia Boyce*, Oxford: University of Oxford, Ruskin School of Drawing and Fine Art, 2007, pp.42–51. Emphasis original.

8 Eddie Chambers, *Black Artists in British Art: A History since the 1950s*, London and New York: I.B. Tauris & Co, 2014, p.142.

9 *Ibid*., pp.1 and 105.

Sonia Boyce, *Six Acts*, 2018, wallpaper, six-screen video, colour, sound, 15min. Installation view, Manchester Art Gallery, 2018. Photograph: Michael Pollard. Courtesy the artist and Manchester Art Gallery

10   S. Orlando, 'Sonia Boyce: Post-1989 Art Strategies', *Critique d'art*, no.43, Autumn 2014, available at http://journals.openedition.org/critiquedart/15362 (last accessed on 11 September 2019). S. Orlando, *British Black Art: Debates on Western Art History*, Paris: Dis Voir, 2016, pp.76-88.

11   S. Orlando, 'Sonia Boyce', *op. cit.*

12   See Paul Gilroy, *The Black Atlantic: Modernity and Double Consciousness*, London and New York: Verso, 1993; Stuart Hall, 'New Ethnicities', in David Morley and Kuan-Hsing Chen (ed.), *Stuart Hall: Critical Dialogues in Cultural Studies*, London and New York: Routledge, 1996, pp.441-49; Kobena Mercer, 'Ethnicity and Internationally', *Third Text*, vol.13, no.49, 1999, pp.51-62, available at http://dx.doi.org/10.1080/09528829908576822 (last accessed on 11 September 2019).

13   S. Orlando, 'Sonia Boyce', *op. cit.*

14   S. Hall, 'New Ethnicities', *op. cit.*, p.448. Emphasis original.

15   S. Orlando, *British Black Art*, *op. cit.*, p.87.

16   S. Orlando, 'Sonia Boyce', *op. cit.*

17   See an overview of these issues in David M. Bell, 'The Politics of Participatory Art', *Political Studies Review*, May 2015, available at https://doi.org/10.1111/1478-9302.12089 (last accessed on 11 September 2019). In this paper, the author reviews later works of G. Kester and Claire Bishop: *The One and the Many: Contemporary Collaborative Art in a Global Context*, Durham, NC: Duke University Press, 2011 and *Artificial Hells: Participatory Art and the Politics of Spectatorship*, London: Verso, 2012, respectively.

18   G. Kester, 'Conversation Pieces: The Role of Dialogue in Socially-Engaged Art (2003)', in Zoya Kocur and Simon Leung (ed.), *Theory in Contemporary Art Since 1985*, Chichester, WS: Wiley-Blackwell, 2012, pp.153-65.

19   *Ibid.*, p.158.

20   C. Bishop, 'The Social Turn: Collaboration and Its Discontents', *Artforum*, vol.44, no.6, February 2006, p.181. Emphasis original.

21   S. Boyce quoted in Natasha Stallard, 'The Female Artist Who Helped Define the British Black Arts Movement', *AnOther*, April 2018, available at https://www.anothermag.com/art-photography/10704/the-female-artist-who-helped-define-the-british-black-arts-movement (last accessed on 11 September 2019).

22   Allison Thompson, 'Matter Out of Place: Collaborative Performance in the Work of Sonia Boyce', in S. Orlando (ed.), *Sonia Boyce: Thoughtful Disobedience*, Dijon: Les Presses du Réel, 2017, p.83.

23   Okwui Enwezor (ed.), *All the World's Futures* (exh. cat.), Venice: Marsilio Editori, 2015, pp.560-61.

24   Marie-Anne McQuay, 'Like Love, the First Four Chapters', in S. Boyce (ed.), *Like Love*, *op. cit.*, p.61.

25   S. Boyce quoted in S. Orlando, 'Encounters: Sonia Boyce & Sophie Orlando', in S. Orlando (ed.), *Sonia Boyce: Thoughtful Disobedience*, *op. cit.*, p.126.

26   ICA, 'Sonia Boyce: We move in her way', available at https://archive.ica.art/whats-on/sonia-boyce-we-move-her-way (last accessed on 11 September 2019).

27   S. Boyce quoted in S. Orlando, 'Encounters: Sonia Boyce & Sophie Orlando', *op. cit.*, p.126.

28   See K. Mercer, 'Black Art and the Burden of Representation', in *Welcome to the Jungle: New Positions in Black Cultural Studies*, New York and London: Routledge, 1994, pp.233-58.

29   Z. Shearman, 'Desiring-Machines', *op. cit.*, p.69.

30   C. Bishop, 'The Social Turn', *op. cit.*

31   S. Boyce quoted in S. Orlando, 'Encounters: Sonia Boyce & Sophie Orlando', *op. cit.*

32   S. Boyce, 'The Uncertainty of Signs', in S. Boyce (ed.), *Like Love*, *op. cit.*, p.35.

33   Z. Shearman, 'Desiring-Machines', *op. cit.*, p.69.

34   S. Boyce, 'The Uncertainty of Signs', *op. cit.*, p.33.

35   S. Boyce quoted in 'Sonia Boyce and Mikhail Karikis with Tessa Jackson Discussing *For You, Only You*', *Scat: Sound and Collaboration* (exhibition leaflet), London, Rivington Place, 2013, p.17.

36   S. Boyce quoted in S. Orlando, 'Encounters: Sonia Boyce & Sophie Orlando', *op. cit.*, p.128.

37   M. McQuay, *op. cit.*, p.59.

38   Katie McCabe, 'Sonia Boyce: We Move in Her Way', *TimeOut*, February 2017, available at https://www.timeout.com/london/art/sonia-boyce-we-move-in-her-way (last accessed on 11 September 2019).

39   Liese Van der Watt, 'Recouping the remains', *C&*, May 2017, available at https://www.contemporaryand.com/magazines/recouping-the-remains/ (last accessed on 11 September 2019).

40   *Sonia Boyce* (exhibition leaflet), Manchester Art Gallery, Manchester, 2018.

41   Under the title 'Whose Power on Display?', Manchester Art Gallery carried out a series of public discussions and consultations, as it planned to start changing in 2020 some of its displays.

42   In January 2018, as part of a newly commissioned artwork for her mid-career retrospective at the Manchester Art Gallery, Boyce decided with participants and gallery staff to temporarily remove Waterhouse's painting off the gallery walls to generate discussion about gender representation in the permanent collection displays. Many critics and members of the public accused the artist of censorship and engaging in a publicity stunt, mostly assuming the removal was definitive. See, for instance, Charlotte Higgins, '"The vitriol was really unhealthy": artist Sonia Boyce on the row over taking down Hylas and the Nymphs', *The Guardian*, 19 March 2018, available at https://www.theguardian.com/artanddesign/2018/mar/19/hylas-nymphs-manchester-art-gallery-sonia-boyce-interview (last accessed on 19 November 2019).

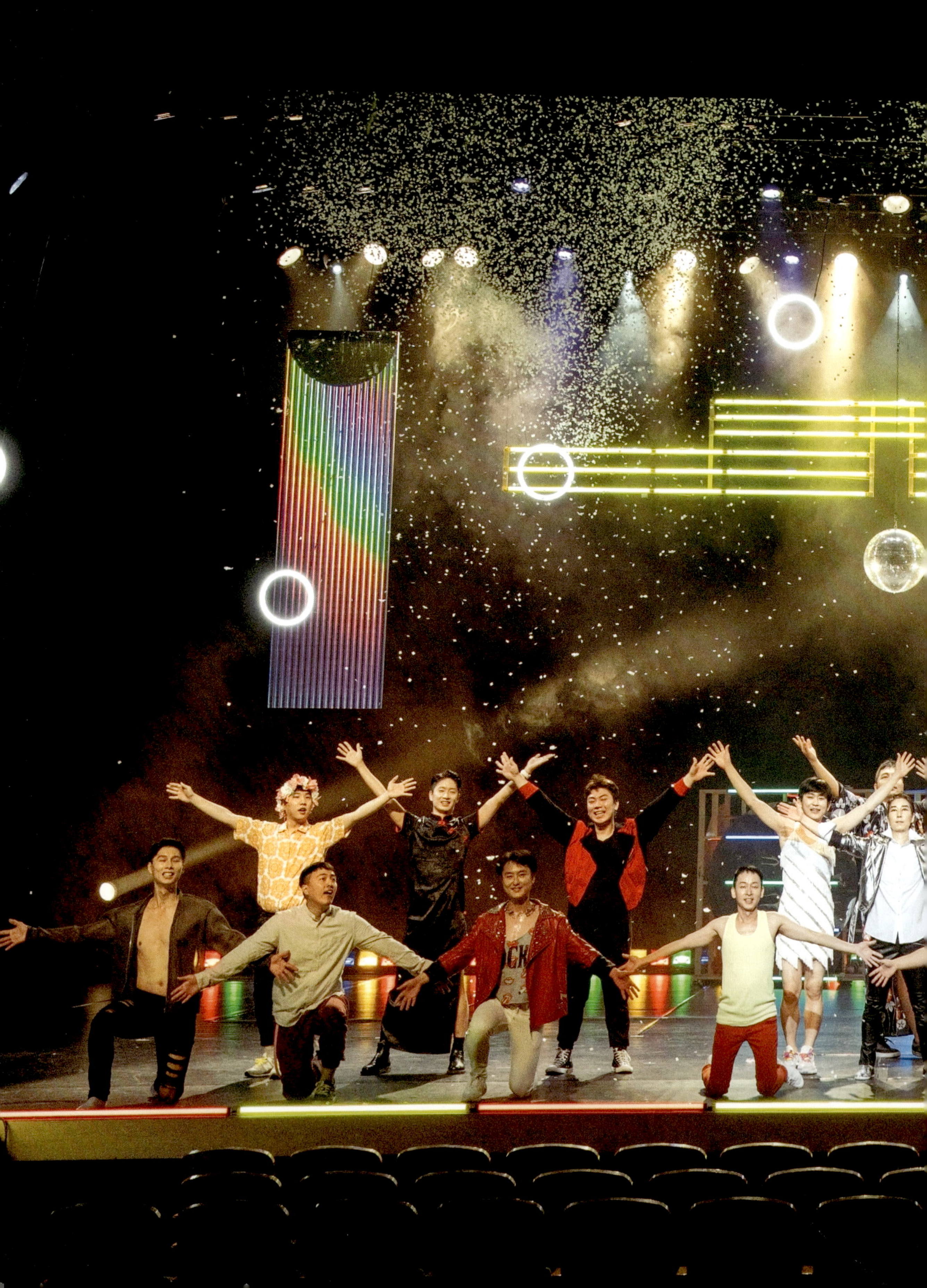

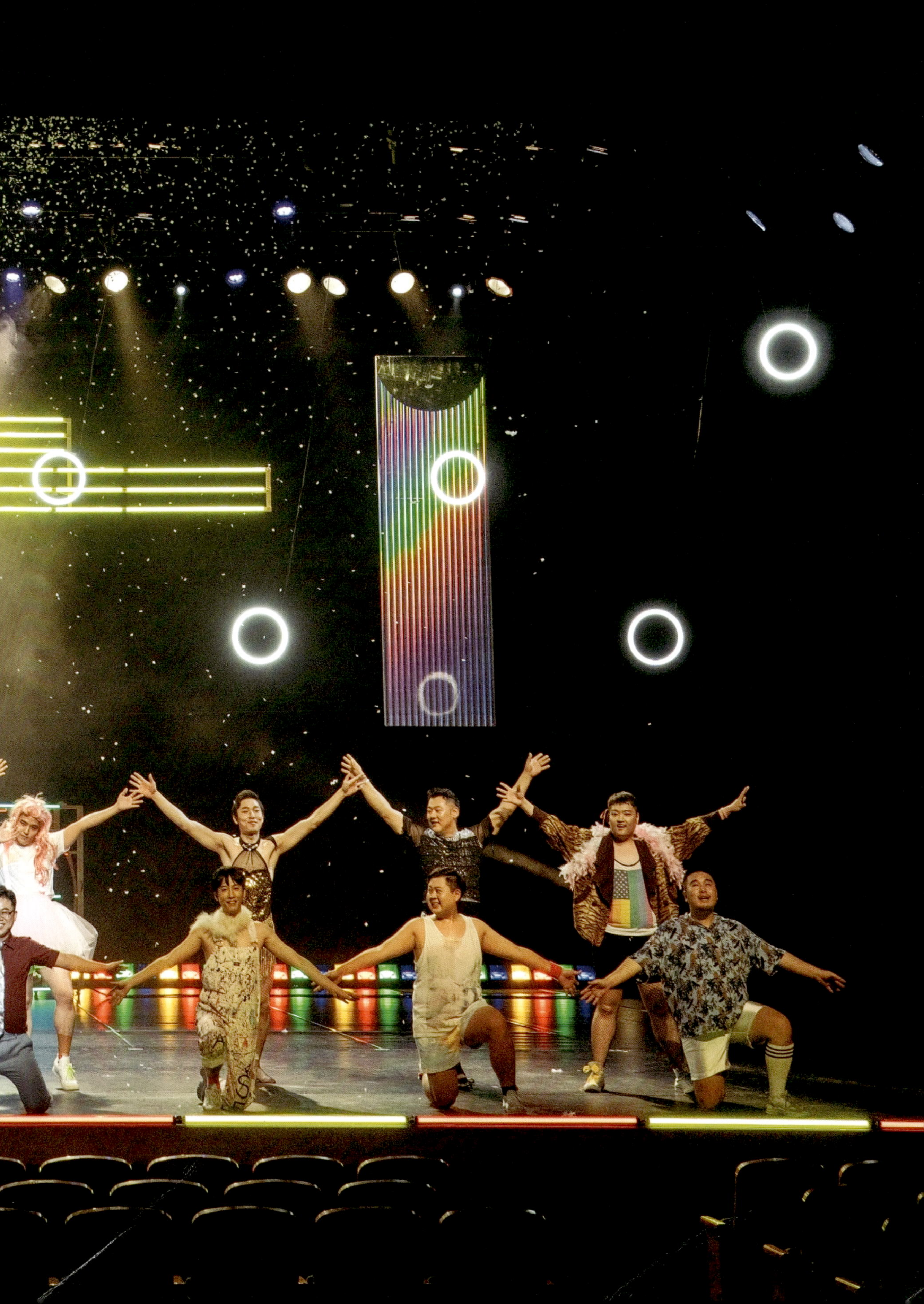

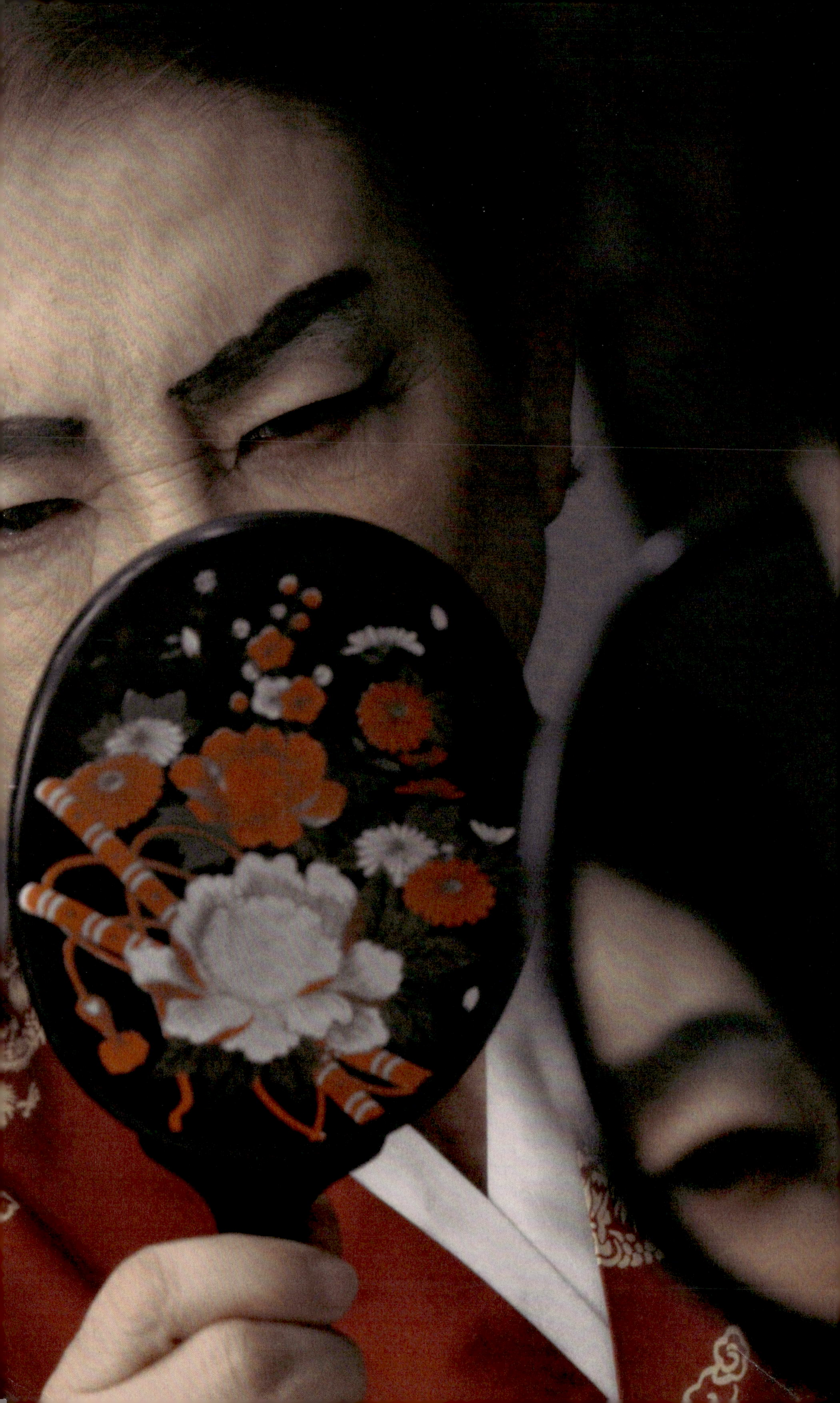

siren eun young
jung, *A Performing
by Flash, Afterimage,
Velocity, and Noise
(part 1)*, 2019, looped
single-channel
video, 4.5K, colour,
sound, 10min 22sec.
Courtesy the artist

Previous spread:
siren eun young jung,
*Anomalous Fantasy
Korea Version (Kyoto)*,
2019, performance,
85min. Photograph:
Yuki Moriya.
Courtesy Kyoto
Experiment

Anomalous Tradition, Queer Enchantment: On the Work of siren eun young jung

– Hyunjin Kim

Hyunjin Kim contextualises siren eun young jung's audio-visual work at the 2019 Venice Biennale in relation to queer performance in South Korean history.

Tense beats echo, and a curtain opens on the entry scene. Soon, as electronic sounds spread out, immensely magnified, a human body becomes visible, divided by oblique lines and light, completely filling the three walls where four performers appear in a specific order. The main part of artist siren eun young jung's audio-visual installation *A Performing by Flash, Afterimage, Velocity, and Noise* (2019) – which represented the Korean pavilion at the Venice Biennale – is a tight black box-like space of $5 \times 5 \times 4$m, charged with beats in which light circulates like laser beams across the three walls that form a U-shape in the square projection room. In this work, overflowing and overwhelming with sound and image, performers reconceive the strange and uncomfortable human body as a language for the stage.

Among the four performers whose images are projected on the three walls, lesbian actor Yii Lee (이리), known for her unique, transgressive, characters in a male-centred theatre world, soliloquises about her floating position and the lack of understanding from family and society. Drag king Azangman, who has been struggling to expand the South Korean drag community, represent the self-renewal of a person who breaks through oppression via explosive primal release within their body. Seo Ji Won (서지원), a person with severe disabilities who is Director and a member of the Disabled Women's Theater Group 'Dancing Waist', creates exceptional performance aesthetics in which she alternates between restricted possibilities for action in a wheelchair and the singular movements such limitations make possible. Finally, electronic musician KIRARA's musical activism translates the bodily dissonance and segmentation of transgender experience and reflects on their body in transcending the constraints of reality.

Based on their physical experiences, these performers bring bodily singularity to the stage. From their position as 'Others' in contemporary South Korean society, these acts escape genre stereotypes through formal challenges in performance. Moreover, the 'anomaly' they perform on stage is of importance to gender politics at large. At the Venice Biennale, their soliloquies, sounds and gestures move between constraint and liberation; in return, the sensations induced by the beats and powerful sounds in the work as a whole overwhelm the audience's visual experiences and bodies. Unaware, viewers start to dance and become one with the performers in the throbbing room.

Installed at the entry to the Korean Pavilion, the three monitors that make up the first part of *Performing by Flash, Afterimage, Velocity, and Noise*'s, show *yeoseong gukgeuk* [여성국극, Korean or National women's theatre] actor Deung Woo Lee dancing solo, performing *pansori* [a traditional form of solo vocal performance] and putting on make-up in a large theatre. The actress's traditional Korean men's costume, shown across the monitors, and the immersive experience provided by the electronic music are somewhat heterogeneous, seeming not only unrelated but almost diametrically oppposed. What bridges them within this context is 'queer performance'. Here, the artist summons and reaffirms *yeoseong gukgeuk* as a forerunner of queer performances. On view is a contemporary aesthetics of anomalousness, which establishes *yeoseong gukgeuk* as the imaginary origin of a modern and historical queer genealogy. In this work as well as in her latest – including *Anomalous Fantasy* (2016–ongoing) – siren eun young jung articulates genderqueer 'anomaly' in the form of uneven, unconventional and anomalous acts and movements.[1] Celebrated by the artist for their aesthetic singularity, the aesthetics and politics of contemporary queer performances are taken from the restricted sphere of the LGBTQI+

community to the stage of 'official' or 'established', performing arts.

A university student in the 1990s, siren eun young jung belongs to a generation who grew up under the influence of campus feminism in South Korea. Since her earliest works, she has attempted to expand feminist language in contemporary art. Through narratives reminiscent of video essays, her early pieces addressed issues including the social violence and oppression inflicted on female Others and their vulnerability as they were ceaselessly pushed out of society. Having brought about some change, feminism in South Korea lost its driving force and dwindled in the 2000s. It nevertheless continued to be a personal concern for the artist, serving as an important ressource and impetus for her work. Encountering aged *yeoseong gukgeuk* actors by chance and beginning to exchange with them around 2008, she initated the substantial *Yeoseong Gukgeuk Project* (여성국극 프로젝트, 2008-ongoing) based on a decade of ethnographic research that approached tradition from the perspective of subversive gender performativity.

A form of musical dance theatre begun in the latter half of the 1940s, *yeoseong gukgeuk* enjoyed great popularity in the 1950s after the Korean War (1950-53). Formally, it is viewed as an offshoot of *changgeuk* (창극), the theatrical staging of a traditional Korean solo vocal performance genre called *pansori* (판소리).[2] However, just as it means 'Korean/national women's theatre', in *yeoseong gukgeuk* female actors play all of the roles. It can thus be seen as an opposite version of traditional Chinese opera, which consists of all male actors. *A Flower in Jail*, staged in 1948 by the Women's *Gugak* (국악, Traditional Korean Music) Association, initiated *yeoseong gukgeuk*. It came out of the women's determination to create their own stage, their antipathy towards the authoritarianism and violence of male artists, and their will to fight back against the prolonged sexual and monetary exploitation of female students by male masters in their training – an apprentice system of oral transmission that predominates in traditional Korean music circles.[3] In spite of a hostile environment, women's awareness expanded during the modernisation process. Although the very first *yeoseong gukgeuk* performance went unnoticed, the genre won great popularity in the 1950s and continued clandestinely when, due to the war, the theatre company was evacuated elsewhere. After the ceasefire, *yeoseong gukgeuk* fostered popular fantasy and allowed the public to forget the pain of war, yielding unprecedentedly large fandom.

From the 1960s onwards, *yeoseong gukgeuk* declined as dictatorial regimes implemented projects to nationalise and officialise traditions involving male musicians, excluding it from institutional support.[4] It also fell behind amidst the influx of cinema and forms of Western theatre and performance into South Korea. But even though the institution failed to train new generations of actors, the experience of *yeoseong gukgeuk* for women in the 1950s was beyond a mere escape from a patriarchal society:

Yeoseong gukgeuk *provided women with positive experiences in being 'outside' at a time when women could not venture beyond the confines of the home. Against gender norms in early modern East Asia that saw women outside the home as potential threats to public morals,* yeoseong gukgeuk *showed that it was possible for women to perform activities* on their own *and to create a same-sex community that produced a sense of belonging and commitment for women.*[5]

Yeoseong gukgeuk is thus primarily reminiscent of modern female subjects, who allow for a glimpse into the subjectivity and realisation of women-centred activities. Furthermore, over the past decade the genre has unceasingly provided new inspiration for siren eun young jung, who has treated its engagement with genderqueer epistemology as an unexplored and evolving multifarious organism. What she has found most fascinating are the aged actors who have become living monuments for the queer community. Behind such fascination is a liberating awareness of gender from an open and non-normative same-sex community, as found inside the ambiguous, complex and transgressive *yeoseong gukgeuk*.

Based on materials, transcripts and video recordings acquired through a long-term exchange with elderly actors, siren eun young jung has presented visual archives in installations such as *Public yet Private Archive* (2015) and lecture performances such as *Gender Bender Fencers* (2014 at Arko Art Center, Seoul and 2017 at HKW, Berlin). Within these archives, her interpretations intervene in intimate accounts based on the actors' oral testimonies, a photograph of a simulated wedding between a *nimai* (lead male) actor and a female fan, and images of

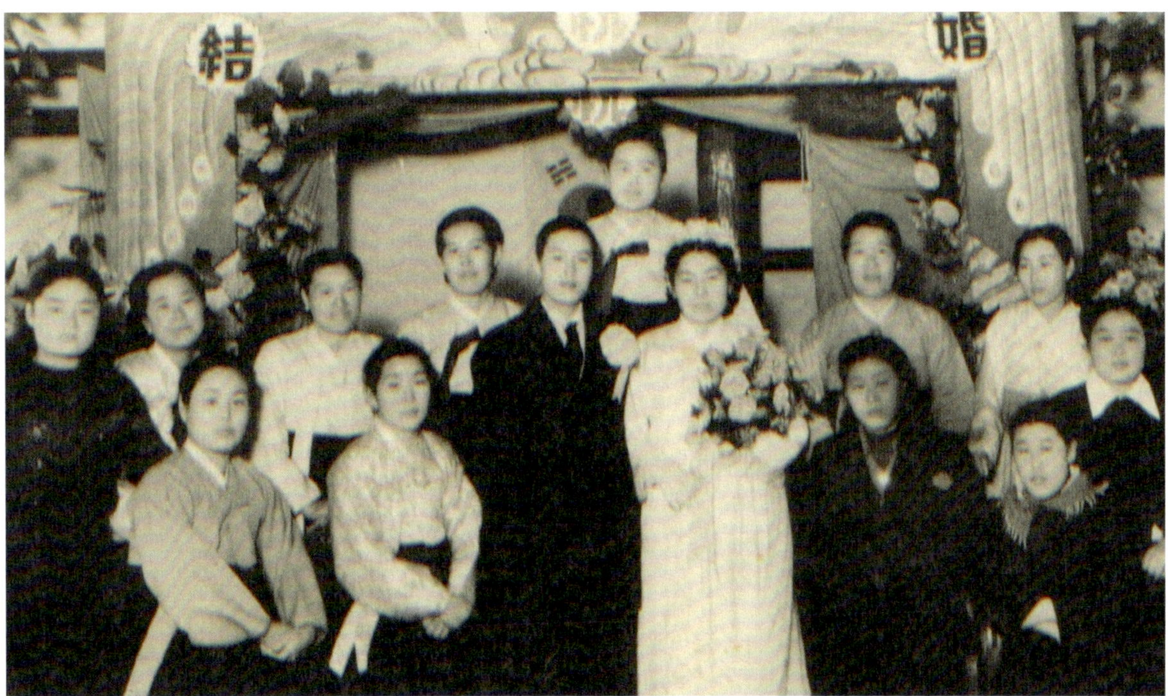

Simulated wedding between a *nimai* (leading male role) and a fan, late 1950s. Photograph: Personal archive of the late Geum Aeng Cho

Following spread: siren eun young jung, *A Performing by Flash, Afterimage, Velocity, and Noise*, 2019, audio-visual installation, full HD, 5.1 surround sound, 27min 36sec. Courtesy the artist

actors impersonating characters who are blind in one eye or staging swordfights. In so doing, she invites the audience in to vivid scenes of homosocial intimacy, which include emotional rapport, passion, sexuality, friendship and affection among women, all common in the little-documented *yeoseong*

Such a tradition calls into question relationships of self-denial, conflict and antipathy towards Korean customs, which have previously been seen as colluding with statism and heterosexism while maintaining the oppressive narratives of the Confucian patriarch.

gukgeuk community.⁶ In *The Masquerading Moments* (2009), the artist focusses on the face of an elderley *nimai* actor. As they put on theatre make-up the performer exists as a gender- and age-fluid being. In works including *The Unexpected Response* (2009), *A Masterclass* (2010) and *Lyrics 2* (2013), the artist presents body-transgressive gender performances – recalling the notion of 'gender-becoming' – while video records the actors' training in 'masculine' acting based on *pansori* dances and songs. These works

are precursors to her latest works, which have moved on to the bodies of queer performers and performance aesthetics.

Pansori is a premodern, traditional genre of vocal performance in Korea that was used to recount the nation's traditional tales in outdoor spaces, or in banquet rooms in traditional houses. In *yeoseong gukgeuk* it is combined with Western proscenium theatre performance, and features women actors only. The artistic community training in and performing this traditional art embraced non-heterosexual relationships and imagination, enjoying complex gender performance without the discriminatory perspectives or exclusions that are based on both Confucian and modern heterosexist gender ideologies. This fascinating and liberating liminal space aroused a powerful imaginary as it transcended the dichotomous ways of establishing boundaries – such as tradition/modernity and female/male – that existed during Korea's transition into a modern society. It is the basis of an epistemological break liberating us from conceptions of Asia's traditions and premodernity only as 'delusions' or 'oppression', with the West positioned as the norm. In other words, siren eun young jung's *yeoseong gukgeuk* works recognise and realise tradition as a liberating threshold and a space of potential intermixing. Such a tradition calls into question relationships of self-denial, conflict and antipathy towards Korean customs, which have previously been seen as colluding with statism and heterosex-

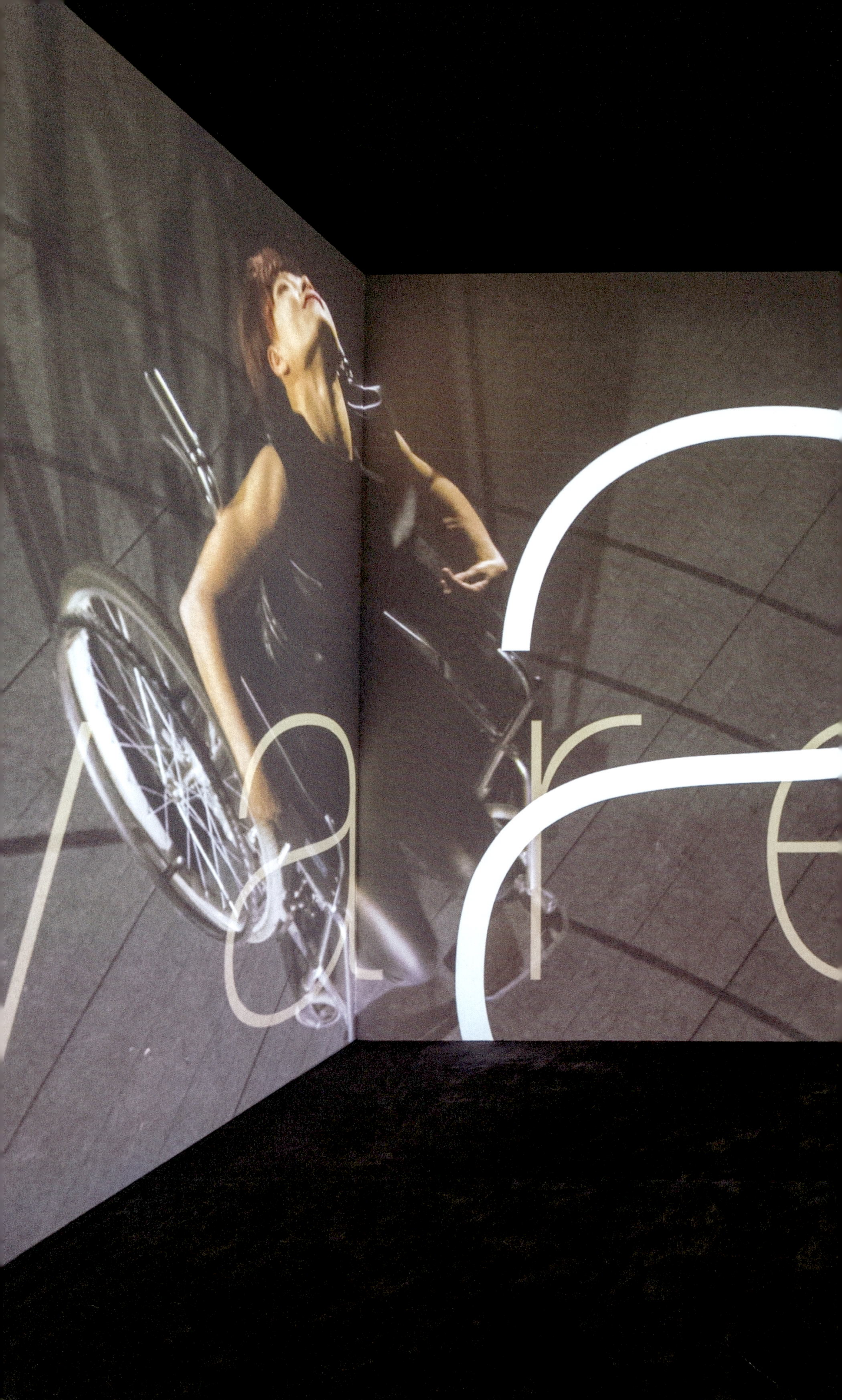

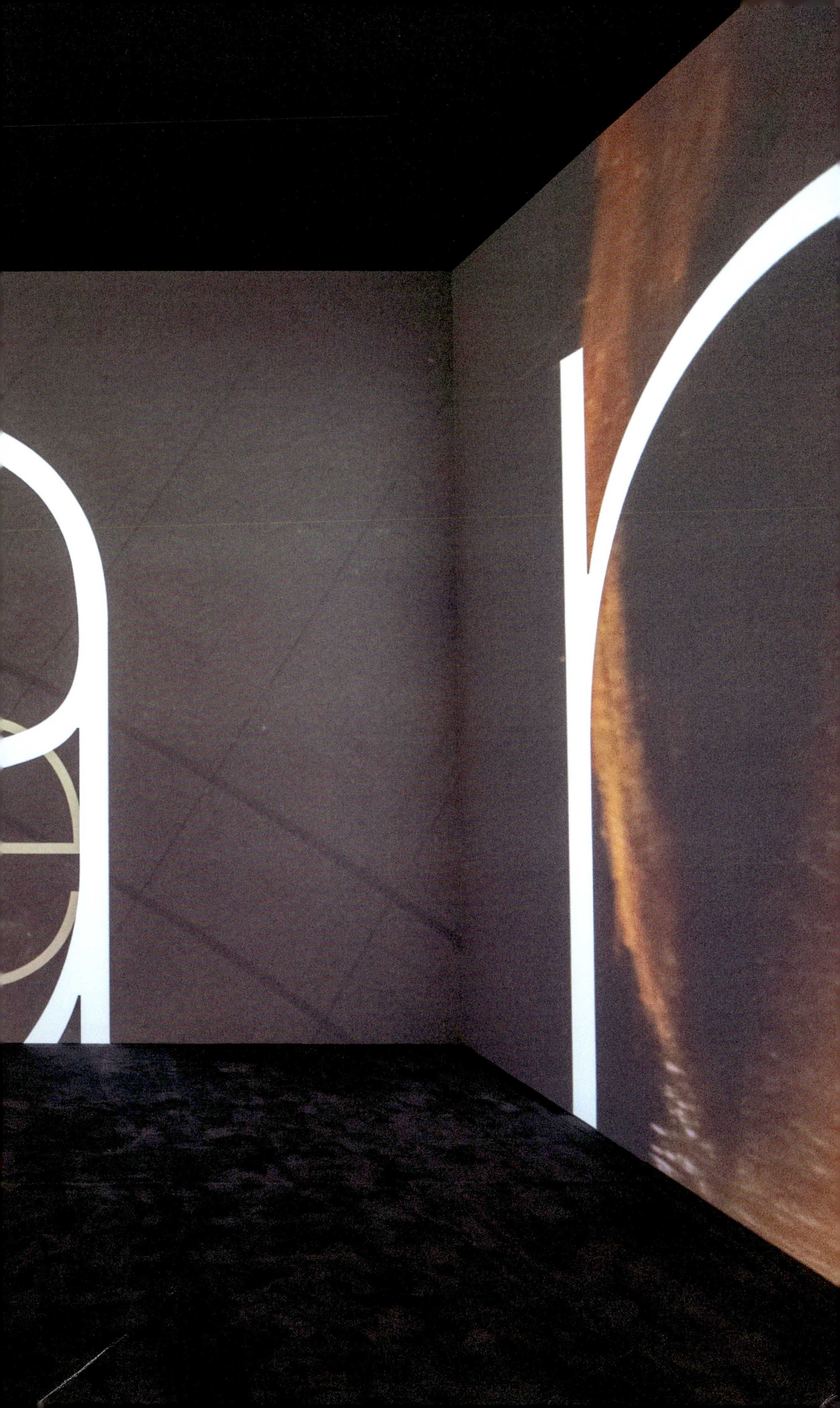

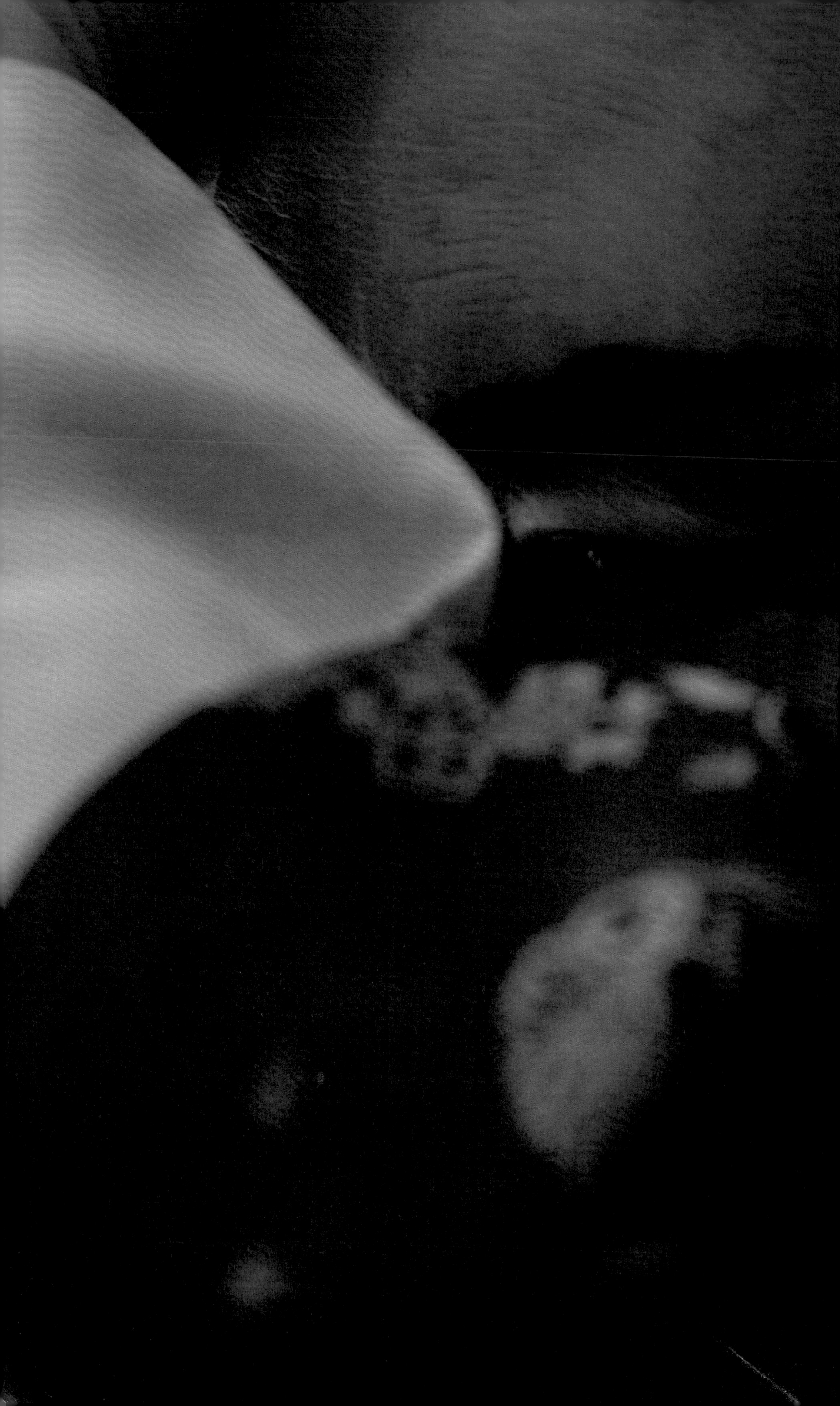

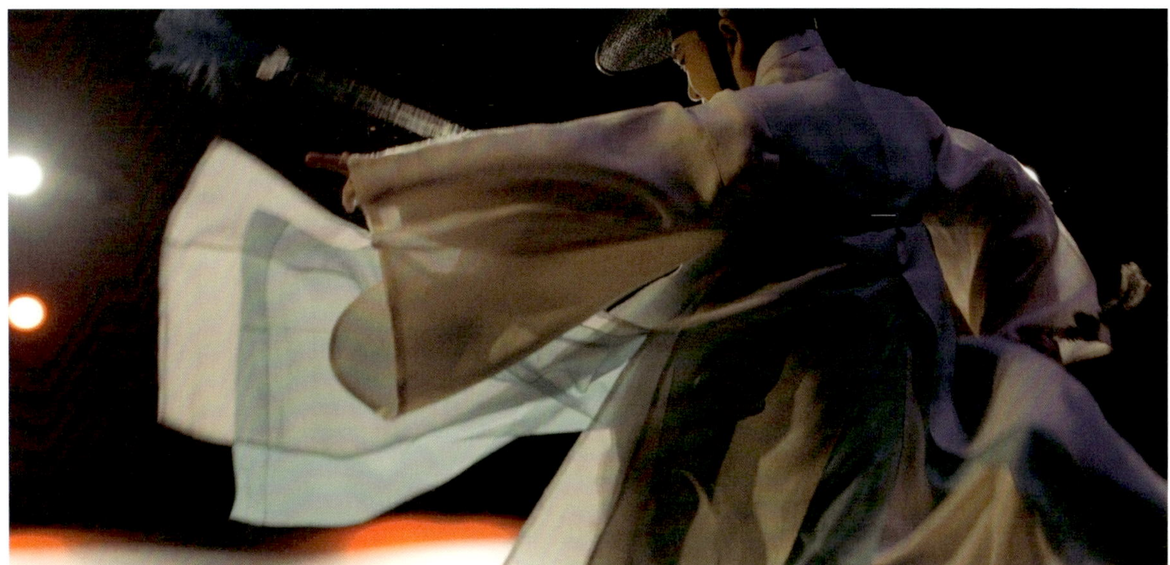

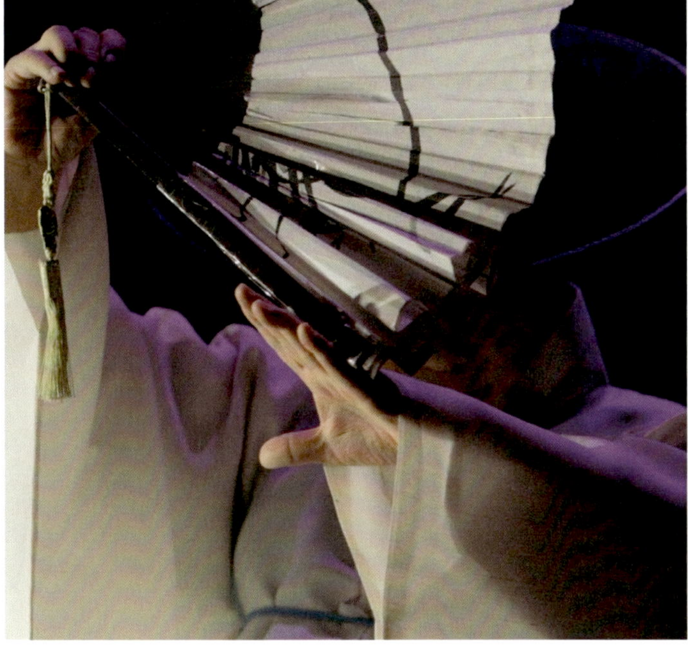

ism while maintaining the oppressive narratives of the Confucian patriarch.

Since 2012, siren eun young jung has expanded on her previous methodology in video, creating outstanding works that transform *yeoseong gukgeuk* into contemporary stage performances, based on her insight into the practice. In the 'docu-stage' work *Off/Stage* (2012), veteran actor Young Sook Cho (조영숙), a long time *sammai* (삼마이, supporting male) actor, recounts her involvement in *yeoseong gukgeuk* and tells anecdotes from her life as a performer, along with a presentation of old photographs. She also laughs, dances and sings, expressing her talents as a National Intangible Cultural Heritage skill holder.[7] *Masterclass* (2012) wittily stages the illusiveness

of biological 'masculinity' through a 30-minute performance that dramatises an acting training process based on the representation of 'maleness' by Deung Woo Lee (이등우), a female second-generation actor who has played leading male roles, along with her pupil. These works are fully-fledged occasions for siren eun young jung. Not only are elderly actors, used to repeatedly performing hackneyed, outdated and conventional narratives, transformed into the bodies of a vivid, non-normative archive on contemporary stages, but the artist herself is expanding her repertoire to works for the theatre played at performance festivals across Asia.

Anomalous Fantasy (2016–ongoing) is a 1h 25min theatre performance on precarity and deprivation, expressed through the melancholic confession of Eunjin Nam, a young *nimai* (니마이) actor training in the *yeoseong gukgeuk* tradition. Oscillating between the frustration and possibility of both the queer, 'camp' sensibility and the liberating and non-normative mentality that vibrates within the culture of *yeoseong gukgeuk*, siren eun young jung gradually replaces the lethargy of a tradition with the songs and dances of an amateur gay chorus, they sing to diverse pieces of popular music, and moving with the sense of empowerment made possible by *yeoseong gukgeuk* and its genealogical imagination. This stage work attempts both to re-inscribe the minority position of LGBTQI+ people in the centre and to queer all norms regarding traditional performances/stages as well as representations of professionalism and gender. More fundamentally, it ponders the unstable positions of Asian traditions

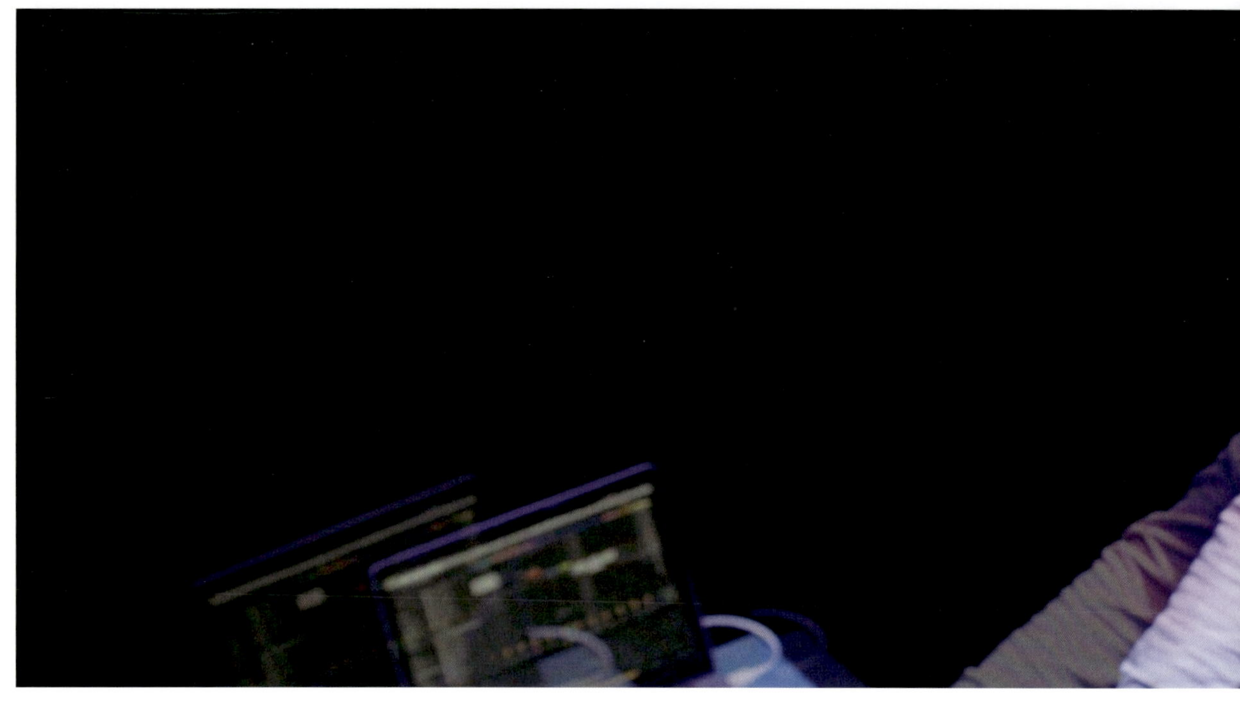

and of the queer, in particular via *Deferral Theatre* (2018).[8] Here siren eun young jung confronts the personas of Minhee Park (박민희) – a renowned performer of *gagok* (가곡, Korean traditional vocal poetry and singing genre), grappling with the narrow possibility granted by tradition; Azangman – a drag king performer who discovers their authentic self through queering; and the melancholia and modulation of gendered identity of Eunjin Nam, the remaining male-role successor of *yeosong gukgeuk*. In doing so she emphasises the potentiality that the decline and instability of *yeoseong gukgeuk* in fact open up:

By creating a triangle of Eunjin Nam, Minhee Park and Azangman, I did want to show how they needed mutual support in such [an] exclusive and disadvantaged genre and how there had been such struggles. I thought that performativity on stage has its core in the 'time' of their performing, where the problematic topics like tradition or sex gradually show themselves, and that it might be necessary to let movements like questions, challenges and resistances be made about the time. So I'd like to contend that this insufficiency, instability and lack could instead be the resources of imagining a new realm. 'The queer' could be 'in/ stability'. When something isn't completely concluded, naturally named, or given authority that we can create unique kinesthetics. It's a view that rather than by being given a name by authority, we can write our own history by deferring it.[9]

Being adrift due to the denial of one's authority can give way to resistance or mobility. siren eun young jung focuses on the queering made possible by the deferral of authority and the non-normativity of a discriminated-against position. The artist stresses that she approaches *yeoseong gukgeuk* from the context of queer performance not because of the queer identities within that community, but rather 'because it lets us constantly question how queerness can be performed, and what its aesthetics as forms and styles are'.[10]

At last, *A Performing by Flash, Afterimage, Velocity, and Noise* is a work that fully addresses the aesthetics of queering inherited from *yeoseong gukgeuk*. The performers' bodies are mobilised, and sound and light elements inherent to the medium are pushed beyond their conventional range, which the artist describes as 'exploiting' the medium. The immersive screens on the three walls that completely fill the room emit intriguing sensory stimuli such as vibrating sounds and extremely slow or fast-paced rhythms. Screens smoothly expose the disparate bodily senses and the intriguing disharmony of the performers. In this situation, however, stimuli never exclude the viewers. Rather, the work wonderfully invites them to a moment of being one with the breathing and dancing of queer bodies. Caught

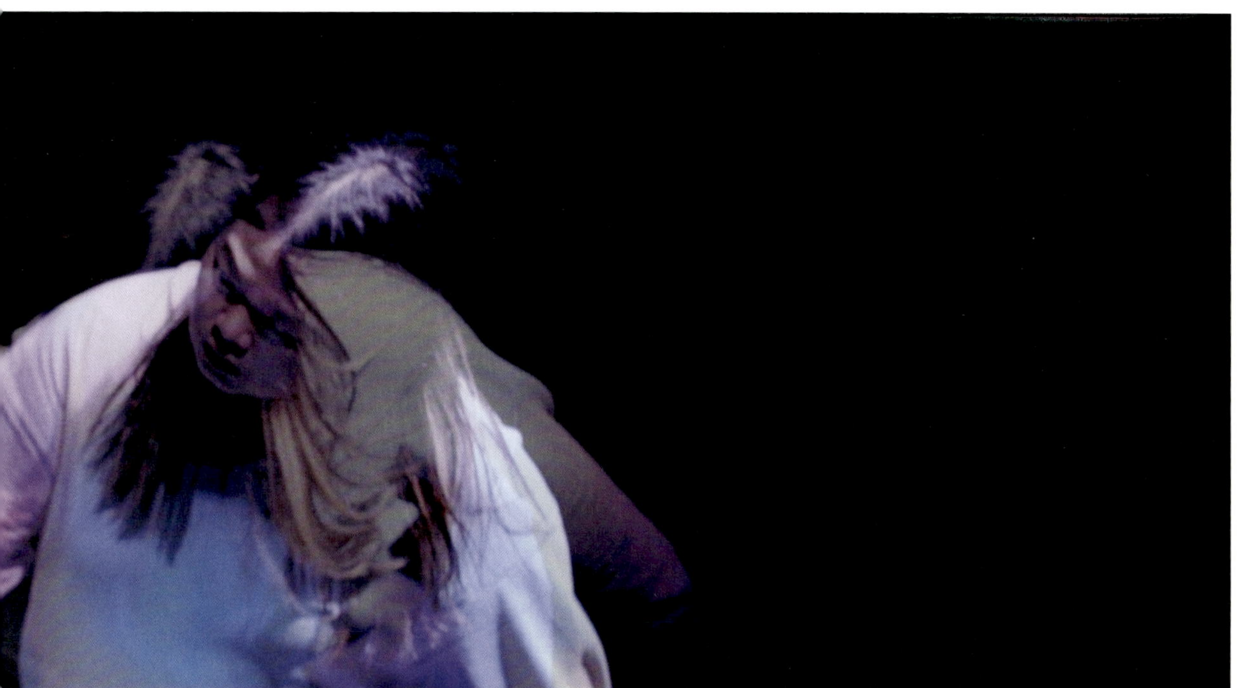

off guard, we face moments that move our hearts amidst KIRARA'S music. The sensory overload that siren eun young jung mobilises in this work constitutes a bold, vibrant action, towards campness and unevenness, and towards one's own anomalousness and enchantment; it is a celebration of one's own non-normativity. Transgender musician KIRARA's 135-bit sounds collide with or lead the performers' movements whose (im)

perfect performing bodies clash with their worlds. This queering of video draws out a transformative moment to which viewers can naturally surrender together to the beat. One finally comes to realise that what always and truly makes us dance lies in nothing else but the emancipatory moment found in utterly anomalous, utterly queer enchantment.

1   *Anomalous Fantasy* was first performed in Korea in 2016 with subsequent versions in Taiwan (2017), Japan (2018-19) and India (2018), and again in Korea in 2019.

2   *Pansori* is a folk music genre unique to Korea where, to the accompaniment of a *gosu* (drummer) playing *jangdan* (rhythmic patterns), a singer orally performs narratives, interweaving them with *sori* (singing) and *aniri* and adding *ballim*. *Aniri* refers to the *saseol* (narration) uttered between songs without adding melodies, as if talking; and *ballim* refers to gestures made with the body or the hands in order to aid in the dramatic development of the singing.

3   siren eun young jung, 'A Brief History of *Yeoseong Gukgeuk*: Birth and Decline', *Trans-Theatre* (ed. s. jung), Seoul: Seoul Forum A, 2016, p.201.

4   See Ji Hye Kim, '1950 nyeondae yeoseong gukgeukui danchehwaldonggwa soetoegwajeonge daehan yeongu (A Study on the Troupe Activity and the Declining Process of 1950's Female *Gukgeuk*)', *Journal of Korean Women's Studies*, vol.27, no.2, 2011.

5   s. jung, 'A Brief History of *Yeoseong Gukgeuk*', *op. cit.*, p.204.

6   Homosocial, same-sex intimacy was the concept used by gender culture scholar Ji Hye Kim in her article '1950 nyeondae yeoseong gukgeukui danchehwaldonggwa soetoegwajeonge daehan yeongu (A Study on the Troupe Activity and the Declining Process of 1950's Female *Gukgeuk*)' in order to explain the level of gender complexity in the *yeoseong gukgeuk* community found in studies on the female subject of this genre.

7   The Korean government has officially announced and protected Intangible Cultural Heritage since 1964. According to the National Intangible Heritage Center in Korea (https://www.nihc.go.kr/english/html/content.html?menu=02_01.html), it refers to traditional cultural heritages where human performance is a medium, for example *Pansori* (traditonal Korean vocal performance) or *Talchum* (Korean mask dance). In contrast, tangible heritages refer to historically valuable inheritance or relics like tombs, pagodas, statues of the Buddha, pottery, books and so on.

8   The work was created on the occasion of her receiving the Korea Artist Prize from South Korea's National Museum of Modern and Contemporary Art (MMCA) in 2018.

9   Ágrafa Society, 'Interview with siren eun young jung: Re-formation and witnessing of performative languages', *Seminar* [online journal], no.2, available at http://www.zineseminar.com/wp/issue02/interview-with-siren-eun-young-jung-re-formation-and-witnessing-of-performative-languages (last accessed on 18 November 2019).

10   *Ibid.*

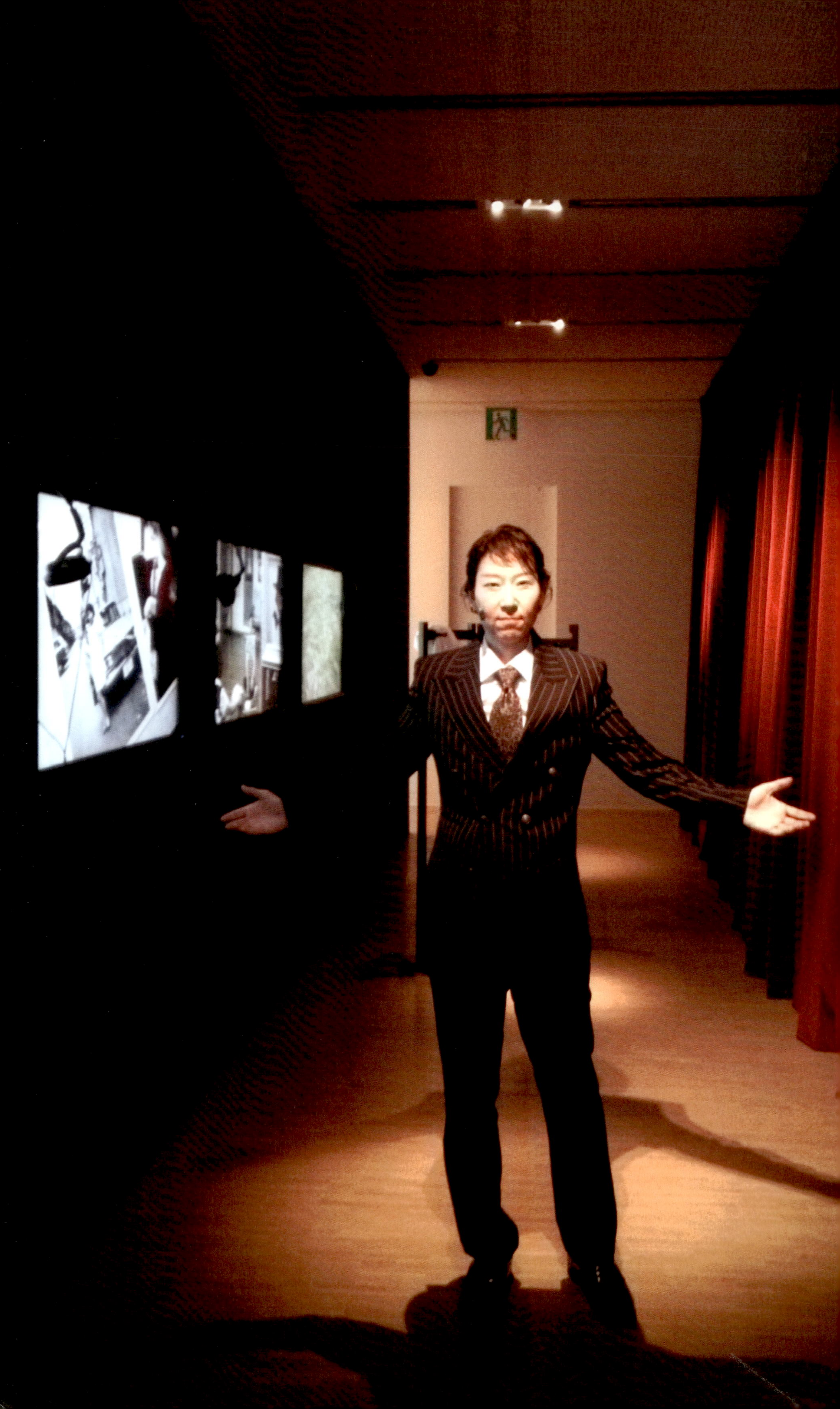

Acts of Affect: siren eun young jung's *Yeoseong Gukgeuk Project*

— Ashley Chang

siren eun young jung's *Yeoseong Gukgeuk Project* (여성국극 프로젝트, 2008-ongoing) attends to the remnants and remainders of *yeoseong gukgeuk* (여성국극), a little-known form of performance that first emerged in Korea during the 1940s. Today, *yeoseong gukgeuk* is on the verge of extinction. With its melodramatic tales of war and romance, set to the plaintive drumming of the barrel-shaped *buk* (북), *yeoseong gukgeuk* resembles a more popular style of Korean opera known as *changgeuk* (창극), usually performed by men. What distinguishes

In *Acts of Affect*, siren eun young jung returns to the disappearing *Yeoseong Gukgeuk* theatre. In her discussion of the project, Ashley Chang examines how masculinity is produced by women.

it from *changgeuk* – and perhaps what consigns it to the peripheries of the Korean performing arts – is its queer regard for the fluidity and fragility of gender. Its ensembles consist only of women who, wearing *appliqué* beards and silken *hanboks* (한복), take to the stage as men in archetypal male roles: the hero, the joker, the villain.

In its approach to gender, *yeoseong gukgeuk* departs somewhat from its analogues in American drag culture. Preferring intense sincerity to the more playful sensibilities of camp and limiting their pursuits of hero/joker/villain realness to the theatrical stage, *yeoseong gukgeuk* performers do not trouble gender by parodying or passing as men; their aim is neither to mock manhood nor to impersonate it. Instead, the women of *yeoseong gukgeuk* push back against dominant forms of masculinity by producing one that is all their own: a masculinity without men. *Yeoseong gukgeuk* performers author, rather than appropriate, alternative manhoods that are no less real than those created by men. In doing so, they embody what

queer theorist Jack Halberstam has called 'female masculinity', a category of gender expression that challenges men's claim to manhood.[1] As Halberstam argues, 'masculinity does not belong to men' and 'has not been produced only by men'.[2] In *yeoseong gukgeuk*, masculinity is neither skewered nor imitated. Rather, masculinity is *generated* – through precise modulations of 'voice, gesture, emotion and attitude', in the words of one of its practitioners.[3] *Yeoseong gukgeuk* demonstrates that gender is both malleable and makeable.

Simultaneously panoramic and kaleidoscopic, jung's *Yeoseong Gukgeuk Project* documents – through video, photography and installation – the time jung spent with several surviving *yeoseong gukgeuk* practitioners as they reflected on the origins and legacies of their craft. Assembled from nearly a decade's worth of exchanges with these women in their homes and at theatres, backstage and onstage, choreographed and improvised, jung's elegiac collection examines gender and its performance; reality and its representation; history and its telling; time and its passing. Death hangs over every piece: the first and second generations of performers are either dead or dying, and once they are gone, the tradition itself might not have much longer to live. In many ways, *yeoseong gukgeuk* is already beyond recovery. jung articulates its ongoing dispersal and disintegration by showing it in fragments, flung across media and gathered into an imagined – a wished-for – whole.

Though most of the women featured in *Yeoseong Gukgeuk Project* are 'grannies' (할머니), as jung calls them, a few are significantly younger than these older performers who are in their seventies and eighties.[4] jung's two-part piece *Act of Affect* (정동의 막, 2013) enlists Eunjin Nam (남은진), a latecomer to the tradition whose expertise lies in playing the romantic male lead, the *nimai* (니마이). Through Nam, who is in her forties, jung examines not just *yeoseong gukgeuk*'s unforeseeable future

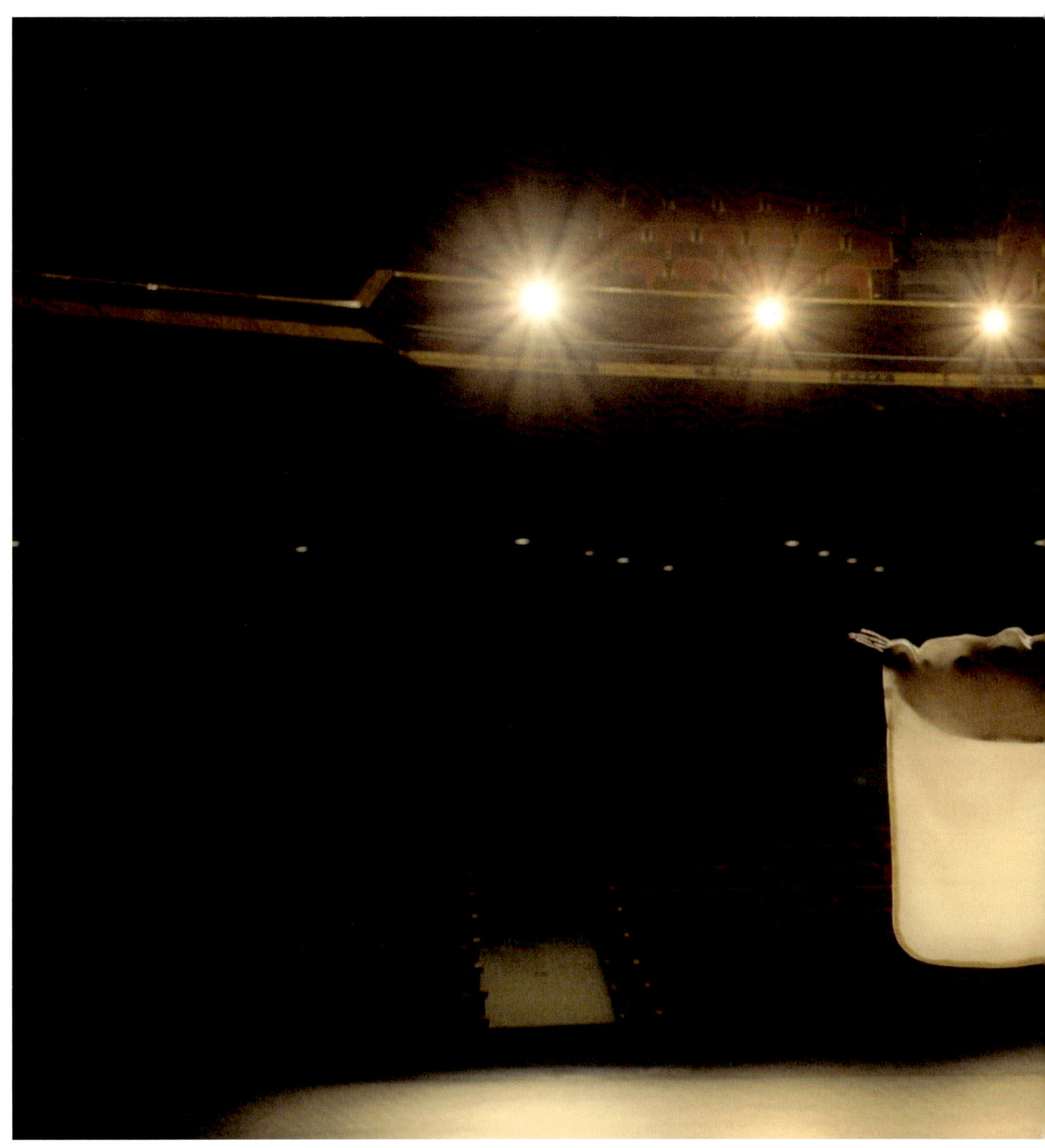

but also the affective intensities that limn its wavering present. *Act of Affect* documents the ruins of *yeoseong gukgeuk* through what literary scholar Heather Love calls the 'forms of ruined subjectivity' created by its gradual loss – a ruination that is, Love says, inescapably part of 'the history of queer experience'.[5] In keeping, then, with the investments in affect that have long informed queer and feminist theory and politics,[6] *Act of Affect* offers an account of *yeoseong gukgeuk*'s decline through an intimate catalogue of feeling: the boredom of rehearsal, the pleasure of becoming a man, the torment of obscurity, the thrill of doing it anyways. Affects, here, give

specific texture and shape to the larger social structures that have worn away at *yeoseong gukgeuk*, its culture and its communities, making it possible to see how the effects of patriarchy and homophobia emerge at the level of individual experience. Nam's delight is marred by frustration and despair, a constellation of affects painfully particular to her experience as an artist whose art approaches its end and, moreover, as a queer figure whose very queerness is at risk of displacement and disarticulation.

By foregrounding affect, jung translates Nam's losses into the language of the body, and of Nam's body in particular. These losses are hard to describe in ordinary

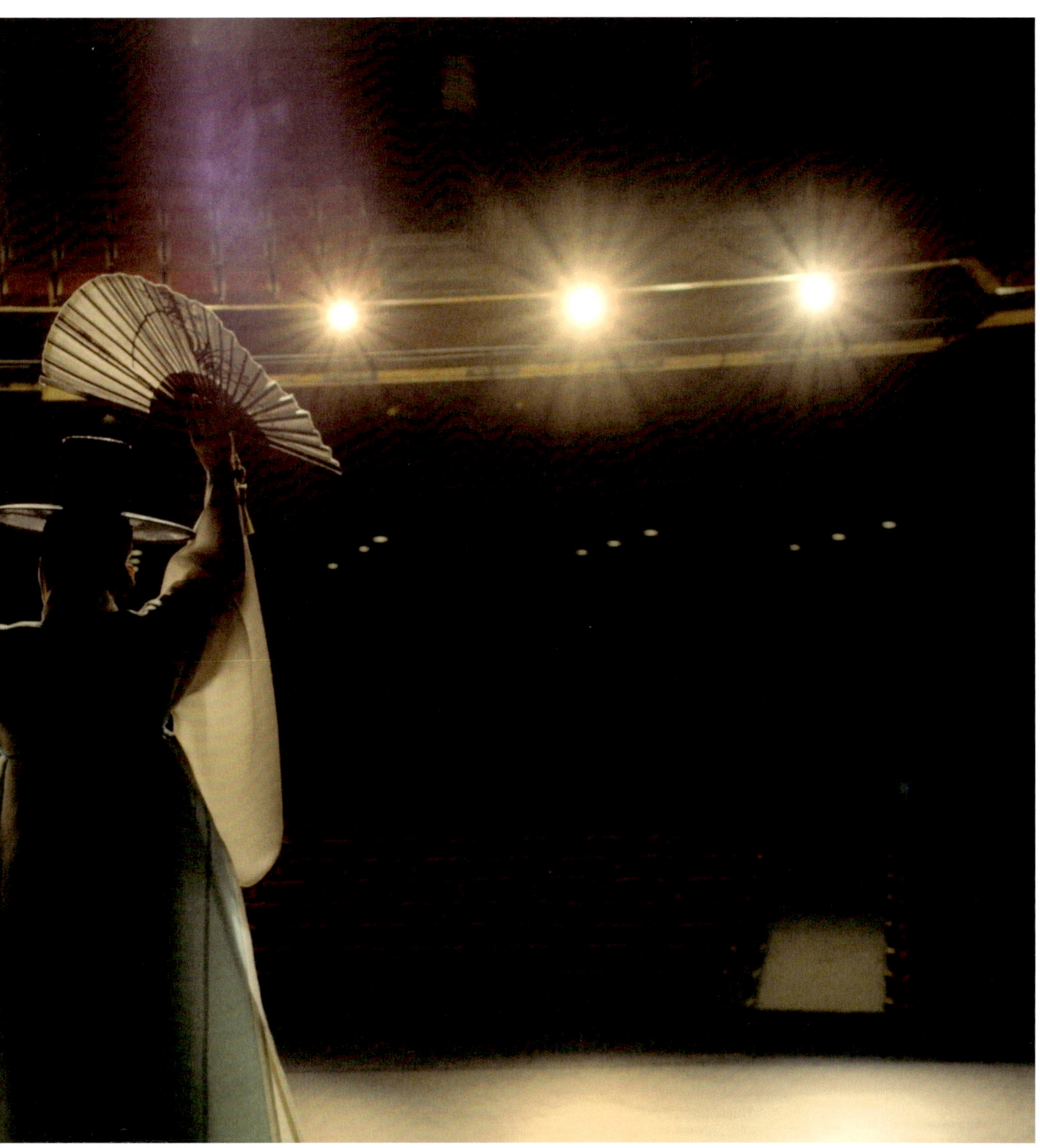

language because the experience that is being lost – the experience of becoming a man in a folktale played before an audience – is rare to the point of lacking much precedent in contemporary Korean culture. There are few references Nam can make to talk about *yeoseong gukgeuk* and what it is like to keep doing it as it disappears. As Halberstam has observed, female masculinity tends to be 'indefinable' and 'unspeakable', standing as 'all that cannot be absorbed into systems of signification, legitimation, legibility, recognition, and legality'.[7] jung's interest in the body – in its affects and its expressions – allows *yeoseong gukgeuk* to remain unassimilable, existing somewhere beyond everyday speech. For jung, explanations of Nam's suffering would only go so far. Better just to let these feelings be felt.

Act of Affect: Performance

The public performance of *Act of Affect* took place in 2013 at Atelier Hermès, an exhibition hall in the Gangnam district of Seoul (서울 강남). Throughout the piece, Nam's voice slips in and out of a masculine register of delivery, with her appearance sometimes easing and sometimes vexing the overall readability of her gender.

This slippage, borne out through careful adjustments to the tone of her voice, underscores the dynamic process of journeying towards and into manhood. To become a man is, for Nam, to shuttle through various iterations of masculinity. She hovers in hybridity and half-tones just as often as she settles someplace stable.

The piece begins with a musical demonstration marked by ambivalence: between masculinity and femininity, between senescence and youth, between performance and rehearsal. As the performance gets underway, Nam starts by singing a Korean folk song: 'I was once a youth', she croons, her voice deep, 'and I am a pathetic old man now, with my snowy hair'. The old man's lament sits at odds with her apparent youth and femininity. This incommensurability comes without pomp or pageantry: the plurality of her identity is casual, even noncommittal. For

She is not between masculinity and femininity, senescence and youth, performance and rehearsal; she is both masculine and feminine, old and young, performing and rehearsing, all at once.

much of the song, she hovers in an empty corner of the exhibition, singing to no one in particular. She appears not to be performing – just rehearsing. As the song goes on, however, she gradually lifts her posture and acknowledges the crowd. She concludes it in the centre of the room, fan gallantly unfurled. What begins as an almost private warm-up becomes a public performance, confident in its multiple dualities. She is not *between* masculinity and femininity, senescence and youth, performance and rehearsal; she is *both* masculine and feminine, old and young, performing and rehearsing, all at once.

Nam shifts, then, to her speaking voice, a soft alto that corresponds more smoothly with her body. She proceeds to give a short talk on *yeoseong gukgeuk*, taking special care to explain that she first took up the craft ten years ago in order to have the honour of creating a character who is, she says, 'female and male at the same time'. She confesses, however, that she is not famous, nor does she have any upcoming shows, nor are

there enough performers to keep *yeoseong gukgeuk* alive. 'There lies my tragedy', she tells the audience, her countenance grim. She is a performer with no opportunities to perform.

Upon sharing these accounts of longing and admissions of failure, she retreats to a clothing rack in a makeshift hallway flanked on one side by a wall and on the other by a red velvet curtain. The audience lingers at one end of the narrow corridor. Facing away from them, Nam takes off her shirt, revealing her bound chest. She dons a buttoned dress shirt, switches out her espadrilles for leather oxfords, unrolls her cuffed slacks, slips into a matching blazer and tightens a tie around her neck.

When she turns back to the audience, her eyes are steely, her demeanour firm and her voice low. Though she moves little, she gives off energy like heat: she simmers, she radiates, she is white-hot. In becoming a man, she produces what Gilles Deleuze and Félix Guattari call 'a bloc of sensations', a bundle of vibrations that escape fixity and convention.[8] With her transformation, made complete by the sonorous timbre of her voice, the whole atmosphere becomes charged and the audience enraptured. There is a 'boiling' in her heart, she says, and not because passion is the purview solely of men but because this is what it feels like for her to become a man.

Her ardour, she goes on, is coupled with a sense of feeling at home in such attire, a sense of *belonging* (a 'comfortable unity') and, at the same time, a sense of *unbelonging* (an 'unexplainable strangeness'). The exhilaration of being both whole and divided is, for Nam, irreducible. 'What can I say?' she asks, by which she seems to mean: 'Nothing can be said, not really.' Her experience eludes easy explanation, so she resorts, ultimately, to metaphor. She tells her audience that whenever she finds herself onstage and the curtains open, she imagines her former self sitting in the audience, a mental picture that always makes her smile: 'I, who is me and not me at the same time, am smiling on and off the stage.' Her two selves – though split across time, split across gender and split, too, across the threshold of the stage – are affectively united, their smiles in impossible harmony.

The harmony Nam shares with her former self cannot shift the course of her tragedy, however, and the smile that concludes *Act of Affect* makes no pledge of

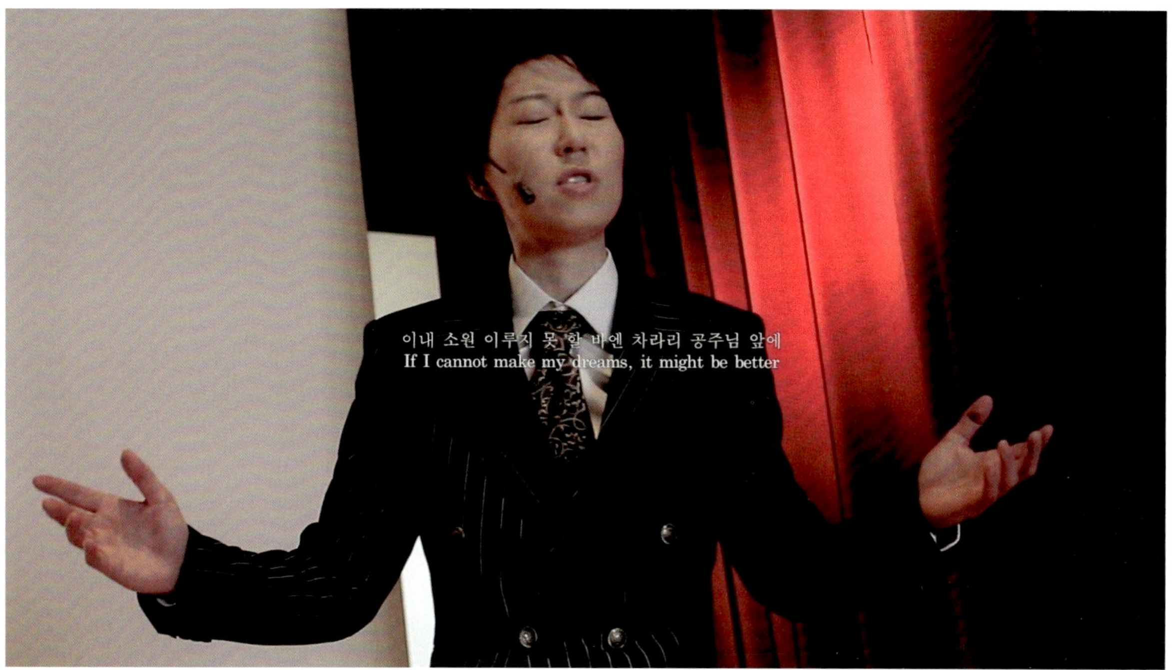

siren eun young jung, 정동의 막 *Act of Affect*, 2013, single-channel video, HD colour, stereo, 20min. Documentation of performance at Atelier Hermes, Seoul. Courtesy the artist

hope. The performance ends, as it began, with a song. This time, her words reveal the perspective of a young man. 'Better to die in front of a princess', she keens. 'That would be my land of happiness. Do not hold back and do not hang on. Living is hell if you don't solve (*sic*) your wishes'. The yearning of the character that she embodies echoes her own yearning for *yeoseong gukgeuk's* survival, for chances to perform, to play the hero. The verse enunciates her character's feelings as well as her own. The verse also underscores the painful reality of her situation: while his wishes might come true, hers are likely never to come to pass. As she sings, she walks away from the audience. Finally, she disappears behind the curtain with an enigmatic smile. She smiles without any great faith that the future might somehow turn out differently. Rather, as if to shift focus to the present or even to the past, she smiles for herself – for *herselves.*

Act of Affect: Video

The live performance at Atelier Hermès explores the complex bundle of feelings associated with Nam's production of masculinity. These feelings find their clearest expression only obliquely, through metaphor, song and gesture rather than through ordinary speech. jung's short film *Act of Affect*, by contrast, attends to the more existential questions of *yeoseong gukgeuk's* inevitable dissolution and impossible reconstitution.[9] In other words, while the performance feels its way through the process of becoming male, the film considers what it feels like to stand inside a fast-collapsing form.

Just fifteen minutes long, the single-channel video begins on the verge of a performance. Nam stands centre stage, behind a closed curtain, in full *hanbok* and make-up. The viewer shares in her excitement and anticipation as she takes several breaths. When the curtain opens, the camera stays on her face. It is not possible to see what she sees – a full house, perhaps, or, more likely, an empty one. For the viewer, the performance is made hypothetical through its indefinite deferral, though for Nam, the conditions of the performance are known and, whatever they are, worth standing. She remains onstage, steadfast.

The video then moves into an extended montage of images and sounds from rehearsal. Here, jung captures the acute sense of loss hovering over *yeoseong gukgeuk*. The impossibility of its restoration and revitalisation is partially reversed through a strategically incomplete and inchoate strategy of collage. Split across four frames, the camera records haphazard close-ups of her fan as it spreads; her torso as she turns; her neck as she sings; her feet as she runs across the black vinyl floor; her body prone on the floor. Moving in and out of frames, Nam is pictured in pieces, her body fractured and her selves multiplied. jung reveals Nam's isolation and, by picturing her in busy company with herself, somewhat relieves it. Though Nam might be lonesome, that lonesomeness is coupled with a discipline and desire that surround and sustain her.

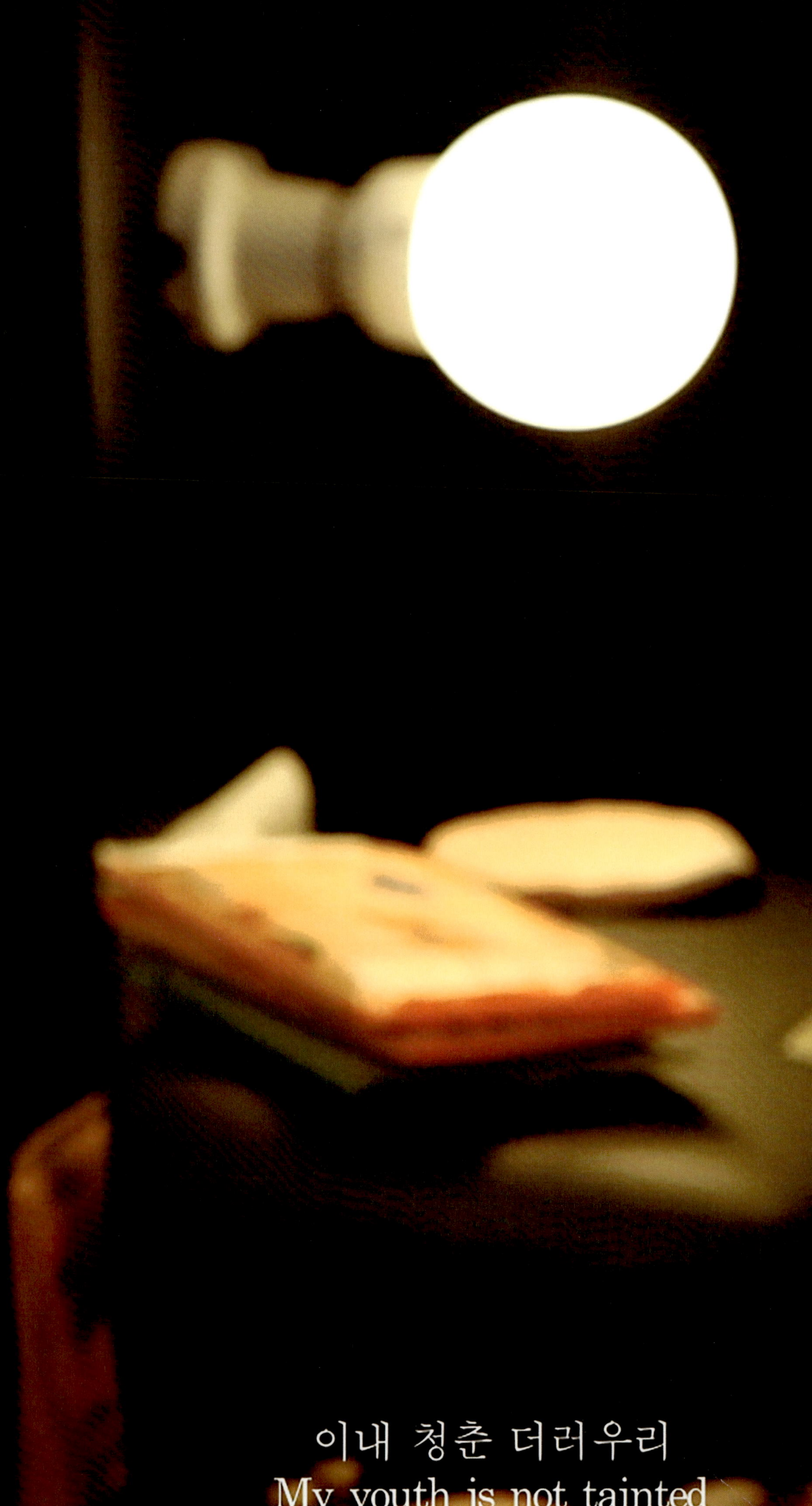
이내 청춘 더러우리
My youth is not tainted

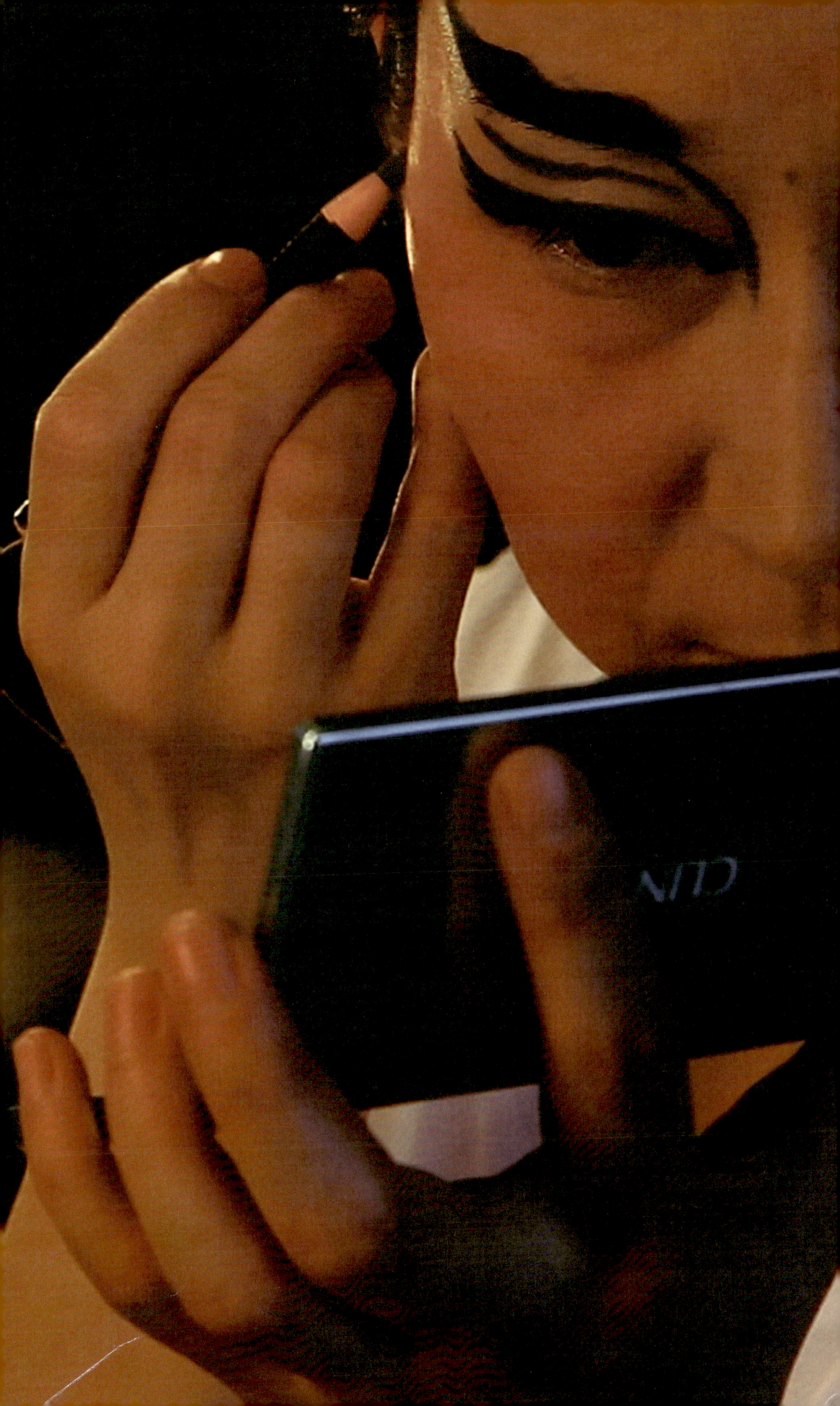

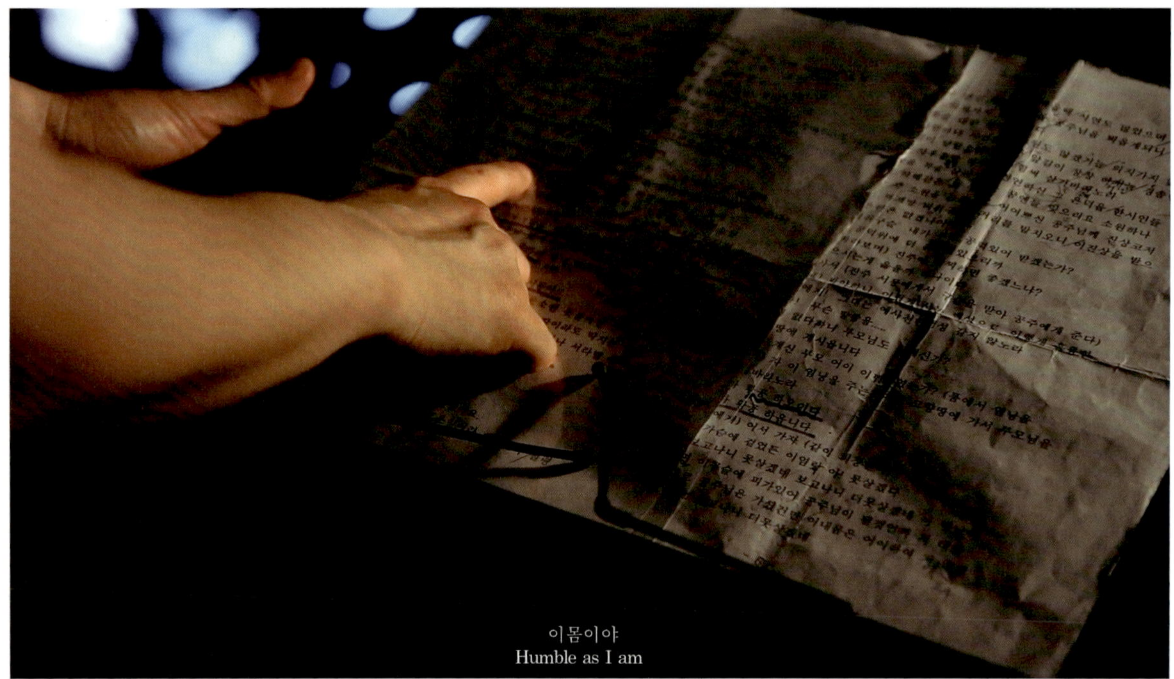

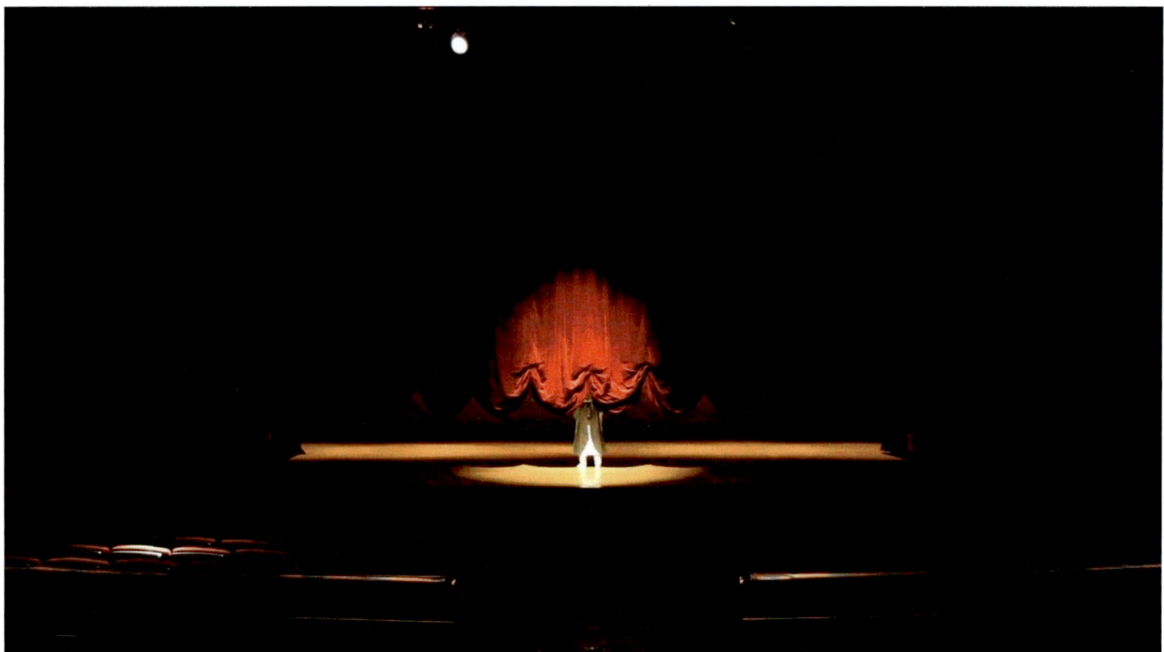

Nam's preparations continue in a dressing room, where the components of her masculinity appear in parts, prostheses separate from body and body severed from voice. As the camera pans slowly across a table, Nam caresses its contents: a fake beard and a roll of cloth bandage. Suddenly her voice breaks through. 'Better to die in front of a princess', she belts off-screen. 'That would be my land of happiness.' Her singing continues as, with deep familiarity, she applies make-up and changes into her *hanbok* before a mirror. Here, again, she is figured multiply – in objects, through voice, in the mirror – as if to compensate for her total isolation.

As the final scene reveals, Nam is alone backstage and everywhere else as well. In the theatre, the audience is entirely absent – except for her. She sits, as the man she has just become, in the empty house, surrounded by a sea of red velvet seats. The stage is empty, too, until she walks down the centre aisle and stands upon it. When she turns back around to face the audience, she sees herself, still as a man, sitting where she had just been sitting. She smiles and, upon smiling, turns her back on the absent audience – and on the version of herself seated there. Then the curtain closes. The camera sweeps through the house, which is now empty.

In contrast to the presentation at Atelier Hermès, which shows a performance before a live audience, the video shows the preparations for performance and, ultimately, the impossibility of performance. Without an audience, Nam cannot perform. Nevertheless, in full possession of her masculinity, she enters the stage. Once she does so, there is nothing to say – nothing is *sayable*. All she can do is be there and, finally, turn away. Her masculinity, which arises only in the context of *yeoseong gukgeuk*, has come to fruition in spite of the failure of that context to receive it. In a gesture of refusal, then, she turns away from the public arena of performance – away from the expectation of attention and the consolation of applause – and retreats backstage, deeper into the theatre, into a space of unreality, the only space that can accommodate her queer reality.

Queer Pasts and Futures

Yeoseong Gukgeuk Project was most recently presented at the 58th Venice Biennale in 2019. Curated for the Korean Pavilion by Hyunjin Kim, the exhibition takes its title – 'History Has Failed Us, but No Matter' – from the first sentence of Min Jin Lee's 2017 novel *Pachinko*, which follows four generations of an impoverished family through the Korean diaspora. Too often, Lee observes, historical archives omit or occlude 'all illiterate people and those who do not have others recording their lives in real time'.[10] Her novel attempts to redress these unjust omissions and occlusions, and the exhibition follows suit.

Though not shown as part of the exhibition, *Act of Affect* also participates in the work of redress. jung submits to the archive an account of *yeoseong gukgeuk*, speaking to its collapse, to its misfires and to its heartbreaks. Though *Act of Affect* is hardly an optimistic contribution, it constitutes a crucial index of queer loss. In *Feeling Backward* (2007), Heather Love proposes embracing the past – with all the 'suffering' and 'abjection' that the past entailed for queers – in order to envision a future that includes more than just pride, celebration and triumph, the mainstays of mainstream LGBTQI politics.[11] 'I insist on the importance of clinging to ruined identities and to histories of injury', Love says, because melancholia, shame and stigma 'cannot be uncoupled' from queer subjectivity.[12] As such, Love's approach to history is neither affirmative nor redemptive nor beholden to the demands of positivity and progress. Instead, it is 'forged in the image of exile, of refusal, even of failure'.[13] Along these lines, jung recognises and reckons with the cluster of negative affects that have become so central to *yeoseong gukgeuk*: exasperation, resignation, loneliness and longing. To allow for experiences of exclusion is to forge a more inclusive queer politics – not by moving on from these feelings of hurt but by making space for them.

1   Jack Halberstam, *Female Masculinity*, Durham: Duke University Press, 1998.

2   *Ibid.*, p.241.

3   *Act of Affect* (performance), dir. siren eun young jung, 2013, 19min 35sec, available at http://www.sirenjung.com/index.php/yeosung-gukgeuk-project/act-of-affect-performance-2013/ (last accessed on 5 November 2019).

4   siren eun young jung, 'In Place of a Preface', *Yeoseong Gukgeuk Project* (ed. Sohyun Ahn), Seoul: Forum A, 2016, p.183.

5   Heather Love, *Feeling Backward: Loss and the Politics of Queer History*, Cambridge, MA and London: Harvard University Press, 2007, p.162.

6   Sarah E. Chinn, 'Queer Feelings/Feeling Queer: A Conversation with Heather Love about Politics, Teaching, and the "Dark, Tender Thrills" of Affect', *Transformations: The Journal of Inclusive Scholarship and Pedagogy*, vol.22, no.2, 2012, pp.124–31.

7   J. Halberstam, 'Preface to the Twentieth Anniversary Edition', in *Female Masculinity*, op. cit., pp.xx–xxi.

8   Gilles Deleuze and Félix Guattari, *What Is Philosophy?* (trans. Hugh Tomlinson and Graham Burchell), New York: Columbia University Press, 1994, p.167.

9   *Act of Affect* (video), dir. siren eun young jung, 2013, 15min 36sec, available at http://www.sirenjung.com/index.php/yeosung-gukgeuk-project/act-of-affect-2013/ (last accessed on 5 November 2019).

10   Elizabeth Flock, 'Min Jin Lee annotates the first page of her bestselling book "Pachinko"', *PBS NewsHour*, PBS, 9 July 2018, available at https://www.pbs.org/newshour/arts/min-jin-lee-annotates-the-first-page-of-her-bestselling-book-pachinko (last accessed on 12 October 2019).

11   H. Love, *Feeling Backward*, op. cit., p.30.

12   *Ibid.*

13   *Ibid.*, p.71.

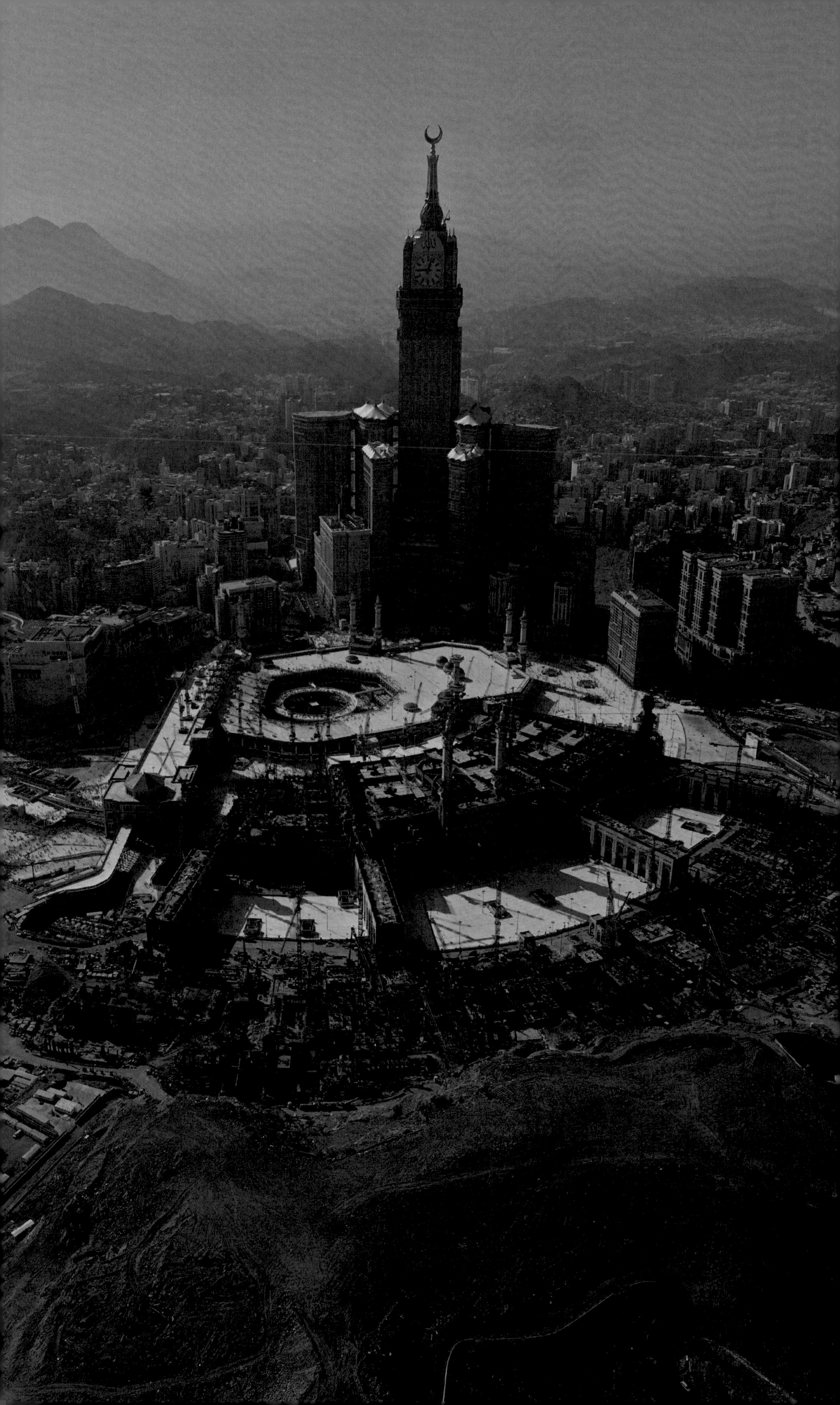

Reconstructing Saudi: A Look into the Short Window of Artist-Led Spaces and Organisations in a Country on the Verge of Change

— Melissa Gronlund

Every few years, someone writes an article about how the art scene in Saudi Arabia is 'opening up', or starting a 'new era'. You don't need to be a mathematician to know that's a logical fallacy. How many times can an art scene start from scratch? In fact, the Saudi scene has resisted historicisation, and what may seem novel or opaque is less a function of the famous Gulf tendency to chase the new than of the country's relative isolation and lack of a critical public culture. Because of restrictions on free speech, much isn't written down, leading to a dominance of rumour and remembrance. Occasional newspaper articles fixate on the qualitative 'difference' of Saudi as a country, rather than recording in detail the development of one of the most interesting art scenes of the region. At this point, contemporary art in Saudi Arabia is twenty years old, and artistic activity in Jeddah, Riyadh and Khobar/Dhahran has grown in concert with global engagement. While artistic milieus there are (for the moment) grassroots, the narratives they fulfil - critical, progressive, subversive, tribal, authentic - are informed, whether in a positive or negative relation, by regional and global art histories.

Part of what is special about Saudi rests on the history, extending back some 40 years, from which it is now emerging. A large proportion of the artists who today comprise the contemporary art scene were raised under the extreme Wahhabi social and religious codes that came into effect in 1979. In a sense, this era is ending before our eyes as Crown Prince Mohammad bin Salman undoes many of the country's most egregious strictures: the prohibition against women driving; the segregation between unrelated members of the sexes; the ban on entertainment in the form of cinemas, music and dancing. Within this whirlwind of reforms, art plays an important role - a fact to which the government's current huge investment in museums, biennials, exhibitions and research initiatives attests. Like other ambitious and wealthy states - the UAE, Qatar, Singapore, Kazakhstan - Saudi Arabia views art as a ticket to a cool globalism, with VIP perks as well as, in this case, the credibility of building on a strong decade of self-organised, spirited art practices.

Melissa Gronlund looks at various artists' initiatives and organisations that have shaped contemporary art in Saudi Arabia, and how artists address sensitive topics in a changing country.

The Early Years

Most people credit the semi-artistic, semi-curatorial initiative Edge of Arabia (2003–ongoing) with introducing contemporary art to Saudi Arabia, on account of its public showing of artworks made privately in studios. The project was founded by the Saudi artists Ahmed Mater and Abdulnasser Gharem, together with the Briton Stephen Stapleton. Mater and Gharem had known each other from the southern state of Asir where they grew up, and had already helped to establish the Al Miftaha Arts Village in Abha, which acts as a centre for art practice and community hub.[1] Edge of Arabia held their first exhibition in 2008, at the Brunei Gallery, part of SOAS in London, with work by Mater, Gharem and other well-known names such as Manal Al Dowayan and Faisal Samra.[2] They then launched an international tour, starting with a pop-up exhibition at a 2010 Riyadh event, and in 2012 presented Saudi's first large-scale public contemporary art exhibition, 'We Need to Talk', in the historically liberal Red Sea port city of Jeddah.[3] 'We Need to Talk' featured 21 artists and was accompanied by an educational programme that reached out to schools and university curricula, emphasising local engagement. It was conceived by Stapleton and curated by Mohammed Hafiz, who had established Athr Gallery - which has gone on to become the major gallery in Saudi - with the artist Hamza Serafi a few years earlier.

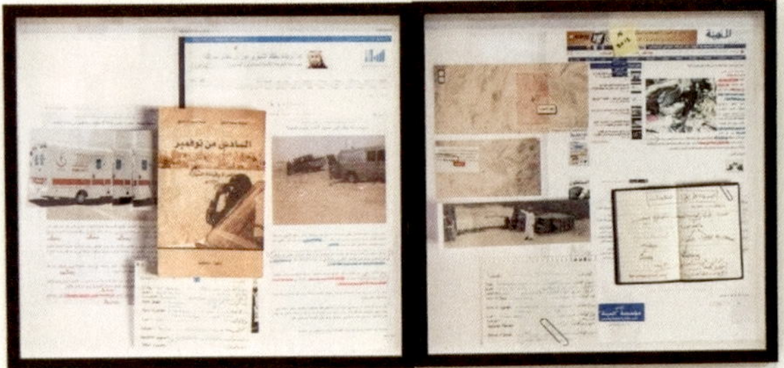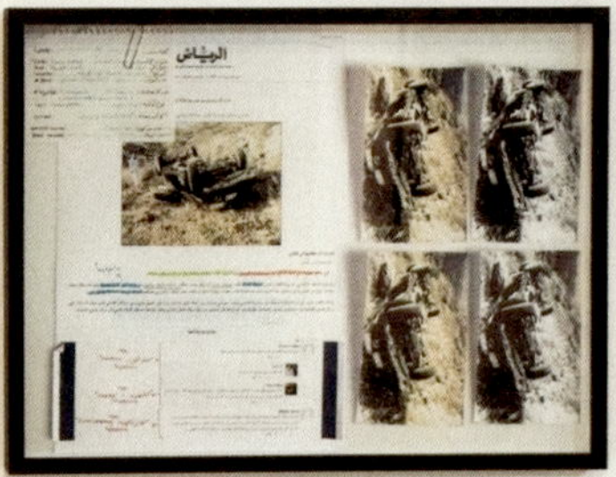

'We Need to Talk' was one of a number of artistic projects in Jeddah that developed in the early 2010s to give the nascent scene wider visibility. Jeddah Art Week, or JAW, which ran from 2013 to 2015, presented a city-wide programme of events and exhibitions of both Saudi and international work. It was initiated by Lina Lazaar and supported by various stakeholders – in the main the Jameel family, who are major patrons of art and social enterprise in Saudi.[4] This included the exhibition 'Kakaibang Jeddah', one of few shows to address the non-Saudi population. Curated by Lazaar in 2014, it showed work by fifteen resident Filipinos who were photographers alongside their domestic labour roles.[5] This was at the height of the country's 'Saudisation' policy, whereby the government tried to tackle its unemployment problem by reducing the percentage of foreign workers to 20 per cent of the labour force. This severely affected the Filipino population, with reports of tens of thousands of domestic workers being abruptly put out of work and facing repatriation.

Strictures against mixed gender gatherings, visual art and entertainment were roundly flouted at this time. Artists describe workarounds whereby they and other artists kept their activities private, including discussions held in private residences, which were subject to different regulations than restaurants or businesses

The event '21, 39' was also launched in 2014: an annual programme centred around a curated exhibition. Named after the coordinates of Jeddah and organised by the Saudi Art Council (a group of fifteen important local families rather than a government body), it has grown into the most important contemporary art offering within the country and the primary means of engagement for international visitors. Its main exhibition is held across disused spaces in the Gold Moor Mall and a crumbling house in the city's historic old town, Al Balad, and has grown into the agenda-setting role of a biennial. Notable editions were 'Safar' ('Travel') in 2017, for which Sam Bardaouil and Till Fellrath developed a pedagogical framework

Manal Al Dowayan, *Crash*, 2017, digital c-type print. Courtesy Saudi Art Council

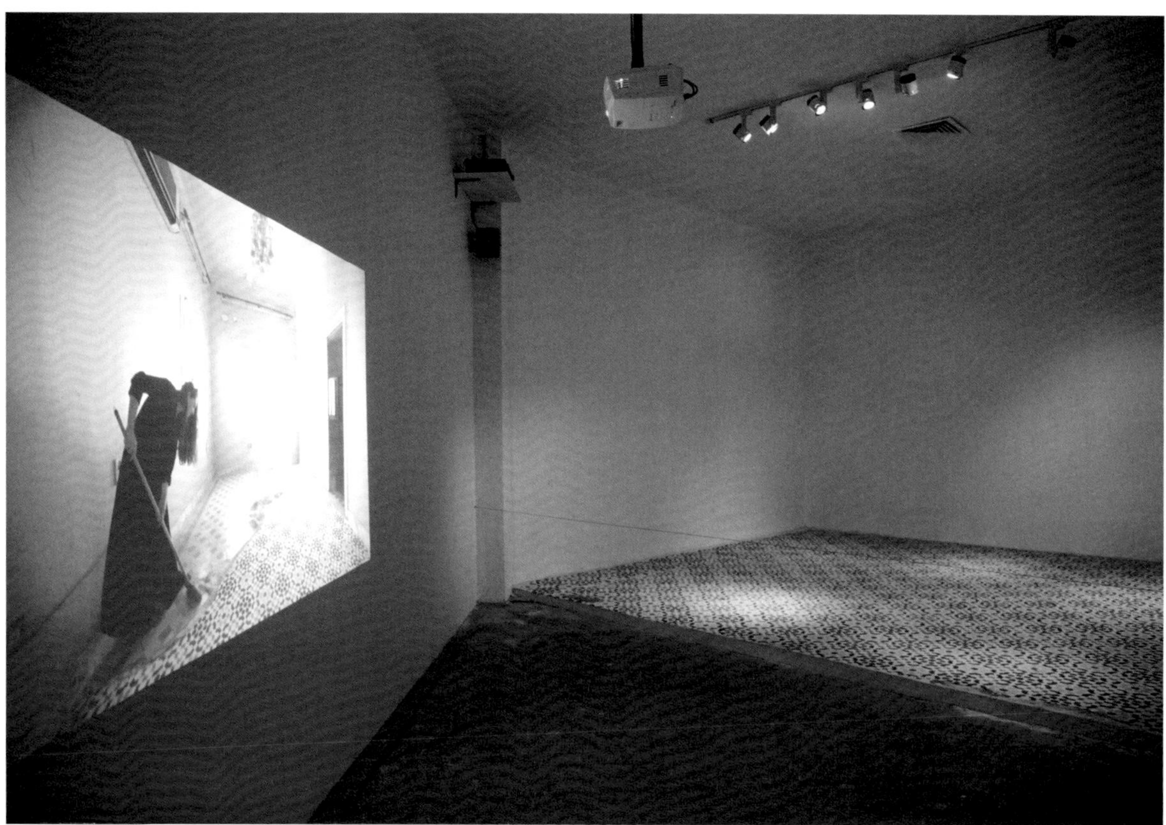

and worked closely with a group of young artists to develop their work, and 'I Love You, Urgently', in 2020, curated by Maya El-Khalil, formerly of Athr Gallery, which presented many of the key young artists of the last five years.

Most of these artists are working in ways unconnected to the modernist art histories that had tried to take root in the kingdom prior to the introduction of the Wahhabi codes. These codes were put into practice after the Siege of Mecca (1979), when a group of religious extremists captured the Grand Mosque, trapping thousands of worshippers inside. The site was besieged for over two weeks, with extremists fighting against the Saudi military and the French corps who had come in their support, in what became a shocking episode for the Saudis. In response, Saudi clerics sought to placate religious conservatives, and throughout the 1980s issued a number of strict proclamations. Before these restrictions, art had been part of Saudi, if only to the extent that any country with little visual arts or European cultural tradition had a painting or sculptural-based art scene. Modernism is principally associated with the Dar Al Funoon Al Saudi (Saudi Art House), founded by the painter Mohammed Al Saleem, which was active as an art school and exhibition site in Riyadh in the 1970s.[6] Many artists were sent by the government to be educated abroad during that time – a common practice among the Gulf states, which had money but no faculties for art education – to places such as Cairo, Baghdad, Paris and London. Some, such as Safeya Binzagr, set up informal art schools when they returned. It is debatable how much impact these have had on the contemporary art scene today, but their existence belies the impression of a Saudi state whose aniconic fatwas and gender hierarchies were fully enforced. In the 1990s Binzagr, together with a Scottish assistant, taught painting to both male and female Saudi and expat students at her Safeya Binzagr Gallery in Jeddah. Binzagr herself collected examples of and painted watercolours of the folk dresses that showed the diversity of tribes and regions before they were united by the house of Al Saud in the 1930s.

But the Wahhabi restrictions should not be underestimated either. They had a determining effect on the art scene that exists now, on the artwork produced as well as on the infrastructure behind it, as most culture was forced underground. Many early works were critical in nature, and this criticality increased as time went on, aided by frustration with the state and restlessness among the young population, as well as excitement over what was possible – particularly after the introduction of the internet, which met a population that had

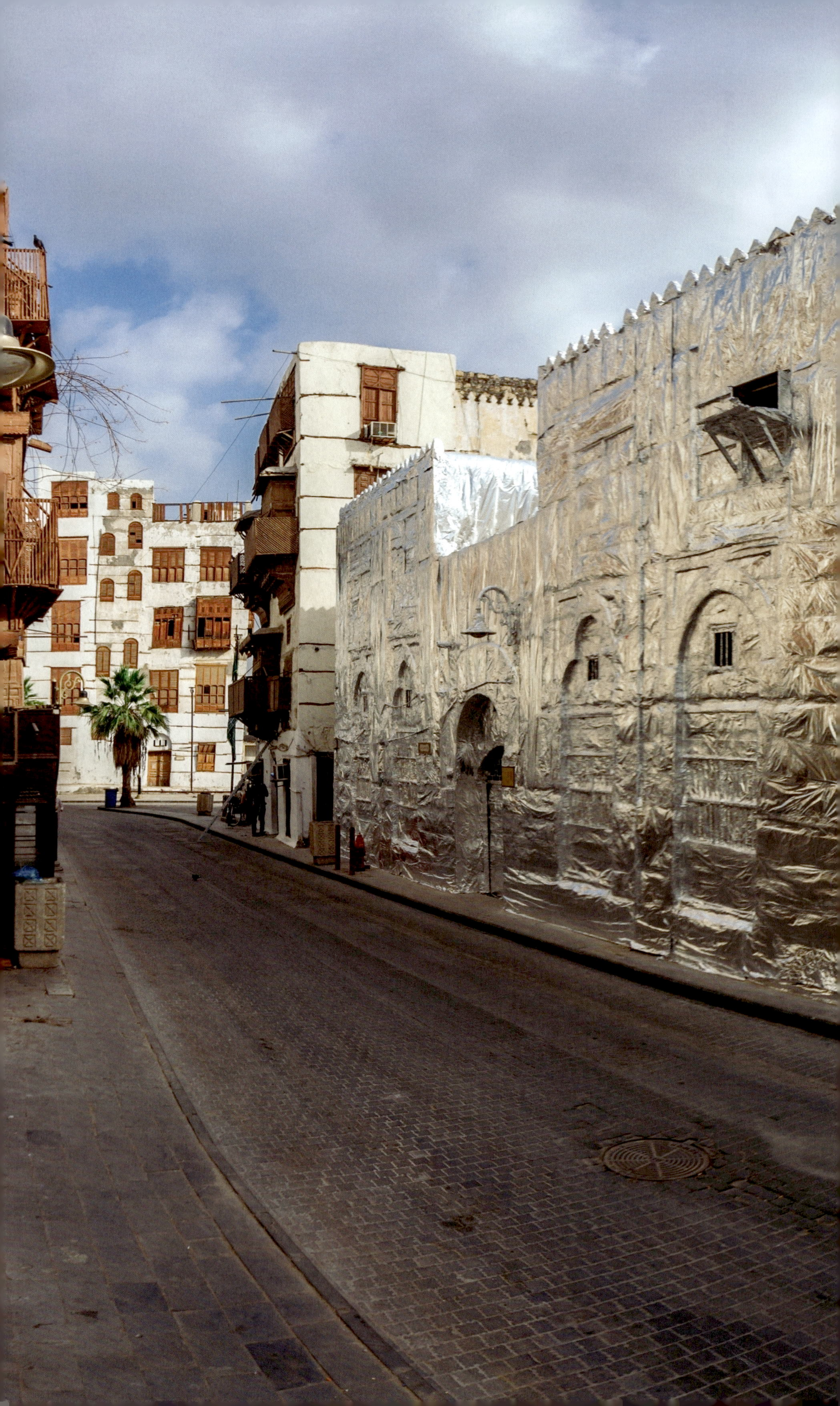

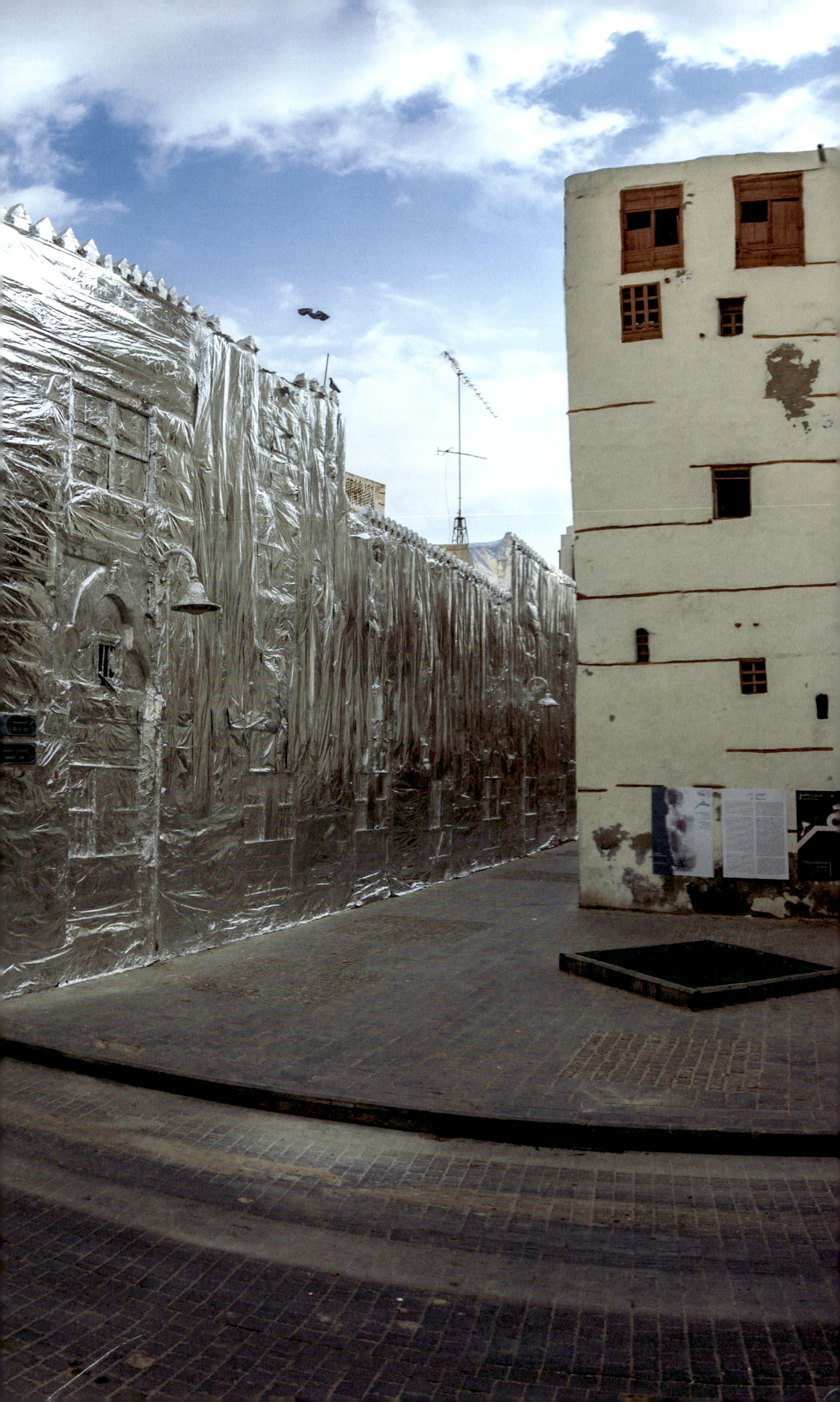

been largely home-bound, whether because of gender restrictions or lifestyle. Social media sites and YouTube played a major role in forming pockets of creativity and community among artists, film-makers, writers, graphic designers, comedians and activists.[7]

Strictures against mixed gender gatherings, visual art and entertainment were roundly flouted at this time. Artists describe workarounds whereby they and other artists kept their activities private, including discussions held in private residences, which were subject to different regulations than restaurants or businesses. The Kuwaiti artist Monira Al Qadiri likened the way information travelled to *samizdat*. Recounting an experience from 2016 in Riyadh, the country's conservative capital, she recalled the circuitous path she took to get to an underground society of film-makers, which was open only to men but had extended an invitation to her. She dressed in men's clothes and followed her friend's instructions, making several turnings and then pushing forward on a door marked with an 'X'.[8]

In Jeddah, Mater's studio operated as a semi-public site for exhibitions, talks, screenings and general discussions. He ran it with the artist Arwa Al Neami, his then-wife, calling it Pharan Studios after the Pharan desert - another name for Jeddah's Hejazi region. Pharan Studios became a crucial part of the Jeddah art scene, welcoming international visitors and open to local projects. The 2017 talks programme 'RAWdah Talks', which Mater organised with the artist and architect Abdulrahman Gazzaz, now of the architecture firm bricklab, discussed topics such as consumer culture, the relationship between public space and freedom of speech, and the idea of the *genius loci*, looking to the street life of Jeddah with its migrant-run shops. The year-long series was open to the public by WhatsApp and Instagram; its audience was mostly artists, students and architects.[9]

Though the art world centred in Jeddah, film-makers and artists also organised in the country's other two main cities of Riyadh and Khobar, in the Eastern Province. Gharem's studio in Riyadh, like Mater's, was a site for discussions and exhibitions with young artists. In 2012, the curator Raneen Bukhari set up the art organisation Loud Art in Desert Designs, a provincial art gallery run by her parents in Khobar. Loud Art aimed to present curated shows - still not yet the dominant practice in Saudi - and was a success among the emerging generation. With her co-founder Najla Al Suhaimi, Bukhari gave significant early shows to a number of now established artists, including Sarah Al Abdali, Ayman Zedani and Muhannad Shono. Prices for work were kept low - around 20–30 US dollars a piece - to avoid an elitist art market. Bukhari then launched a second, more discursive platform, Hunart, which aimed to host one talk per month and broadcast all its activities on Snapchat.

In all Saudi exhibitions at the time, works were vetted by the Ministry of Information beforehand and organisers were careful about which images were posted online. This was not only because images themselves were *samizdat*, but because many of these images seemed to have been shocking by any measure: reports in the Western press suggest they addressed sensitive topics head-on, in areas including gender identity and LGBTQI+ rights, sex, and religion. There were numerous run-ins with the religious police. Ashraf Fayadh, the Palestinian poet and artist who grew up in Abha with Mater and who also moved to Jeddah, was in 2015 sentenced to death for apostasy - a charge widely regarded as illegitimate. A public outcry led to the sentence being commuted, but he remains in jail.

Works attained different lives inside and outside the Kingdom. Gharem's photograph and video *Siraat* ('The Path', 2009), for example, addresses an episode from 1982 in the village he grew up in Asir, in which a group of villagers and their livestock took shelter from flooding by gathering under a bridge. As the rainfall became a deluge, the bridge partially collapsed, and the villagers were swept away. Many died, and the incident became well-known locally, but was never officially acknowledged. In 2003, Gharem and 24 friends and associates spray-painted the cracked bridge with the word '*siraat*' (from *siraat al-mustaqim*, or 'the straight path', repeated during Muslim prayers), by way of a memorial.[10] The work has grown into an example of censorship: for many years it was exhibited abroad (at Los Angeles County Museum of Art and the British Museum in London), but not in Saudi. Mater's endorsement by the government (he briefly served as director of Misk, the art foundation set up by Mohammed bin Salman) has also meant his once controversial works are now more widely seen. His cell-phone video series *Ground Zero I-II-III* (2012) captured images of migrant labourers, and his suite of images titled *Desert of Pharan: Unofficial Histories Behind the Mass Expansion of Mecca* (2011–ongoing) also highlighted the fast pace of development of Islam's most holy site, the spiritual nature of which many felt was sold out to real-estate concerns. These were all exhibited in 2018 in Mater's first solo exhibition in the Kingdom, part of '21, 39'.

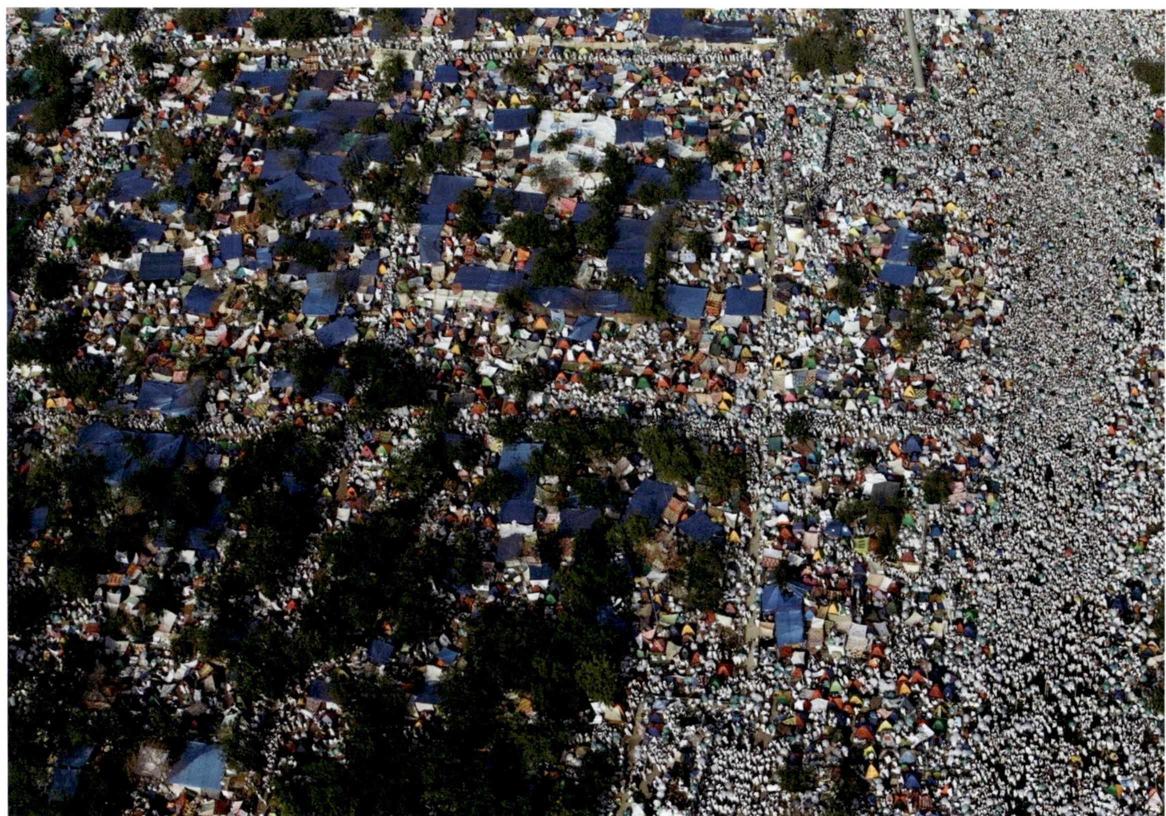

Ahmed Mater,
L'Ouverture from the
'Desert of Pharan'
series, 2012, laser
chrome print
on KODAK real
photopaper, 140 ×
210cm. Courtesy
the artist and Athr
Gallery, Jeddah

Previous Spread:
Abdullah Al-Othman,
Suspended, 2017,
part of 'Safar', 21,39
Jeddah Arts, 2017.
Photograph: Majed
Angawi. Courtesy
Saudi Art Council

Other artists challenged the restrictions on women. Al Dowayan made *Esmi* (My Name) in 2012, a series of enlarged prayer beads that hangs from the ceiling, in response to the common injunction in Saudi against women's names being said aloud; many conservative households hold that women shouldn't be seen or even spoken of publicly. Al Dowayan pointed out that the Quran and King Abdul Aziz, the father of Saudi Arabia, both spoke the names of their female relatives in public. She gathered together groups of women, each of whom spoke her name aloud and wrote it on a bead; Al Dowayan later strung these into the work. Sarah Abu Abdullah, in the video *Saudi Automobile* (2012), shows herself painting an old, disused car pink. 'This wishful gesture was the only way I could get myself a car – cold comfort for the current impossibility of my dream that I, as an independent person, can drive myself to work one day', she wrote.[11]

These acts of resistance have been frequently discussed in the Western press, where they fit with narratives of the artist as dissident genius, or of the eventual triumph of Western-style democracy over Eastern oppression, particularly that of women. It is unclear how widespread the truly provocative practices were, as is the exact nature of what it was that artists were rebelling against – boredom seems as much a potential enemy as illiberal politics. Some practices appear as pointed acts aimed at changing civic society, while others appear more like adaptations to a restrictive environment. It's also important to underline that many of these works were not anti-Saudi; many artists remain invested in the religious, historical and cultural specificity of Saudi identity. Arguably, these concerns have made Saudi artists more anti-colonialist than artists in other Gulf countries. When Al Dowayan, for example, wrote her master's dissertation at the Royal College of Art in London, she pointedly moved away from secondary material from Western sources, using mostly Middle Eastern material instead – a performative project in its own right. Dana Awartani, who studied at Central Saint Martins, rejected the role – of oppressed woman or exiled Arab – she felt forced to play in London, and in Turkey undertook an *ijazah*: an apprenticeship in traditional illumination. Her practice now marries Sufi influences and traditional craft with Western contemporary art strategies such as narrative and site-specificity. There is also a strong recuperative ethos, even in the most critical of practices. Like Mater's *Mecca* series, many of the works from the 2010s were produced less by artists rushing forward towards a new liberal order than by artists seeking to halt a pace of change that had begun with

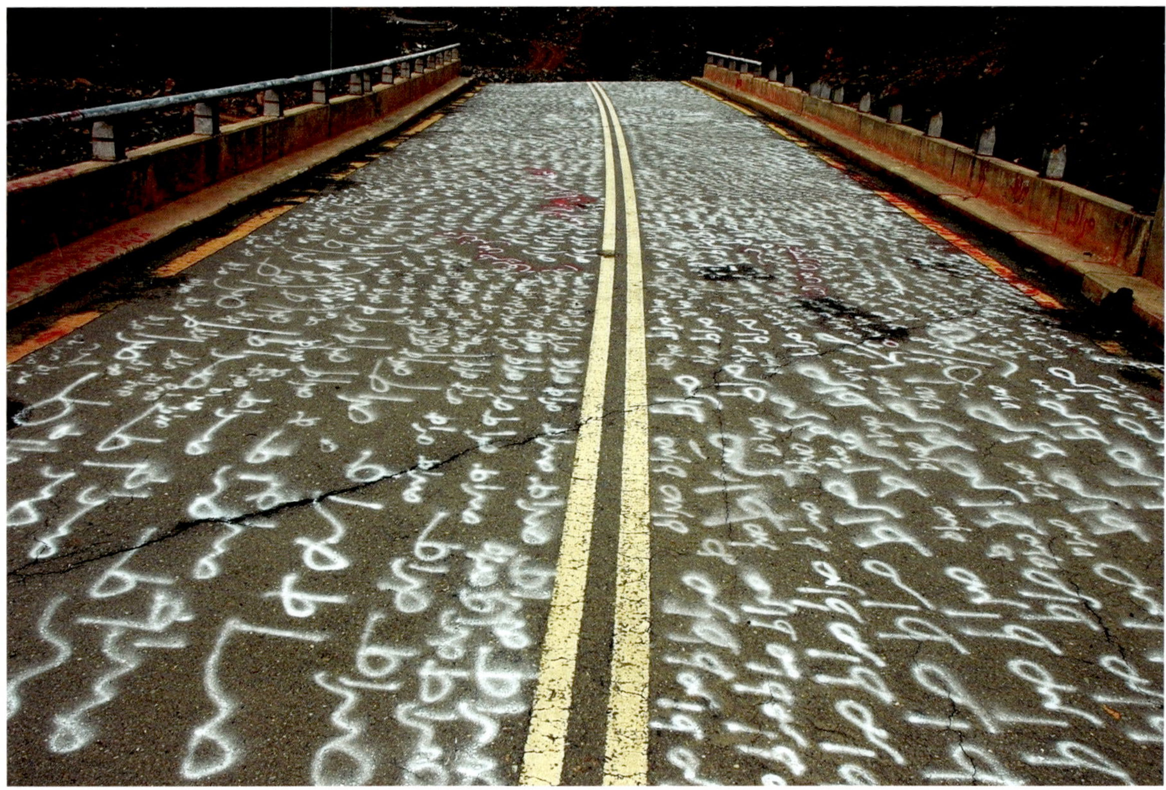

newfound wealth. In the series *Doors of Barlik* (2017) Moath Alofi captures images of series
of doorways in his native Medina that were being destroyed as the city was renovated. These
were made of worn wood and cheap metal, sometimes with crumbling steps – the un-new
part of the Gulf already fast receding.

The Short Window

It is strange to write these words about the mid-2010s as if those years were in the far past.
Most of the 'young' artists working today were already working then, and yet the rapidity
of change in Saudi seems to have pushed that era far afield, aided perhaps by the sheer
visibility of reform. Until 2019, women in Saudi still wore the abaya, the robe covering their
clothes. Landing at the airports would generate a hubbub of sartorial switcheroos as women
headed to the bathrooms or rustled in bags for their cover-ups. At the entrance to houses,
clothing racks were set up for abayas, which did not have to be worn in private homes. On
leaving, queues clogged up all exits. These practices are now a thing of the past for visitors
and non-Saudis, and have the effect of dating the whirlwind of the last few years, incidentally
separating the artist-organised years from the present of large-scale investment and
governmental priority.

A hallmark of the Saudi art scene has been its glorious imbalance between artists and
infrastructure, and its success shows the importance of home-grown networks and self-
organisation – buoyed, to be sure, by a financial stability for artists that does not have a
correlate in the West. All this, however, is set to change, as the new Ministry of Culture is
establishing an infrastructure of museums, biennials, festivals and arts organisations. These
are all positive developments, but how exactly they will affect the art world at large is yet to
be seen. The spotlight on the visual arts curtails its former freedom to criticise, and I have
heard from numerous sources that one is no longer sure of the rules, which can make the field
of artistic production more difficult to navigate. Others point to the breakneck speed with
which shows and institutions are being set up, as well as a reliance on outside international
consultants, such as Kearney, Deloitte and PWC, all of which are paid enormous sums of
money to advise on an art world that lies beyond their field of specialism.

International collaborations, which appear to be the hallmark of these consultant
projects, have also proven difficult politically. Many foreign art organisations have
taken stands against working with Saudi, and for good reason. Saudi Arabia has a poor

track record on human rights, gender equality and LGBTQI+ issues. The authoritarian government gives vastly different treatment to its citizens versus its substantial labour migrant population. Mohammed bin Salman most likely ordered the killing of the journalist Jamal Khashoggi. At the same time, it's difficult to properly construct a recent art history of Saudi, or to support its artists, when engagement is constantly stymied by political opposition to the state. It feels important to note that the conflation between individuals and state is too quickly made in a Saudi context, for a host of reasons – most charitably, the desire to find a stable moral high ground in difficult times.

Many of the artist-led initiatives mentioned here have now closed. Some of the founders are working to build up the 'new' scene; others have moved out to typical Saudi hideaways such as London and Dubai, or to places less typical, including LA. Investment is soaring but free speech remains elusive. There is now a certain nostalgia for the Pharan Studios years, which is easy to understand. The artist Arwa Al Neami told me that within the studio was a feeling of support that existed nowhere else. 'Everyone said you were nothing', she says she told the artists, 'but I said: you are everything'.[12]

1   Asir, which borders Yemen and has a verdant, mountainous terrain, has a reputation in Saudi for its creativity; the houses are all brightly painted and the men of one tribe wear flower crowns on their heads. These men, of course, are now becoming a tourist attraction.

2   'Edge of Arabia', Brunei Gallery, SOAS, 16 October–13 December 2008. Edge of Arabia was initially partially funded by Art Jameel, the Saudi family foundation that is an important supporter of traditional and contemporary art. Other early partners included the British Council, the Saudi Arabian General Investment Authority (SAGIA) and Abraaj Capital. In 2011 they developed a commercial strand, EOA.Projects, which mostly sold prints.

3   'Global Competitiveness Forum', Riyadh, 1 January–2 February 2010; 'We Need to Talk', curated by Mohammed Hafiz with Stephen Stapleton, Al Furusiya Marina, Jeddah, 20 January–26 February 2012.

4   Other entities involved included Athr Gallery, Ayyam Gallery, Arabian Wings, Rochan Fine Arts Gallery, Hafez Gallery, Edge of Arabia and Sotheby's. The final edition was largely stalled because of the mourning period declared after the death of King Abdullah in January 2015.

5   'Kakaibang Jeddah', Al Furusiya Exhibition Hall, Jeddah Park Hyatt Hotel, 31 January–6 February 2014.

6   Two of the best introductions to this period are in sites associated with commercial activity: the market has outpaced traditional scholarship when it comes to the Gulf art scene. See Sam Bardaouil and Till Fellrath (ed.), *That Feverish Leap into the Fierceness of Life: A Look at Five Artist Groups in Five Arab Cities across Five Decades* (exh. cat.), Dubai: Art Dubai Modern, 2018 and Ahmed Mater, 'Fifty Years of Modernism in Saudi Arabia', *20th Century Art / Middle East* [auction catalogue, April 2019], London: Christie's, 2019, available at https://www.sothebys.com/en/auctions/ecatalogue/2019/20th-century-art-middle-east-l19228/lot.38.html (last accessed on 10 February 2020).

7   Some of these people have expanded into the entertainment sphere that is also burgeoning in Saudi, such as Faisal Al Amer and Malik Nejer, who now run the Myrkott Animation Studio, or the comedian and social activist Hisham Fageeh, whose video *No Woman, No Drive* from 2013, about the law against women driving, went viral on social media. He later co-produced and starred in the Oscar-submitted film *Barakah Meets Barakah* (2016) and has become a well-known actor.

8   Monira Al Qadiri, 'Future Imperfect: The Saudi New Wave | Digital Landscapes and Future Institutions', *Ibraaz*, 9 December 2016, available at https://www.ibraaz.org/publications/77 (last accessed on 13 February 2020).

9   The title references Rawdah, the working-class area in which Pharan Studios was located.

10   This work was due to be in Edge of Arabia's 'We Need to Talk', but could not be shown in Saudi.

11   See the work's documentation on Athr Gallery's website: https://www.athrart.com/artist/Sarah_Abu%20Abdallah/works/2577 (last accessed on 13 February 2020). Abu Abdallah's *Saudi Automobile* and Mater's *Ground Zero*, as well as a number of works by other artists in this story were on view at Athr in 'Durational Portrait: A Brief Overview of Video Art in Saudi Arabia' – one of the few shows to shed a historical light on this period. Curated by Afia bin Taleb and Tara Aldughaither, it sets out a typology of stages of Saudi video art development, from 'Beginnings' to 'Identity' to 'Connections' to 'Recovery', or the current reform era. It also takes in the importance of contextual events, such as the September 11 attacks (where fifteen out of nineteen attackers were Saudi), as well as the Arab Spring.

12   Conversation with the artist, 11 February 2020.

salmon today
would be grey,

but salmon can also
be red, or pink,
or even salmon

The dramatic rise of open net salmon fish farms have created a new season of polluted oceans that emerged in the 1970s. Salmon today would be grey, but salmon can also be red or pink, or even salmon. The fish are heavily dependent on antibiotics and pork- and fish-based feed pellets. Since salmon in farms are not allowed to swim free, they cannot feed on krill and shrimps, which would give them their natural salmon colour. Farms replace the pigment with synthetic additives that can be chosen from 15 salmon pantones. Grown in open-net cylinders containing about one to two million fish per farm, salmon environments have a dramatic effect on both the body of the fish and the seabed. Hundreds of kilos of salmon manure are deposited into the sea every minute, devastating the ecosystem underneath while stimulating outbreaks of parasites and disease, like lethal sea lice.

Unlike how intensive salmon farming produces an excess of nitrogen, other aquacultures clean water by breathing and eating. One mussel is able to filter up to 25 litres of water per day and one oyster can filter up to 125 litres. So do other bivalves like clams, scallops, and razor clams, as well as a wide range of seaweed, especially kelp, which has a great appetite for carbon dioxide. In addition to being crucial agents in removing pollutants from coastal seawater, these creatures provide a good source of protein without the need for irrigation or fertilisers.

Bloody Oyster Cocktail

Materials
30 ml Vodka
90 ml Tomato juice
1 celery stalk
1 cucumber stick
Horseradish
1 oyster
Ice

Method
Over ice pour vodka and tomato juice into a highball glass. Shuck your oyster and immediately spill all the water inside the shell into your glass. Release the oyster from the muscles with your shucking knife and gently skewer it. Put the skewer, oyster facing down into the glass and stir a couple of times gently. Add the celery stalk, cucumber stick and grade a bit of horseradish. Don't throw the shells! Instead, distribute them along your flowers and vegetables growing outside as fertiliser; they also act as a snail deterrent. Your garden will be thankful.

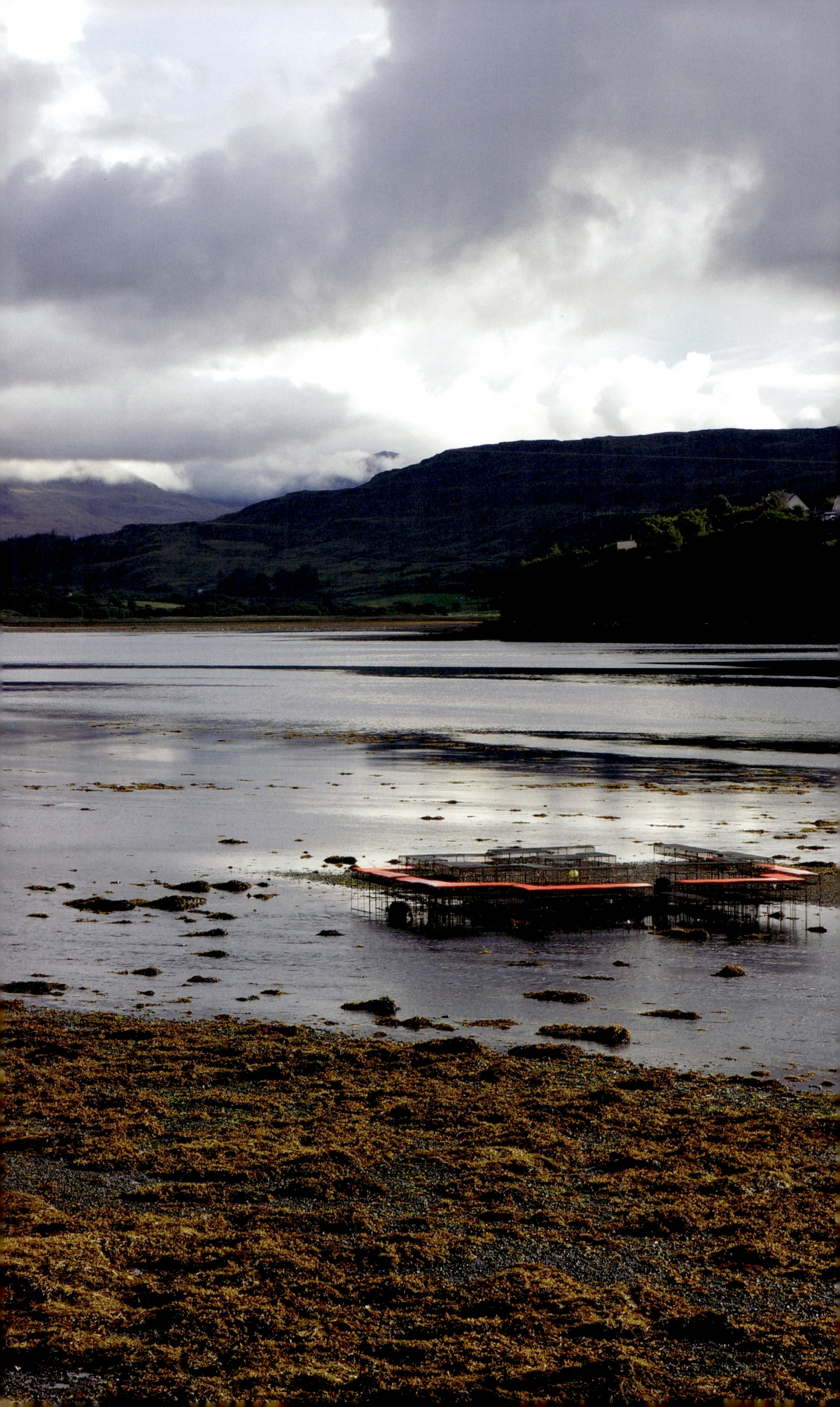

On Cooking Sections

— May Rosenthal Sloan

Oyster bloody Mary, Christmas pudding and Japanese knotweed ice cream. These might just sound like features of a chic midwinter menu, but in fact, these dishes are punctuations in a growing body of richly researched work by Alon Schwabe and Daniel Fernández Pascual, aka Cooking Sections, who describe themselves as 'spatial practitioners'. Informed by their backgrounds in architecture and performance, the duo practices the kind of interdisciplinary, idealed work that stubbornly resists definition, intersecting subjects of food, space, ecology, politics, history and culture.

Cooking Sections' projects might at first appear somewhat esoteric, with research that takes as its starting point such varied subjects as colonial pudding ingredients, aquaculture practices, pantone shades of salmon flesh and Ukrainian soil

May Rosenthal Sloan explores the culinary works of Cooking Sections, whose research in questions of ecology, capital and power culminates in transformative interventions.

health. But the beauty of this work is the way in which it makes clarifying links between seemingly disparate subjects, making history, the contemporary and the future part of the same question. That Cooking Sections use food – that most universal material, imbued with complicated symbolism – as a way to address apparently disconnected spheres is no coincidence. Using cooking and eating as ways to communicate, the duo ensures that viewers (eaters) almost inevitably insert themselves into a broader narrative, seeing with clarity how their experience and choices fit into the systems and dynamics at play around them.

To take a first example, *The Empire Remains Christmas Pudding* (2013-ongoing), a performance that was part of the broader project *The Empire Remains Shop* (2013-ongoing), made use of a 1928 Christmas pudding recipe from the Empire Marketing Board, an organisation set up to promote and celebrate the consumption of goods produced within the British Empire. The recipe calls for

Australian currants, South African candied peel, eggs from the Irish Free State, nutmeg from the British West Indies and brandy that might be Cypriot or Palestinian. Over time, however, many of these geographical and political boundaries have shifted. Supply chains have become more tortuous, and Britain's relationship with its own colonial and imperial past has become something to grapple with rather than take solipsistic pride in. Cooking Sections traced these shifting dynamics by recreating that original Christmas pudding recipe. Charting the modern origins of the ingredients used in 1928, and 'turning the locations in the new recipe for the pudding into an edible map', they made tangible the changes in Britain's political, economic and cultural network of supply.[1] Their pudding signals a changing awareness of the former British Empire, and the enduring ghosts of colonial and imperial abuse.

The project *Climavore* (2015-ongoing), much like *The Empire Remains Shop*, reflects on serious global issues, however, this project also faces the future, proposing a new form of eating that plays on the idea of the 'locavore' (who eats according to what can be locally grown and acquired). Unlike a locavore, the 'climavore' would eat according to climate events, their choices not just inflicting less damage on the natural world, but actually improving the ecological health of the land and sea around them. Incorporating detailed research, recipe writing, performance and site-specific installations, this concept is as bold and interesting in its scientific and political outlook as its artistic output. As with *The Empire Remains Christmas Pudding*, a focus on cooking allows the participant or viewer to consider how their own eating experiences and choices link their bodies and minds to various spatial and temporal contexts.

As the earth and its human and nonhuman inhabitants suffer from the harsh and unpredictable effects of climate change, there are difficulties in rendering the relevant academic research intelligible to a general public audience. One such issue is visibility. For example, while the image of the world's forests as giant lungs is a familiar one (and one that gathers potency as we witness the combination of rainforest clearances and rampant wildfires that have been ravaging our collective breathing apparatus), less familiar is the idea of the oceans and marine life as vitally important oxygen producing resources. The acidification of oceans is not as troubling a visual as the dramatic burning of plant life and yet it poses a significant risk to our planet.

A recent study has produced evidence that the mass extinction that occurred some sixty-six million years ago was likely to have been caused in part by a sudden, dramatic drop in oceanic PH levels following the meteorite collision that wiped out the dinosaurs. The study takes an in-depth look into the long-distant past, providing new perspectives on our present ecological situation.[2] The authors suggest that we urgently need to address the current acidification of oceans, caused by the absorption of man-made carbon emissions. Dr Michael Henehan, citing the drop of 0.25 PH units that his co-authored report claims has destroyed marine life on a colossal scale, states: 'ocean acidification can precipitate ecological collapse. [...] If 0.25 was enough to precipitate a mass extinction, we should be worried.'[3]

Worrying, however, feels like a painfully passive activity in the context of such evidence. But how can non-specialists begin to consider this kind of research? One issue is that of linking the vastness of academic knowledge with the kind of everyday action, demanding widespread participation,

---

By invoking the power of storytelling, prototyping and poetry, artists can convert meaningful words on a page into visual, audible imaginings of better worlds and actions – cultural calls to arms.

required to make change. The role of artists and designers, as cultural interventionists, is crucial here. By invoking the power of storytelling, prototyping and poetry, artists can convert meaningful words on a page into visual, audible imaginings of better worlds and actions – cultural calls to arms. And by incorporating rigorous ecological research in tangible, sensory, presentations, Pascual and Schwabe's work allows ideas to be ingested (sometimes physically) and understood. It also responds to the political, social and cultural contexts surrounding that science in new and compelling ways that would be difficult to achieve from within the academy. In the context of food research, the power of this work can be immediate because food is something with which we all engage on a daily basis.[4]

It is much more widely understood today than it was 50 or even 10 years ago that how we eat impacts on the world around us. But what if questions around how we engage with food could be framed less as damage limitation than in terms of possibilities? What if we could move away from the inconvenient tweaking of diets (being asked to eat less of what we like) and towards positive acts of eating in ways that will improve the health of the planet? With a project like *Climavore*, Cooking Sections look at what is possible and what could be beautiful, rather than examining perceived behavioural failings. Rather than admonishing, they intrigue, inform and delight. Early iterations of the project saw the development of recipes that utilised drought-resistant ingredients in the context of a temporary water shortage, or seaweed and filtering bivalves in response to polluted shorelines. Not only did Cooking Sections develop a methodology for in-depth research into specific man-made climate and landscape alteration, they also went on to envision entire growing and eating cultures that would respond to these phenomena.

In 2017, Pascual and Schwabe began to experiment with how to turn the philosophy behind the *Climavore* project into something more physically tangible. A long-term installation off the Isle of Skye, *CLIMAVORE: On Tidal Zones*, reacts to the island's changing coastal environment, and particularly the acidification of the local Scottish seas, by encouraging the cultivation and consumption of bivalves and seaweeds, which have a cleansing effect on water. Functioning as both a farming and dining space, the installation emerges from the glassy water of Bayfield like an elegant metallic sea monster, its low-slung wire mesh angles delicately trailing seaweed against a gorgeously moody mountainous backdrop. *CLIMAVORE: On Tidal Zones* pushes the concept of remedial diets, articulating the idea that a particular geographic and ecological zone can become the recipient of a positive human impact that in turn provides the basis for their nourishment (nutritional, cultural and social). It is a beautiful but practical realisation of the artists' ideas.[5]

This work resists the logic of market-driven over-production, instead using ideas, research and artistic practice to positive,

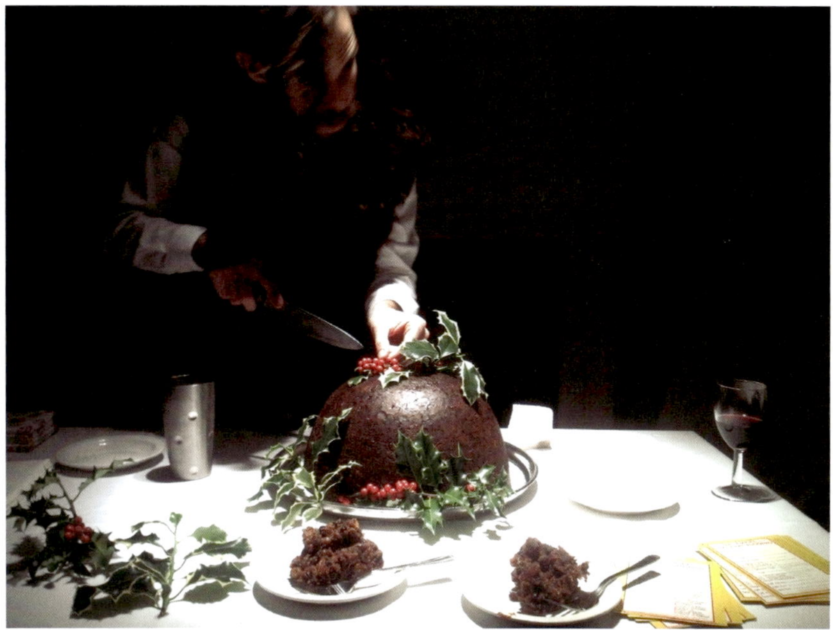

even transformative effect. It must be noted that this can only be expected to come about through thoughtful and well-funded commissioning of work, that allows (and pays) for the time of both artists and curators to engage in meaningful research and development.[6] Cooking Sections have discussed the importance of research and presentation bearing equal weight, acting as reciprocal agents in the dissemination of ideas.[7] This is something that many artists and designers working with food appear to be putting at the core of their practice.

For example, designer and materials researcher Nienke Hoogvliet has been finding ways to render the issue of value gut-wrenchingly tangible through pared-back presentation of research. Her project *Bare Bones* (2018–ongoing), a collaboration with curator Jorn Konijn, highlights the physiological differences between factory-farmed and organic chickens. Most people know there is a difference between these two kinds of bird in the quality of both life and of meat, yet for many of us this is easy to ignore as abstract, and therefore only mildly uncomfortable knowledge. With *Bare Bones*, Hoogvliet presents two sets of bones, primarily distinguishable through slight differences in size. She then takes each set through the process required to make bone china, displaying the results. Two small pots of ground bone sit next to two tiles and two tiny bowls. One set has the smooth, pale, delicate characteristics of fine bone china; the other looks pitted and crumbly, as though the material has refused to coagulate. One can guess which set of

samples comes from the factory-farmed chicken. While Hoogvliet shows what you already knew, her presentation makes this knowledge inescapably felt.

Bare Bones is a tender, stark representation of the way that animal bodies are valued in large-scale industrial agriculture, in which the lives of birds are made to fit with factory methods. The quality (or lack thereof) of those bones also points to human exploitation of other humans – the squeezing of certain lives to the point where only cheap food is affordable. Humans need to eat and the brutal inequity of people going hungry anywhere in the world when there are enormous profits being made in the food industry is plain. But when food becomes 'cheap', the cost does not go away; rather it is transferred elsewhere in the system of production, in the form of exploitative labour or ecological damage. This transferal of cost and value is reflected in artist Asunción Molinos Gordo's work *Hunger is a Man-Made Object* (2016). Her neon sign, displayed in Cooking Sections' *Empire Remains Shop* flashes a phrase used by traders on the stock exchange: 'BUY THE RUMOR, SELL THE NEWS.' It reminds us that in global markets, food becomes something to be speculated upon, rather than primarily a means of nourishment. Investors like foodstuffs because buyers for them can almost always be found, whatever the price. Since the financial crash of 2008, investment in food markets has grown enormously, in turn causing volatility in food prices globally, with a knock-on effect of hardship for both producers and consumers.

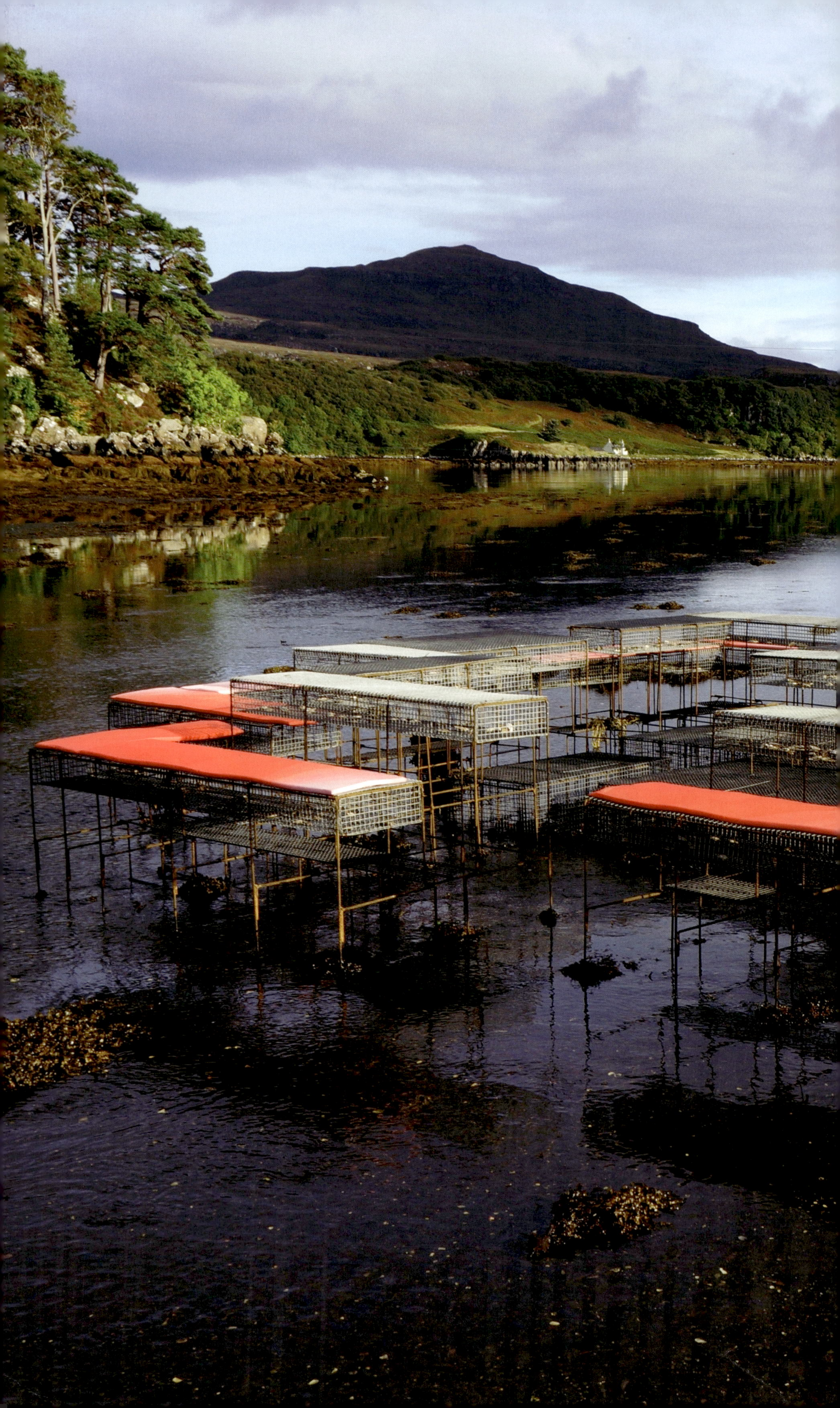

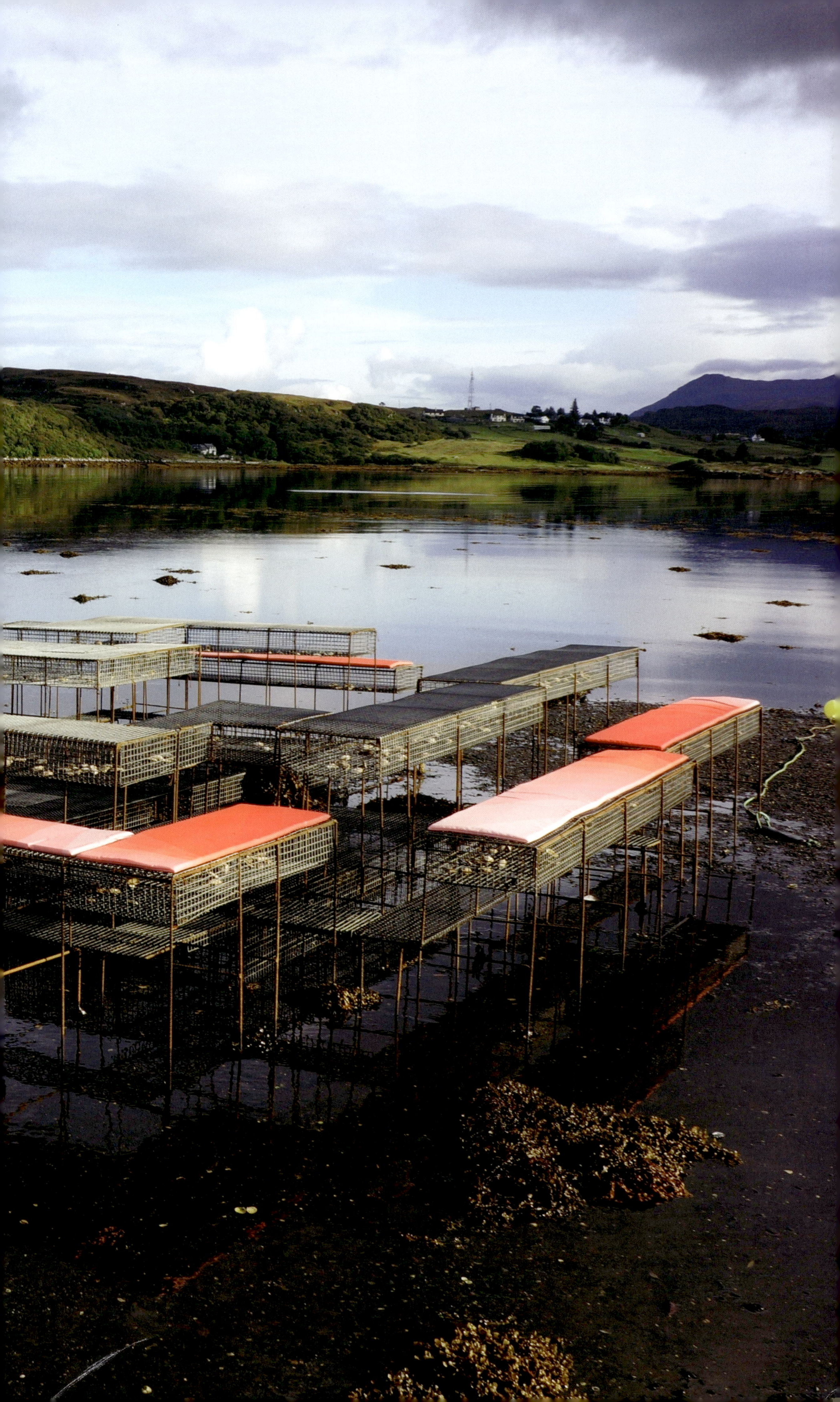

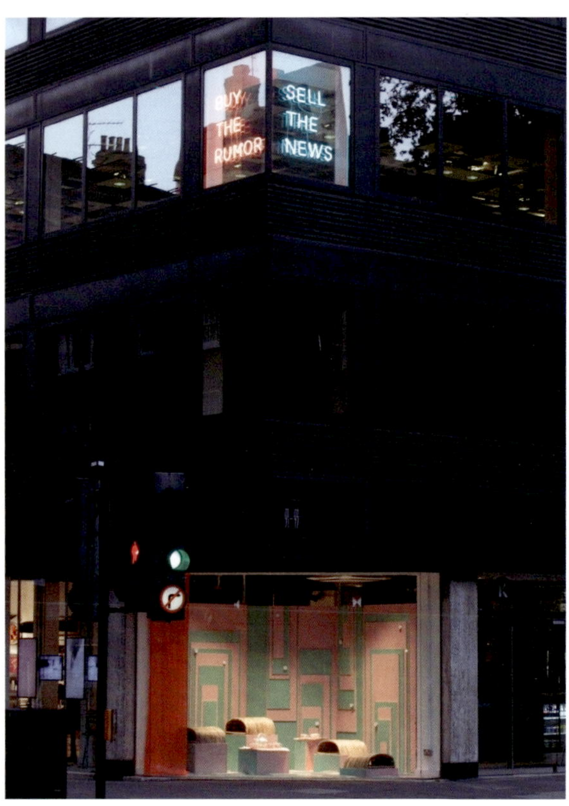

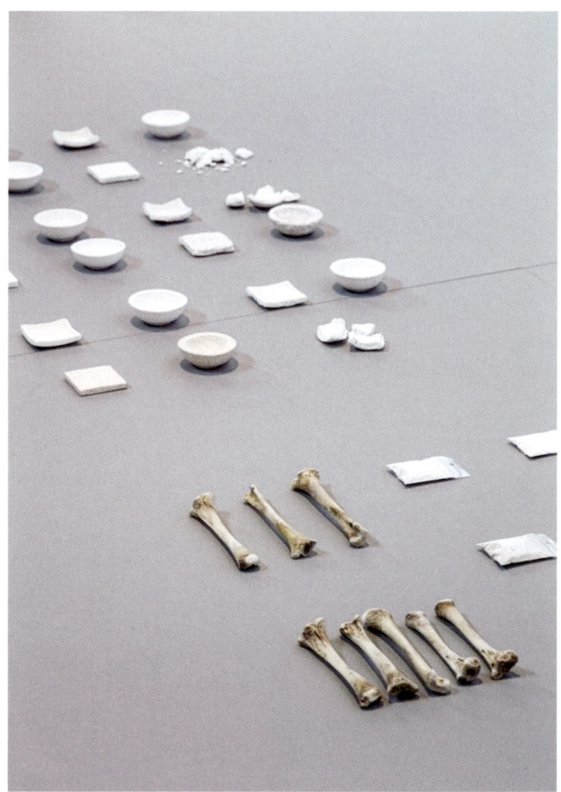

As Nat Muller puts it in her introduction to Cooking Sections' work, 'it is clear that whomever controls the supply and demand of food, has power [...]. [Cooking Sections] map out – often playfully and deliciously – that what we eat and how we eat is in fact never innocent.'[8] I would go one step further and say that, in this context, there is no such thing as innocence – only ignorance, and that much of the modern industrial food system relies on mass-ignorance, facilitated by a complexity of supply that most of us fail to get our heads around. This is a dynamic that began to develop in earnest as those dual forces of industrialism and colonialism entrenched themselves. It continues to bear destructive fruit today.

The relationship of power to production has throughout history led to the exploitation and disenfranchisement of humans. In 1924, W.E.B. Du Bois described the economic incentive of those in power in the American South to divide and conquer, in relation to working class whites and formerly enslaved blacks. His astute analysis starkly identified a reliance of industrial capitalism on populist racism that feels every bit as relevant today, nearly a hundred years after it was written.[9] Comparably, the grand colonial project allowed for a double-sided exploitation of poor Britons and colonial 'subjects' made even smoother by a lack of geographical proximity (and thus detailed knowledge) of those whose lives and bodies were being exploited. This allowed the colonisers to control the narrative with projects like the Empire Marketing Board. Of the Board's propagandistic promotion of foodstuffs from British colonies between 1926 and 1933, the artists themselves write that:

As familiar as these imports became, most citizens could neither experience in the flesh nor imagine the production sites of those same foodstuffs. Visual propaganda in the form of posters, films, and recipes enhanced a geographical gap between two realities: a relative proximity to the site of tropical foodstuffs and a relative distance from the abusive and violent labor conditions of their productions. Indeed, the planet was transformed into a 'highway' connecting and dividing sites of production from sites of consumption. A cycle of capitalist exploitation required enslaved workers to extract sugar, tea, or coffee in the tropics so that industrial workers on the other side of the world could work more hours for less pay. The idea of the overseas as an abstract endless source resulted in images that reshaped the built environment and natural landscape to fit external expectations – that is, to serve the needs of both local elites and foreign corporations.[10]

Substances like sugar and caffeine, imported from the colonies, profoundly impacted on the bodies of industrial workers in Britain, speeding them up and masking the signs of exhaustion.[11] At the same time, the ravaging of land and brutalisation of people in colonised countries had devastating effects that are still being felt today. It is no coincidence that the people suffering most today from the effects of climate change are the same people who suffered most from colonial projects – individuals with little financial means, people of colour and indigenous communities are disproportionately affected. While the industrial food system has resulted in affordable food for some and large profits for few, the cost of production still never goes away.

Cooking Sections have articulated the way in which complex geographical power dynamics can be brought to light through food: 'We are used to perceiving maps as knowledge-objects that inform us about unfamiliar territories. By making them into an edible object that can be made, ingested, and digested over and over we suggest that one can change the interaction with space.' Similarly, 'sourcing, cooking or eating all the ingredients in a given recipe creates awareness of existing power structures and their direct connection to the environment'.[12] The idea of the climavore, for instance, is apparently simple, and yet the *Climavore* project shows how the simplicity of eating in accord with the changing climate is underpinned by great complexity – by systems of control, profit and manipulation traceable through various histories. What Schwabe and Pascual do so deftly is to render these interlinked systems and structures understandable (and edible) through their presentation in a way that both informs and invites further exploration and debate.

Cooking Sections are unsentimental about the use of food in their practice, commenting: 'We see food more as a project than a practice; for now, food is a tool that works to convey our research until we will find a better one.'[13] But they have found a rich seam of potential in the subject. Food is a magic connector. Both as substance and subject, it is a stubborn, enduring thing that refuses to stay still, instead bleeding between disciplines and across temporal and physical boundaries. It is the central point that connects nature to culture, economy to physiology, politics to biology. It moves over national borders and over oceans, sculpting the landscape and marking our bodies as it goes, according to power structures and financial systems. It has inherent value as nourishment and cultural meaning; but this value can also be monetised, turning the most everyday into gold, and into cultural or political weaponry. Food's value is a complex, compelling question, traceable from the soil through economies, kitchens and bodies, and back to the soil itself.

1   Cooking Sections, 'Empire Remains Christmas Pudding', available at https://empireremains.net/agenda/empire-remains-christmas-pudding/ (last accessed on 24 December 2019).
2   Michael J. Henehan et al., 'Rapid ocean acidification and protracted Earth system recovery followed the end-Cretaceous Chicxulub impact', *PNAS*, vol.116, no.45, 5 November 2019, pp.22500-04.
3   'Study reveals ocean acidification has caused mass extinctions', available at https://www.oceanographicmagazine.com/fossil-study-ocean-acidification/ (last accessed on 31 October 2019).
4   See the work of the Center for Genomic Gastronomy, who describe human eaters as 'planetary sculptors' on their website in '5 Years of the Planetary Sculpture Supper Club', available at http://genomicgastronomy.com/texts/5-years-of-the-planetary-sculpture-supper-club-2015/ (last accessed on 24 December 2019).
5   See the description of the project at https://climavore.org/place/isle-of-skye/ (last accessed on 24 January 2020).
6   Among other residencies, Cooking Sections have taken part in the Delfina Foundation's 'Politics of Food' programme from 2 February-6 April 2014, a brief on which is available at http://www.delfinafoundation.com/in-residence/cooking-sections/ (last accessed on 30 January 2020); *CLIMAVORE: On Tidal Zones* (14-24 September 2017) was commissioned by Atlas Arts, with more information available at https://atlasarts.org.uk/projects/climavore-on-tidal-zones-cooking-sections/ (last accessed on 24 January 2020).
7   Nat Muller, 'Tasting Power, Tasting Territory. Nat Muller in Conversation with the artistic duo Cooking Sections', in Nina Levent and Irina D. Mihalache (ed.), *Food and Museums*, London: Bloomsbury, 2017, p.340.
8   *Ibid.*
9   W.E.B. Du Bois, 'Georgia, Invisible Empire State', *These United States, A Symposium* (ed. Ernest Gruening), New York: Boni and Liveright Publishers, 1924, pp. 325-29.
10 Cooking Sections (Daniel Fernández Pascual and Alon Schwabe), *The Empire Remains Shop*, New York: Columbia University Press, 2018, p.20.
11 See *Ibid.*, p.19.
12 N. Muller, 'Tasting Power, Tasting Territory', *op. cit.*, pp.340-41.
13 D. Fernández Pascual, quoted in Zeno Franchini and Franchesca Gattello, 'Cooking Sections: food is culturally invasive', *Domus*, 8 June 2018, available at https://www.domusweb.it/en/speciali/manifesta/2018/cooking-sections-food-is-culturally-invasive.html (last accessed on 21 October 2019).

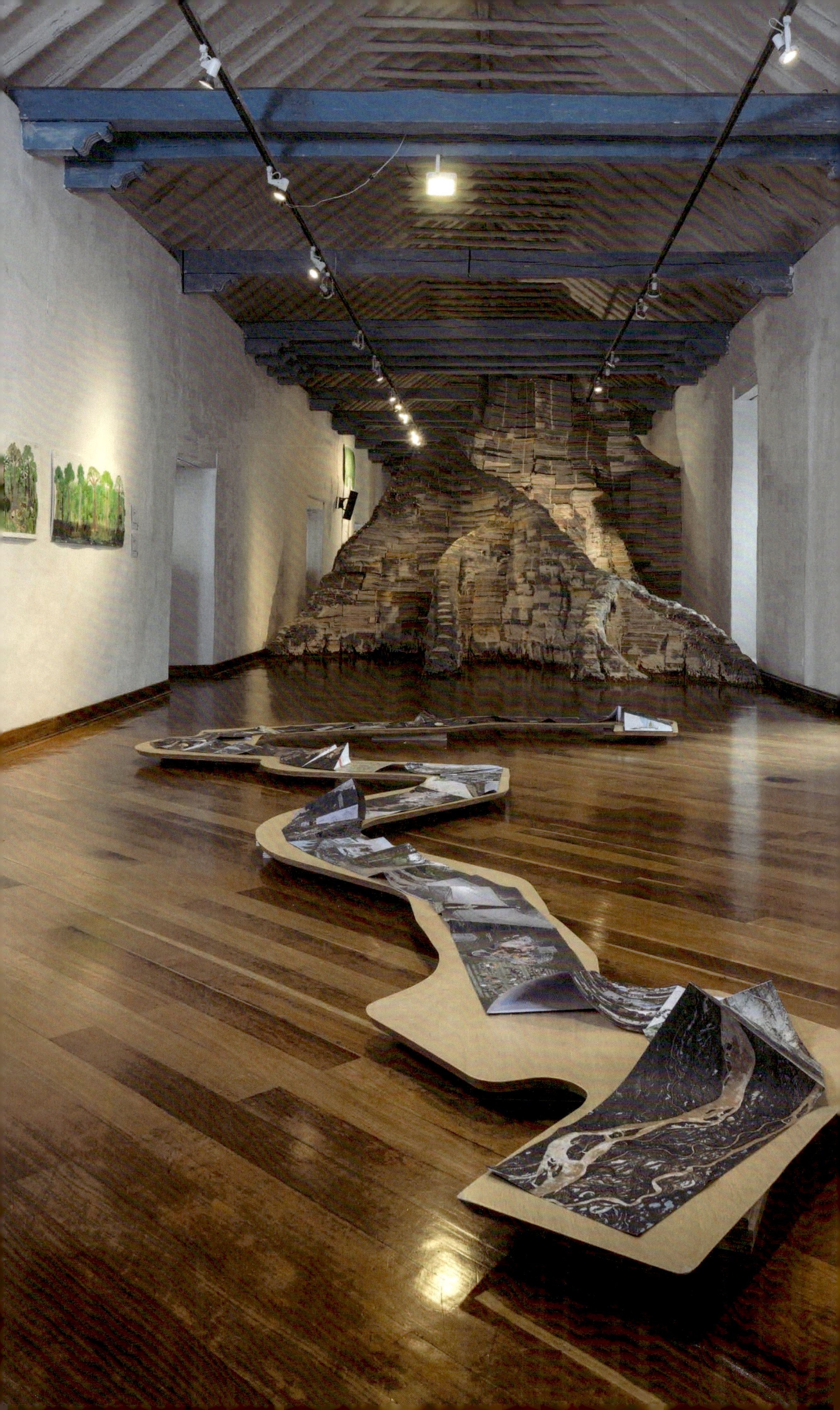

When Walls Become Rivers: Carolina Caycedo's *Serpent River Book*

— Lisa Blackmore

In 1982, the Brazilian writer Carlos Drummond de Andrade published a full-page poem in the newspaper *Jornal do Brasil*. In this heartfelt elegy, titled 'Farewell to Seven Falls' ('Adeus a Sete Quedas'), he paid tribute to the Guaíra waterfalls near the border of Brazil and Paraguay. This stunning hydro-geological formation was situated at a narrow gorge where the Paraná River was funnelled into eighteen cataracts clustered in seven groups that cascaded down more than one hundred metres. Such was the power of the Sete Quedas that the sound of the water could be heard 20 miles (32 km) away. However, to create a huge dammed body of water that would feed the Itaipú hydroelectric plant – a joint venture with General Alfredo Stroessner's dictatorship in Paraguay and still the second largest plant in the world – Brazil's military dictatorship mandated the flooding of the land where the falls were located. Once submerged, the Brazilian government exploded the waterfalls' rock face to ensure smooth passage for any vessels across the reservoir. A natural monument had been reduced to rubble. The river had become a wall.

Lisa Blackmore examines dynamics of hydropower and its contestation by visual, spatial and participatory means in the work of Carolina Caycedo.

In his poem, Drummond de Andrade lamented the waterfalls' destruction, criticising the instrumentalisation of the falls as a mere resource, its flows reduced to a series of numbers for electricity generation. By appropriating and inverting the transactional language of costs and benefits used to justify infrastructural projects, he countered the hydroelectric company's claims that the dam was 'building the big Brazil' and instead alleged that the loss of Sete Quedas was detrimental rather than favourable to well-being:

> And [this monument] crumbles
> due to technocratic intervention.
> Here seven visions, seven sculptures
> of liquid profile
> dissolve among computerized calculations
> from a country that is no longer human
> to become a chilly corporation, nothing more.
>
> Movement becomes a dam,
> from the agitation comes corporate
> silence of a hydroelectric project.
> We will offer every comfort
> provided by the light and energy sold
> at the expense of a priceless good
> that cannot be rescued, impoverishing life
> in the fierce illusion of enriching it.[1]

The poem describes how the concrete wall that dammed the River Paraná stunted its free flows and replaced their thundering noise with 'corporate silence' as the reservoir drowned geology, communities and the ecosystem in the name of national progress and development. The engulfed landscape lost beneath the reservoir is what Rob Nixon in *Slow Violence: Environmentalism of the Poor* calls the 'submergence zone', a political and spatial realm created through the physical and imaginative displacement of communities considered out of sync with industrial and urban modernity. Reading the rise of megadams as the symptom of a drowned commons, Nixon criticises the 'discourses of environmental and

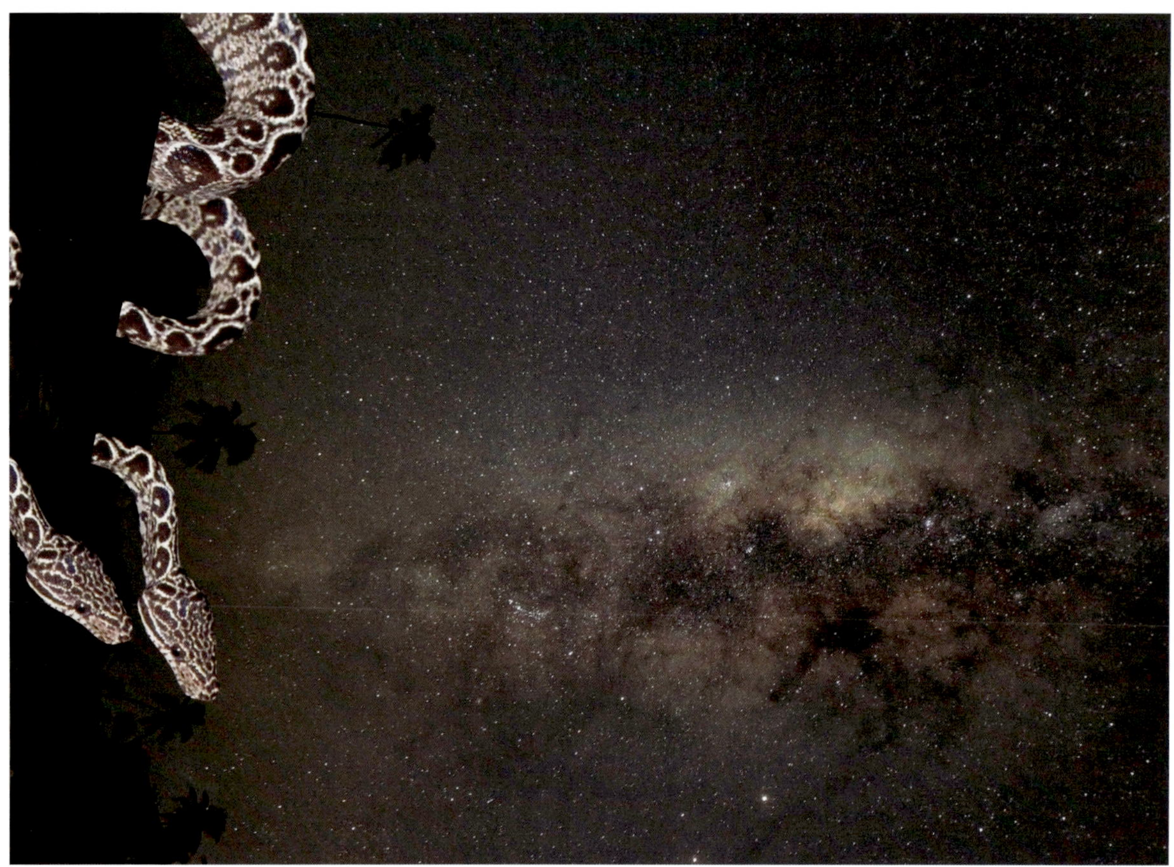

cultural utilitarian control, whereby the convergent unruliness of "irrational" river people and an "irrational" river must be straightened out and channeled into a national culture of rational development.'[2] The developmentalist ideology that justifies the treatment of river communities as anachronisms that inhibit globalisation and economic growth is buttressed by the military-industrial complex of visuality, a set of optical technologies and modes of representation that render the landscape as *terra nulis* – an unpopulated resource carved up by maps, plans, and satellite photographs that reflect the high modernist optics of macro-planning and the legacy of colonisation.[3] Today, there can be no doubt as to the enduring hegemony of hydropower. The cumulative weight of dams has tilted the planet's axis, generating perhaps the most compelling proof of the impact of the Anthropocene. At the same time, catastrophic failures of dam infrastructure, like the twelve-million-cubic-metre river of mud unleashed by the fatal collapse of the Brumadinho tailings dam in Brazil in January 2019, call for a revision of human impact on the environment and the role of transnational capital in ecological disasters.

In her ongoing project *Be Dammed*, the Colombian artist Carolina Caycedo intervenes in the submergence zones and visual regimes linked to megadam projects, exploring the politics and economics of hydraulic systems in her native Colombia and in other Latin American countries, as well as in the global context of transnational capital and the international development agencies that finance major projects in the Global South. Interwoven through her practice are a variety of media, including performance, installation and collaborations with social movements and communities affected by dam projects and infrastructural disasters. Caycedo seeks to decolonise river ecologies by creating countervisualities to the imaginaries that frame rivers as passive resources to be commodified and put to work by human capital and labour. The immersive audio-visual works, performance-based and tactile works insist on the ways that disobedient bodies act as counterflows to structures of containment mobilised by regimes of extraction and mechanisms of social control writ large. Caycedo's work brings to the fore an understanding of rivers as dense liquid ecologies where human and more-than-human material worlds are entangled and where indigenous knowledges persist even amid the imposition of Western 'reason'.

Carolina Caycedo,
Serpent River Book
(detail), 2017.
Courtesy the artist

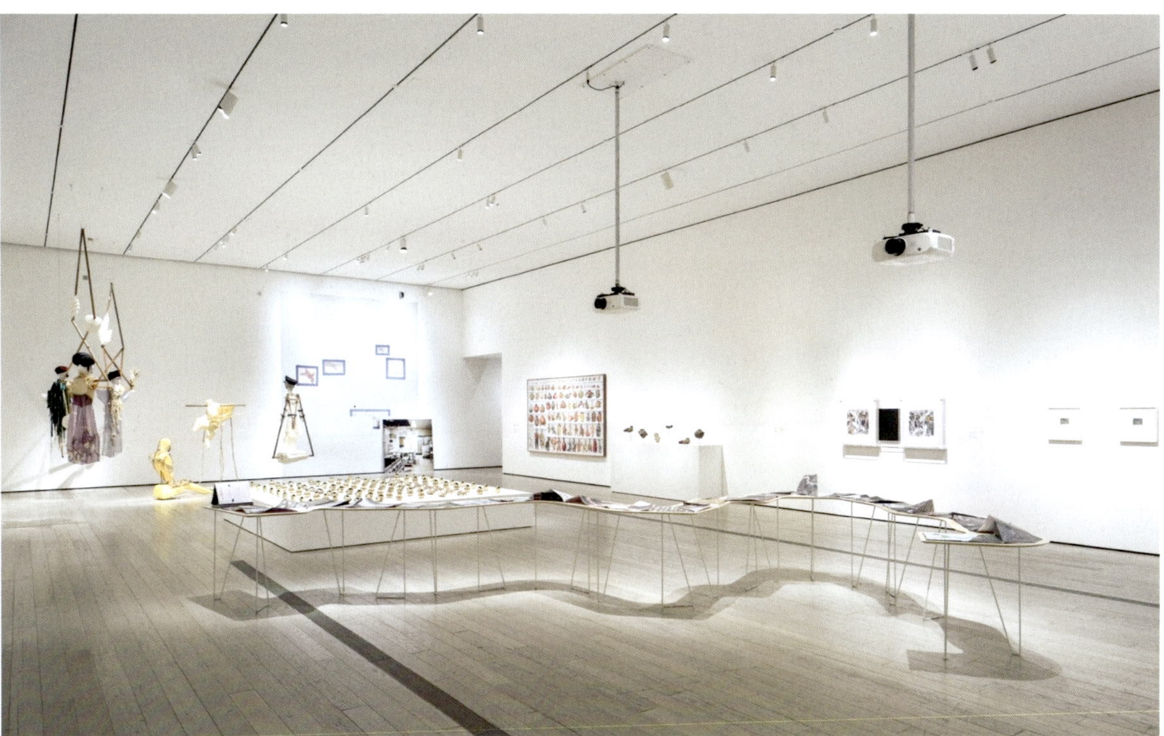

Walls and rivers are motifs for thinking hydraulic order in an expanded sense that goes beyond their literal physical condition. Systems of flow control invite reflection about the built infrastructures that regulate the movement of bodies and matter; the economic models through which capital flows, trickles down or stagnates; and the structures and disciplines through which ideas and media circulate. At the same time, thinking about hydraulics calls attention to those marginal communities and residual ecologies that exceed dominant socio-spatial structures and circuitries that channel material, economic and cultural flows.[4] This tension between containment, overflow and counterflow runs through *Be Dammed*, where apparently solid and structured walls and masses repeatedly take fluid forms of 'rivers' that overflow the logics of hydraulics and productivity. In the performance work *Beyond Control* (2013–16), even as a group of people is corralled tight into the corner of the gallery, individual bodies continue to agitate and move together.[5] In the *Geochoreographies* (2014), a series of community initiatives intersecting 'social justice and environmental practices with creative, collaborative and aesthetic praxis', bodies occupy river spaces in leisure activities orientated toward solidarity not profit, and leisure not work.[6] Rivers are also made to defy containment in the series of *Water Portraits* (2016) where they appear in mirrored photographs printed onto long draped canvases that cascade and unfurl into the gallery space, and in the video work *Land of Friends* (2014) where a hand traces a line of ink over a satellite view of a river's course to signal its detours and alternate routes beyond the fixity of the photograph.[7]

The physical and metaphorical transformation of walls to rivers is precisely the premise of one of the most widely exhibited works from the *Be Dammed* project.[8] *Serpent River Book* (2017) is a two-sided artist book that condenses years of materials Caycedo has accumulated through her fieldwork, archival practice and research into dams and other forms of social control. Unfolding as two streams of pages, where the top side is mainly formed of images and the bottom of texts, its contents range from satellite photography, infrastructural plans and corporate documents related to dam building worldwide, through to poems, origin myths and photographs of the *Geochoreographies*. The book is multi-lingual – with texts in Spanish, English, French and Portuguese – and plurivocal, including the voices of the artist, of poets, activists, people affected by dams and non-human beings that populate rivers. Its form was inspired by an accordion-fold map of the Berlin Wall held in an archive in Germany, which, when folded, reconstructs as a paper circle the perimeter of the wall, signalling the presence of sanitation pipes that ran through it, connecting East to West. Caycedo explains that she immediately thought of rivers when she began manipulating the

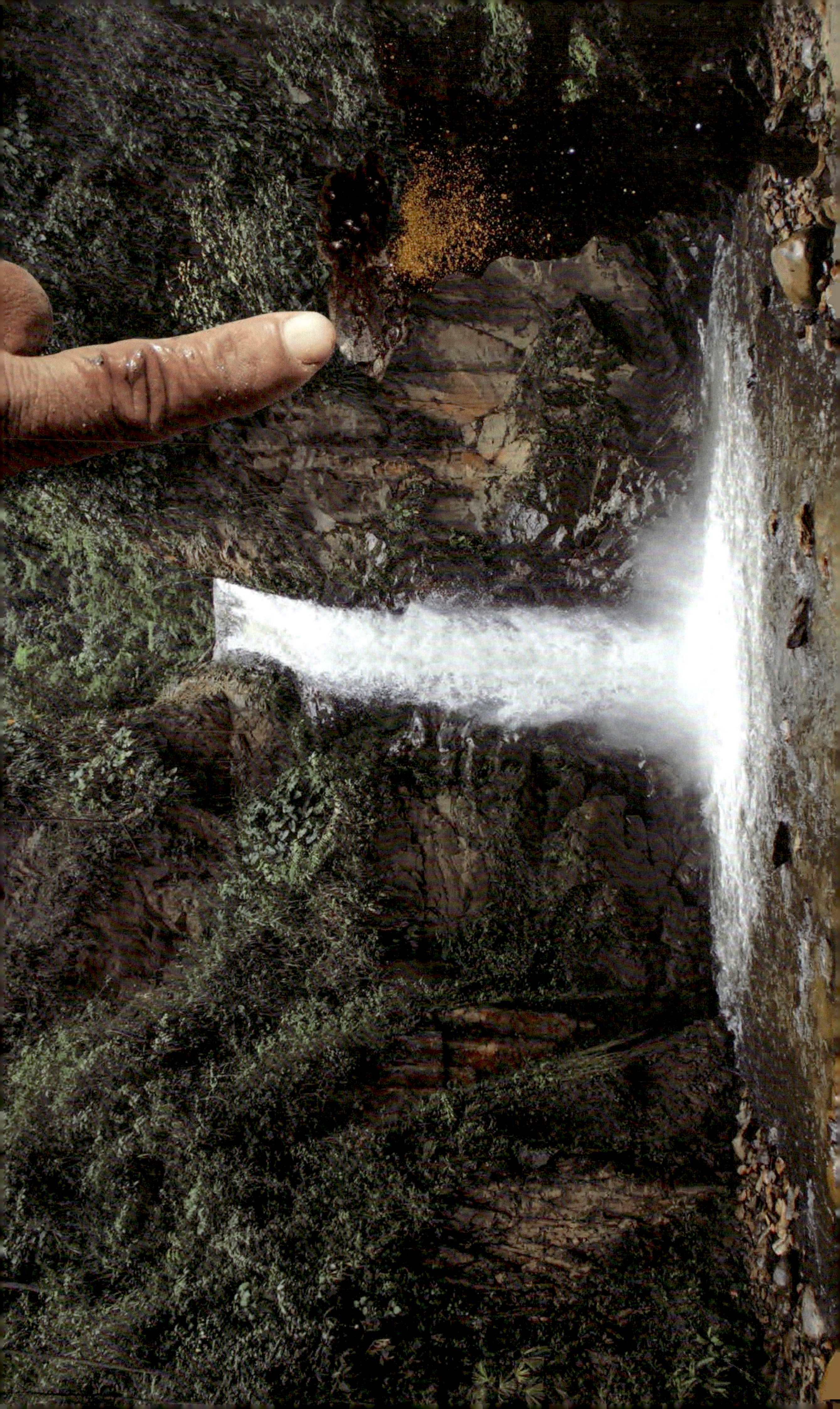

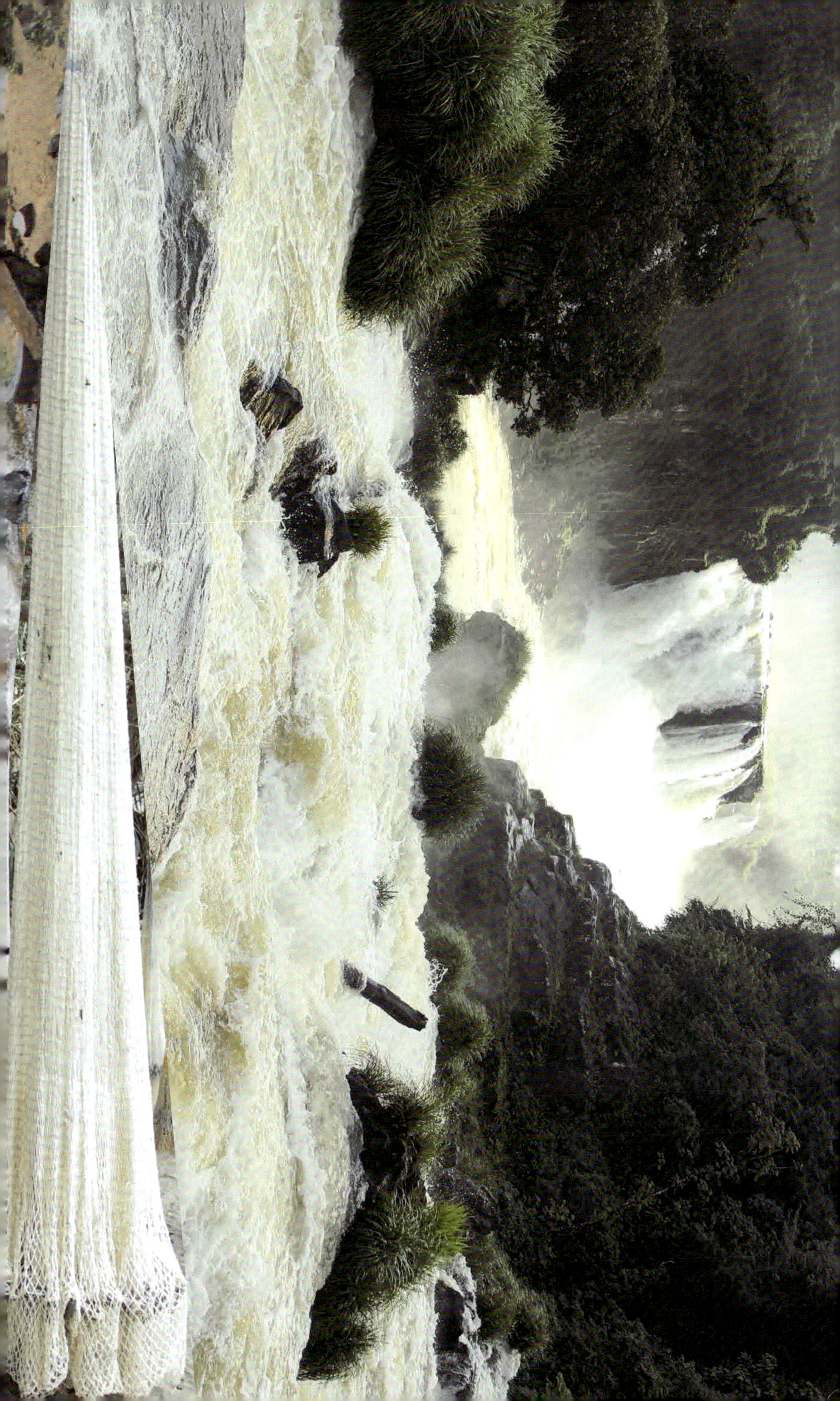

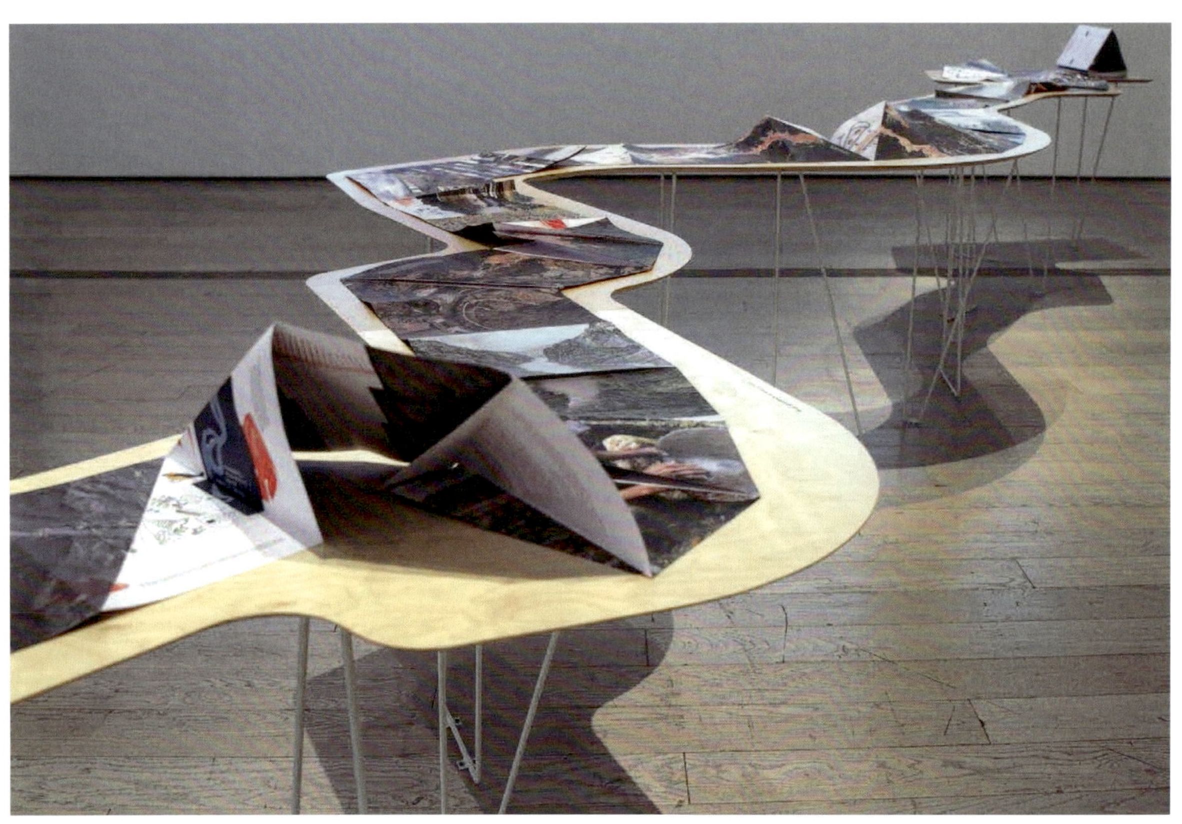

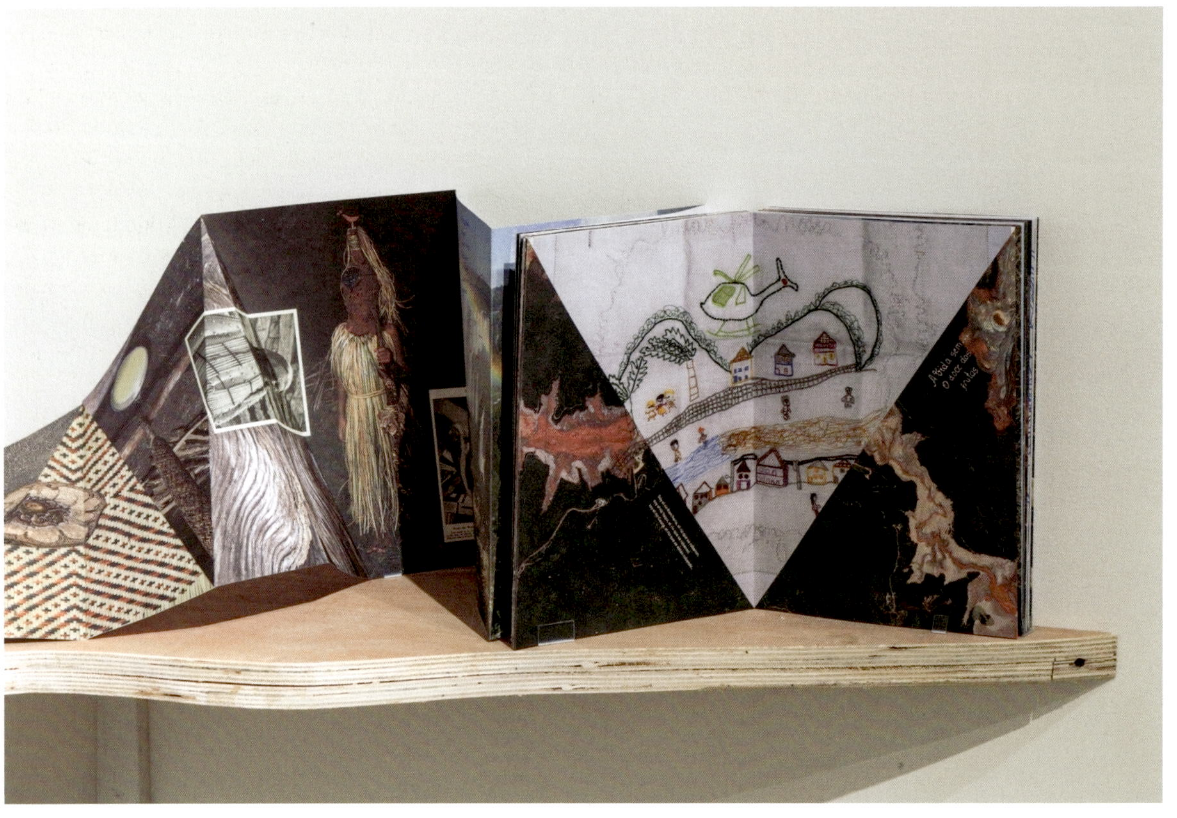

map because of the meandering form it took: 'And I said, "I have to appropriate this format to do a river book," and what I did is that the middle page of the map – it's a 72-page accordion fold – the middle page I did 180 degrees so that the map instead of closing on itself, it opens, so from a wall it became a river'.[9]

The 'river' unfurls as a linear hydrology as the book's component sections move from the sources, through the upper, middle and lower courses, to a delta. These sections in turn move through different epistemologies that shape human relations to rivers, beginning with ancestral Amazonian mythology, in which the river is one of the four serpents that make up the universe, traversing the cosmos, air, water and the underworld. The next section centres on peasant knowledge and artisanal industries linked to indigenous traditions while developing small-scale extractive enterprises such as panning for gold and fishing, which are displaced by large-scale infrastructure projects and industries. The next section shifts to a corporate vision of territory comprised in conventional maps, structural plans for dams, and images of real infrastructure such as the contested El Quimbo dam in Huila state. The subsequent chapters trace ruptures in extractivist engagements with rivers through images of collapsed dams and rivers that breach their banks, followed by documentation of community initiatives that contest the instrumentalisation of environmental resources by big businesses and nation-states.

This linear unfolding of the river, however, is open to constant negotiation, since the book's reception cannot be governed by a single logic. Its form encourages interactive engagement as a mode of exploring unpredictable flows, since the pages can be variously configured – folded and unfolded, stretched out or closed, or pleated along triangular folds to bring the book's two sides together. As Caycedo explains, this means 'that anyone that grabs the book and plays with it can imbue their own narrative into the book', bringing images of Amazonian sources into contact with photos of ruptured dams, for instance, or artisanal fishing into dialogue with images of anti-dam resistance. The book's ludic and shape-shifting dimension is announced from the outset

> *The immersive audio-visual, performance-based and tactile works insist on the ways that disobedient bodies act as counterflows to structures of containment mobilised by regimes of extraction and mechanisms of social control writ large.*

through a series of tongue-in-cheek 'instructions' provided inside the hardback cover. These prime the 'reader' with the challenge of creating through the publication a form of 'hydrocommons' – that is, to confront through embodied experience of the printed matter the question that *Serpent River Book*'s instructions set out: 'How can we make sure the river is not *my* river or *your* river, but the river of everyone, the river of no one?'

This question speaks to timely environmental issues that traverse a range of disciplines, from creative practices and natural sciences through to post-humanist philosophy and climate activism. In the latter, Vandana Shiva has called for a water culture based on 'ecological democracy' where all life, not just human life, has its rightful share in the planet's water.[10] Imagining rivers as simultaneously everyone's and no one's contravenes the logic of capitalist commodification that approaches the environment as a repository of resources for profit generation. It also denaturalises the idea of 'natural' resources by drawing attention to the way that the cultural meanings and economic regimes attached to rivers are themselves the products of the socio-symbolic processes of resource-making, initiated in the *longue durée* of colonial capitalism and intensified in the extractivist economies that dominate the Global South to this day. The *Serpent River Book*'s form and content engages with the extractivist matrix in which water, along with minerals and fossil fuels, are imagined as passive matter that requires human intervention to be commodified and traded to synchronise territories with the speed-time of modernity.

Against the visual regime of hydropower that reduces rivers to stream flow records, used to predict optimal energy production capacity, the *Serpent River Book*'s pages hold within them the densely layered cultural meanings sedimented in rivers. The book foregrounds the indigenous knowledges in which rivers are sacred spaces and deities, attesting to their endurance in (rather than replacement by) modernity. In so doing it exposes the 'epistemicide' enacted by the 'cognitive empire' that, as Boaventura de Sousa Santos writes, imposed through violence Western rationalism on indigenous knowledges of the South.[11] One example of how this strategy of decolonisation plays out on the book's pages occurs in a series of black and white photographs of the River Magdalena – a long-standing industrial artery for the Colombian economy – which is overlaid with a photograph of a snake, along with a meandering sentence in which the *Yuma* (the indigenous name for the Magdalena) speaks in the first person of its course from the Andean highlands to the Caribbean Sea and the diverse cultural meanings it holds along the way. Against the abstract notions of space and time that shore up industrial capitalism, Caycedo uses digital collage as an aesthetic strategy to compose an alternate temporality, one in which the present terrain is represented by satellite images over which phrases like '*Soy el hilo dorado que conecta a los ancestros con los que han de nacer*' ('I'm the golden thread that connects ancestors with those who are yet to be born') snake along the page, connecting ancestral past, to present, to future.

Details such as these can be grasped by looking at the pages of *Serpent River Book* laid flat, but the book is designed to become a series of folds. This adds further complexities to its visual and temporal logics, as well as to the ways in which bodies interact with its pages. Contrary to conventional imagery and Heraclitean philosophy, rivers do not only flow forward. They loop back, eddy, ramify and dry up. They overflow and burst through channels designed to contain them. Hence a river's movement and temporality are not linear but turbulent and unpredictable. In *A Thousand Plateaus* Gilles Deleuze and Félix Guattari argue that State power works to 'subordinate hydraulic force to conduits, pipes,

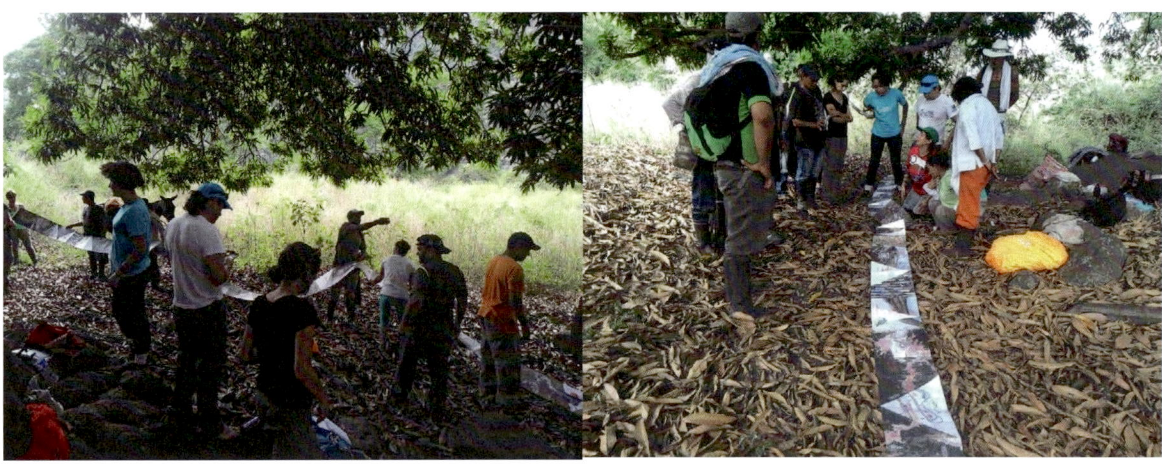

embankments, which prevent turbulence, which constrain movement to go from one point to another, and space itself to be striated and measured'. [12] It is this striation and flattening of the space-time of rivers, their inhabitants and knowledges that the folds in the *Serpent River Book* interrupt. In one of the folds, for instance, a hand-drawn, diagram and notes about the Doctrine of Prior Appropriation (the US legal instrument that determines that the first person to use or divert water can acquire individual rights to it) appears, when folded, alongside the first-person testimony of Francisco Cabrera, a family of artisanal fishermen on the *Yuma* whose land was expropriated by Emgesa (the Colombian hydroelectricity company) to flood the El Quimbo reservoir, and topographical diagrams of German hydraulic infrastructures. Enfolding and bringing into contact these geographically remote sites – the US, Colombia and Germany – evinces the global dimension of the flow control imposed on the world's rivers, two thirds of which are subject to hydroengineering.

Nearly half a century after the Itaipú dam trapped the Paraná River behind a wall, the final pages of *Serpent River Book* revisit that same river delta, selecting a richly detailed satellite image of its meandering courses to depict the end of the river's course overland as it splits into myriad channels, each seeking out the ocean. The gaze moves along the sinuous lines of the sediment-loaded waters, tracing their nomadic flows in and out of each other, here joining together, there looping back to form islands. Caycedo selected this image to evoke a continuous water cycle and sacred union, which reframes the river's outlet into the ocean not as an end but as an instance 'when two bodies of water connect and touch and become something else or become bigger'. [13] It is not only an aquatic encounter staged here. Emerging from the satellite image are the eyes of a jaguar, embedded digitally into the image in a transparency that makes its presence subtle and easy to miss. The image is followed by a quote – 'I am the jaguar, and when I look into your eyes, you stop being prey and become

Serpent River Book workshop with community members of Sabanalarga town affected by the Hidroituango hydroelectric project on the Rio Cauca in Antioquia, Colombia, January 2018. Courtesy Movimiento Rios Vivos Colombia and Movimiento Rios Vivos Antioquia

another jaguar' – that borrows from the anthropologist Eduardo Kohn's book, *How Forests Think* (2013), which moves beyond anthropocentric anthropology to explore more fluid ontologies of human and non-human lifeforms.[14] The inclusion of the quote and the jaguar's gaze suggest the need for a paradigm shift in the ethics of care where human exceptionalism yields to horizontal modes of co-existence. In Caycedo's words: 'We cannot remain in this Western tradition that says: "I think, therefore I exist", which means that you don't need anything else in the world to be a human, when actually it's the total opposite. We need the other to exist. It's only until [*sic*] the jaguar looks into your eyes, when the river touches your body, when you breathe the air, when another entity of the territory perceives you, that's the moment when you become'.[15]

The river, released from the stasis of the wall, has come a long way in the *Serpent River Book*. More than a physical hydrology, its intersecting waters have served as a figure of thought, an environment in which to liquidise the anthropocentric thinking that renders water and other non-human lifeforms as resources and commodities; a medium to loosen the hold that Western epistemologies of reason have had on forms of knowledge that resist reduction to the binary strictures of human/animal or nature/culture. If dams are the tombstones of rivers, the delta is an opening onto liquid ecologies that seek new routes through the philosophical and material worlds we inhabit.

Special thanks to Carolina Caycedo for her receptivity to dialogue and for her generosity in sharing ideas, research materials and images.

1   This fragment from the original poem in Portuguese reads as follows:

        E desfaz-se
        por ingrata intervenção de tecnocratas.
        Aqui sete visões, sete esculturas
        de líquido perfil
        dissolvem-se entre cálculos computadorizados
        de um país que vai deixando de ser humano
        para tornar-se empresa gélida, mais nada.

        Faz-se do movimento uma represa,
        da agitação faz-se um silêncio
        empresarial, de hidrelétrico projeto.
        Vamos oferecer todo o conforto
        que luz e força tarifadas geram
        à custa de outro bem que não tem preço
        nem resgate, empobrecendo a vida
        na feroz ilusão de enriquecê-la.

        See Carlos Drummond de Andrade, 'Adeus a Sete Quedas', *Jornal do Brasil*, Caderno B (9 September 1982), p.8. Translation the author's.
2   Rob Nixon, *Slow Violence and the Environmentalism of the Poor*, Cambridge: Harvard University Press, 2011, p.164.
3   On these optics, see Nicholas Mirzoeff, *The Right to Look: A Counterhistory of Visuality*, Durham and London: Duke University Press, 2011.
4   I have developed these ideas in a series of recent texts, including: 'Colonizing Flow: Hydropower and Post-Kinetic Assemblages in the Orinoco Basin', Jens Andermann, Lisa Blackmore and Dayron Carrillo Morell (ed.), *Natura: Environmental Aesthetics After Landscape*, Zurich: diaphanes, 2018, pp. 171-197; 'Contraflujos: Orden hidráulico y ecologías residuales en el paisaje dominicano', *Iberoamericana. América Latina - España - Portugal*, 19, no.72, 2019, pp.57-80; and 'Hubristic Hydraulics: Water, Dictatorship and Urban Modernity in the Dominican Republic', *Latin American and Latinx Visual Culture* no.2, 2020, pp.115-125
5   Videos of the performance *Beyond Control* are available at http://carolinacaycedo.com/beyond-control-2013 (last accessed on 14 March 2020).
6   Carolina Caycedo, 'Be Dammed', MFA thesis, University of Southern California, 2014, p.iv.
7   All of these works can be viewed on Caycedo's website at http//carolinacaycedo.com (last accessed on 14 March 2020).
8   As well as shows at the Royal Academy, London and LACMA, Los Angeles, recent exhibitions include the solo show titled, like this article, 'When walls become rivers', curated by the author at Art Exchange, University of Essex from February to March 2020, to mark the acquisition of the *Serpent River Book* by the Essex Collection of Art from Latin America (ESCALA), following a successful proposal by students from the MA in Curatorial Studies and MA in Art History and Theory.
9   Interview with the artist, 28 September 2018. For a full record, see Lisa Blackmore, 'When walls become rivers: Interview with Carolina Caycedo', available at https://vimeo.com/381328453 (last accessed on 14 March 2020).
10   Andy Opel and Vandana Shiva, 'Dr Vandana Shiva, an interview by Andy Opel. From Water Crisis to Water Culture', *Cultural Studies*, 22, no.3-4, 2008, pp.498-509 and 501.
11   Boaventura de Sousa Santos, *The End of the Cognitive Empire. The Coming of Age of Epistemologies of the South*, Durham, NC and London: Duke University Press, 2018.
12   Gilles Deleuze and Félix Guattari, *A Thousand Plateaus*, London: Bloomsbury, 2013, p.363.
13   Interview with the artist, 28 September 2018.
14   Eduardo Kohn, *How Forests Think: Toward an Anthropology Beyond the Human*, Chicago: University of Chicago Press, 2013.
15   Interview with the artist, 28 September 2018.

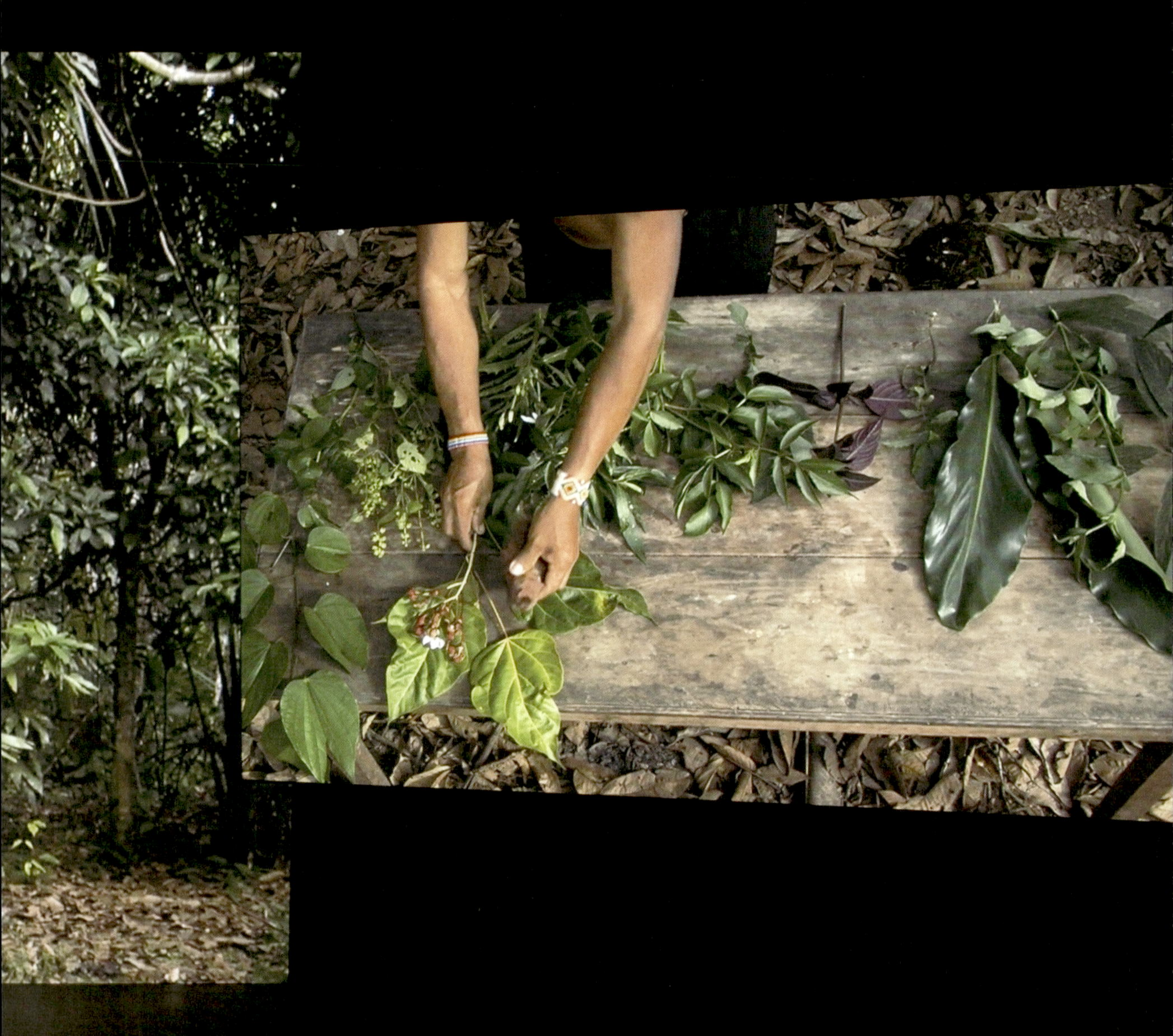

The Occupied Forest

— Macarena Gómez-Barris

The forest is a living organism and a complex space that possesses its own logics. In the time of the Anthropocene, it lives with the human and has been decimated by it. Rather than seeing the forest frontier as a space of purity, or a space of exploration, we might consider how the colonial/modern forest is actually a densely occupied space of harsh and discordant activities.

For instance, Mapuche director Francisco Huichaqueo's 38-minute experimental film *Mencer: Ni Pewma* (2011) represents the forest as an affective space of confusion, elision and disappearance, rather than as an intact ecological wonderland. The film refers to the physical occupation of Mapuche land by military and police forces, as well as the project of land and water defence. But another kind of occupation is also at play: invading the forest are foreign tree species grown for export – rows and rows of radiata pine and eucalyptus plantations. These have replaced the original Pehuén (monkey puzzle tree) in ancient forests now several hundred years old. The film depicts a history of Indigenous uprising in the face of forces of dispossession that date back to the Spanish militias of the sixteenth century.[1]

This powerful film shows what is at stake in current violence against the forest. Like other semi-tropical and tropical forest biospheres throughout the Americas, the original Pehuén forests of the Wallmapu region were dramatically reduced through forest laws of the 1990s that privatised Indigenous territories, with devastating consequences for those who continue to live with the ongoing consequences of reduction, enclosure and removal. In *Mencer: Ni Pewma*, we hear the confused echoes of lamentation as emanating from ancestors from the other side of the colonial divide, as though the charred landscape of ubiquitous monocultural plantations of radiata pine and eucalyptus is demanding retributive justice. As they search for anchor points in the depleted forest, these ancestors mourn the near extinction of the native Pehuén forests.

Forest Law (2014), a 38-minute video projection by Ursula Biemann and Paulo Tavares shot from two different perspectives, considers similar themes of the forest's occupation. The video contends with the inability of human representation to address the world of the forest, reflecting on the failures of institutions to represent nature in general. In the history of the Americas, the law has served as a blunt tool for forest protection, as it has often instead been weaponised in the interests of national elites as well as local and global capital. The violent terrain of occupation enters the frame differently in *Forest Law* when compared with Huichaqueo's work. Although *Forest Law* is quieter, the cacophony of occupation

Macarena Gómez-Barris looks at the work of Francisco Huichaqueo and of Ursula Biemann and Paulo Tavares, identifying their potential to resist extractivist capitalism through alternative representations of the forest.

is omnipresent. We are shown instruments of measurement, management and cataloguing, and hear from scientists who understand the forest as an endless source of knowledge, genetic and medicinal production. In the layers of lush forest life, we see how the scars of oil drilling diminish the capacity of Eastern Amazonian biodiversity. Extractivism is present both inside and outside of the frame, yet it is not the main subject. Instead, the central figure is the living forest and its interactions with humans like the narrator Franco Viteri, who describes his rich life in Sarayaku, made possible through a sustained relationship with the local habitat.

Seeing *Forest Law* for the first time on my small laptop computer in 2017, and later at a private screening at Mary Porter Sesnon Art Gallery, University of California, Santa Cruz, I was moved by the saturation and myriad green colours on the screen, as well as the multi-tiered architectural environment of the forest. Having spent time researching and living in the Amazon, I could relate to how its spatial structures, its clustering shapes and the various views that produce a natural built environment were rendered visually in the installation and its two components. The two-channel film captures the variety of spatial openness and closure that characterises the Amazonian forest with its the multidimensional forms. Verdant forest is shown on the two sharp screens in the foreground, while on the side a photo-text assemblage in a glass case gives contextual information about the history of extraction in Ecuador.

As described on the exhibition website:

> *Forest Law*, 2014, is a 38-minute video essay and book drawn from research carried out by Biemann and Tavares in the Ecuadorian Amazon. It considers the legal cases which plead for the rights of nature against the dramatic expansion of large-scale extraction activities in the region, including the trial won by the Indigenous people of Sarayuku based on their cosmology of the living forest. The project creatively maps the historical, political, and ecological dimensions of these trials on behalf of the forest and the people who cultivate the forest, tracing the entanglements and frictions between the ethical and epistemic stakes these cases raise.

In making the film, the directors acknowledge philosopher Michel Serres' book, *The Natural Contract*,[2] which proposes the emergence of nature as a social, legal and ethical agent, challenging and complementing Rousseau's idea of the social contract. It also calls for human negotiation with the Earth to find a balanced dynamic, respectful of the natural world rather than rapacious in relation to it. It is interesting to note the publication date of 1990, still a moment of possibility at which capitalism's broken pact with the nonhuman was made visible by Indigenous social movements. Indeed, throughout the Americas, 1992 marked the beginning of Indigenous resurgence, five hundred years after Columbus' 'discovery', when many Indigenous peoples began to organise more formal collective responses for a new contract with nature – one that revalued the forest and the network of living relations within it.

Representing the Forest
In the late 1990s, a report titled 'The Last Frontier Forest: Ecosystems and Economies on the Edge' by development researchers Dirk Bryant, Daniel Nielsen and Laura Tangley found that more than half of the world's original forests had already been eradicated.[3] The objective of the report was to describe the status of the world's forests, pointing to the Global South as the area of the planet that contained 'the large, ecologically intact, and relatively undisturbed natural forests *that still remain*'.[4] Noting that the frontier evoked romantic imaginaries of fecund, if extractible, geographies, the report addressed the need to protect and conserve the world's remaining tropical forest. It also expressed the fragility of many ecosystems in the face of intensifying frontier capitalism, or the acquisition of new territories, in particular areas previously unexploited by capitalist extraction.

Written during the pivotal era of neoliberal structural transformation, 'The Last Frontier Forest' used the phrase 'that still remain' to position forest systems within an increasingly catastrophic global picture of deforestation, bringing into analytical relief a critical anteriority. In other words, we might read this phrase as an alert to the continuing impact of environmental disasters, with extinction already looming large on the near future horizon of what I have elsewhere described as 'The Colonial Anthropocene'.[5] The term 'remaining forest' poignantly illuminates how colonial violence operates through language that presumes elimination.

Though the emergency described by World Resources Institute is real and the language precise, there is epistemological violence hidden within its pages.[6] Like much of conservation discourse and its material practice, the primary concern is with the remaining forest rather than Indigenous peoples, or those most directly impacted by the political economy of frontier capitalism. The forest and the people of the forest are inextricably linked, and such entanglement cannot be described through the logics of the remainder.

From the vantage point of frontier capitalism, the non-renewable resources that still remain represent a source of profit and surplus that squeeze 'virgin' territories for raw and primary materials. Writing in the 1990s, anthropologist Anna Tsing described this temporal structure as one of the 'not yet regulated'.[7] Yet, it was precisely during this period that privatisation and deregulation dismantled protections for Indigenous territories, including eliminating Article 27 from the Mexican Constitution, which had protected the Indigenous *ejido* land communal system since the 1910 revolution. Such dismantling and counter-revolutionary legislation led to widescale dispossession in Mexico and throughout the Americas, as well as widespread collective resistance, such as the Zapatista uprisings. It is this dialectic of elimination and refusal, the death drive of capital and the living force of those who resist its incursions that lies at the heart of the occupied forest.

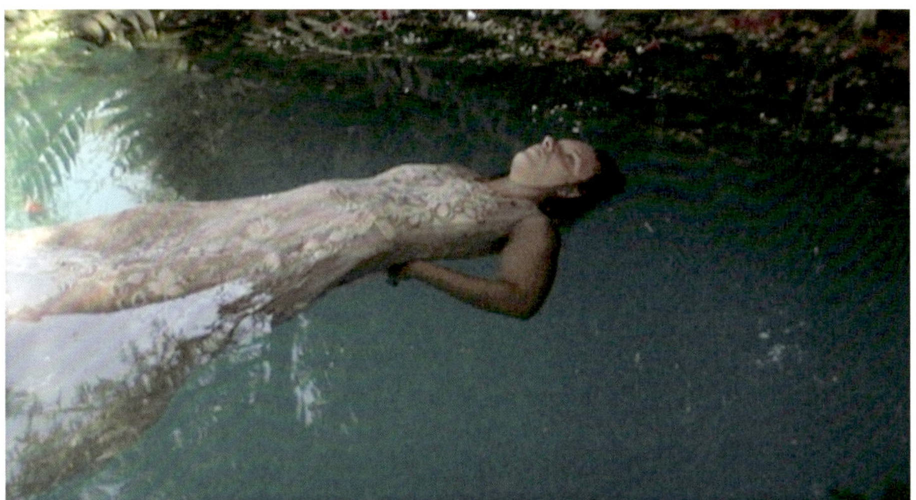

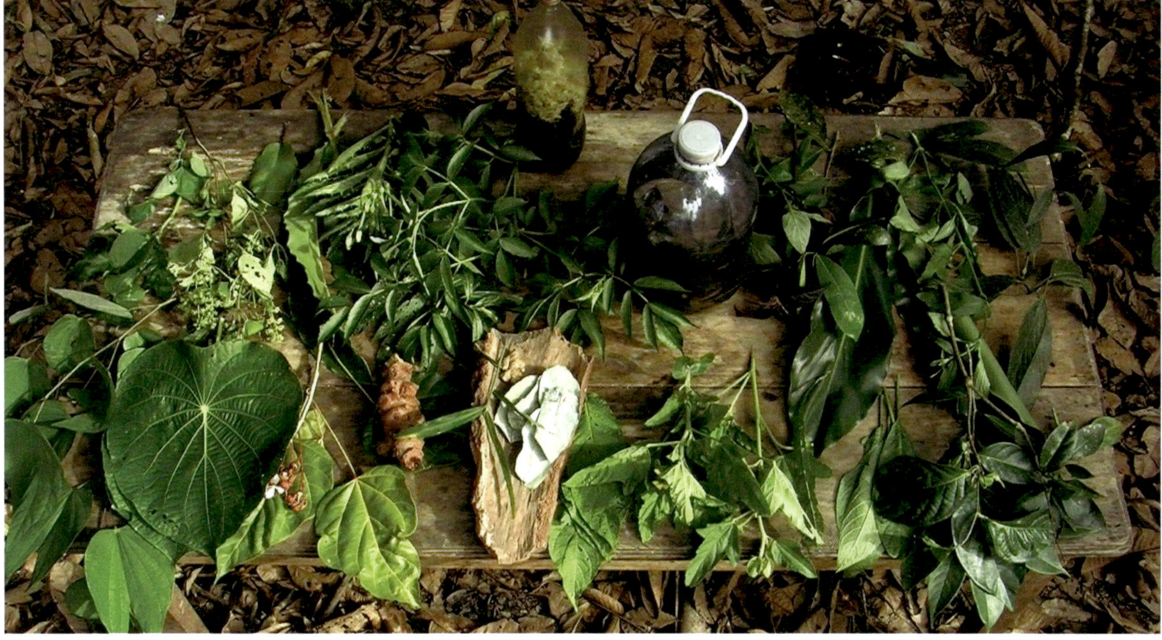

In hindsight, the phrasing, 'that still remain' also referred to those that were 'not yet extinct', or to the not-yet-fully realised futurity of the Anthropocene's localised and planetary genocidal and ecocidal destruction. As Latin America, Asia and Africa entered into increasingly unequal agreements with the International Monetary Fund, the World Bank and the Washington Consensus, the rise of debt economies and expansionist practices produced devastating consequences for the forest, and all those living within and on its peripheries. In the geographies of the Global South, suffering has been disproportionate for those living in the ecotones of clear cutting, those in the peripheries of rural and urban zones, and those situated in the shadows of extractive capitalism. Indeed, the frontier has closed in on the untamed forest and those who inhabit it, intensifying the environmental crisis by appropriating and extracting primary materials for commercial enterprises, feeding the voraciousness of the colonial divide.

Since the 1990s, with renewed intensification over the past ten years, the Americas have experienced a new period of what writer Eduardo Galeano first called the 'open veins of Latin America'.[8] Though it is rarely framed this way, fracking, hydroelectricity, mining, tourism, petroleum extraction and forest monoculture follow the logics of elimination and dispossession that constitute colonialism. In the resource-rich territories of the Global South, extractive projects dominate territories with their sheer scale.[9] Environmental testimonies and visual evidence of dispossession are documented on personal mobile phones, sometimes taken on a single camera, to show what otherwise would be disappeared from the public view. Largely

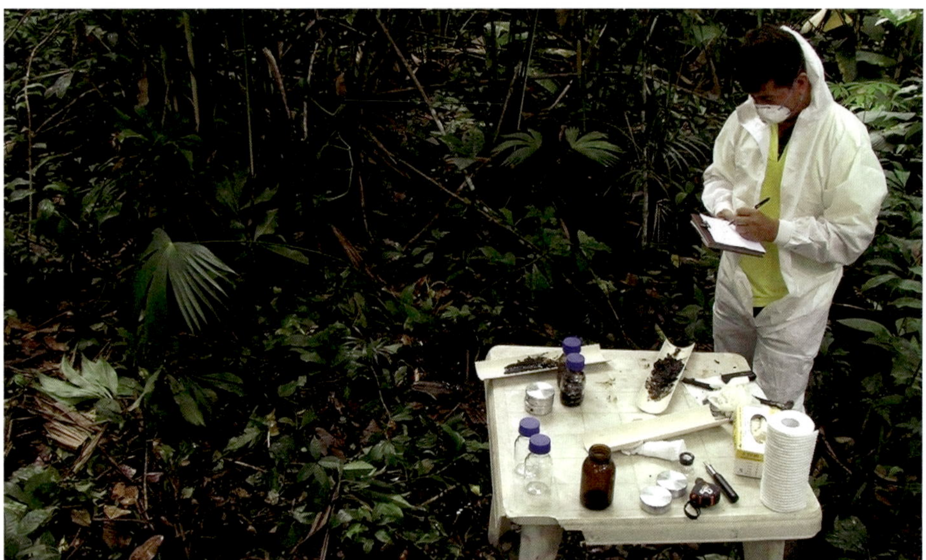

hidden from the domain of urban consumers, biodiverse geographies in the Global South are the shadow spaces of corporations. Such geographies have been unreflexively dubbed as possessing the 'resource curse', a terminology that normalises and facilitates the violent processes of extraction. There are racialised undertones in such a terminology that must be consistently challenged, reworked and subverted.

To work against the normalising language and the extractive view, I propose to use of the concept of *the occupied forest*. By 'occupied forest', I am referring to territories of struggle over biodiversity that have been increasingly militarised, and that have become violent geographies of land and water defence in response to corporate and state encroachment. The occupied forest is a space of war, loss and bereavement in times of mass extinction and rebellion, such as what the Brazilian Amazon forest currently experiences under Bolsonarism. These are also geographies of scientific investigations that 'race for time' to catalogue biodiversity, often bringing their own extractive infrastructures with them as yet more actors of coercion and interrogation within, for the most part, Indigenous- and African-descendent territories.

Environmental testimonies and visual evidence of dispossession are documented on personal mobile phones, sometimes taken on a single camera, to show what otherwise would be disappeared from the public view.

Deforestation is a pivotal issue of the climate crisis. Philosopher Kyle White offers three ways to consider the impact of the climate predicament upon localised territories of struggle, which have relevance to the occupied forest. First, he notes that anthropogenic (human-caused) climate change is an intensification of environmental change imposed on Indigenous peoples by colonialism. Second, he suggests that renewing Indigenous knowledges, such as traditional ecological knowledge, can bring together Indigenous communities to strengthen their own self-determined planning for climate change. And third he observes that Indigenous peoples often imagine climate change futures from their particular perspectives: first, as societies with deep collective histories of having to be well-organised to adapt to environmental change; and second, as societies who must reckon with the disruptions of historic and ongoing practices of colonialism, capitalism and industrialisation.[10] Indeed, in such theorisations, indigeneity is not an afterthought, but rather a central axis and episteme for understanding occupation as an extractive settler condition. Indigenous peoples know how to collectively manage the forest, and understand the historical significance of land, river and tree defence. The ecologies of the forest cannot be disconnected from those of forest peoples. Indeed, one source of our current climate predicament is the colonial condition that reduces territories to things and indigeneity to the remainder.

What can we learn from films that try to represent the forest differently? From the works I have discussed, by Francisco Huichaqueo and by Ursula Biemann and Paulo Tavares,

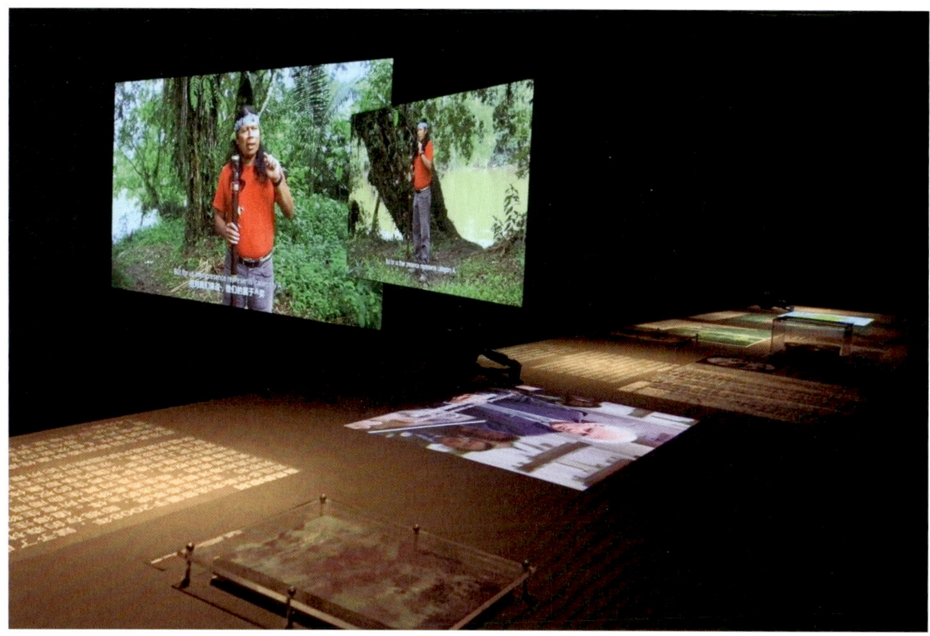

Ursula Biemann
and Paulo Tavares,
Forest Law, 2014,
two-channel video,
colour, sound, maps,
documents, objects,
publication, 38min.
Installation view,
Shanghai
Biennial 2018–19.
Courtesy the artists

we can sense how the forest is a multi-tiered source of life, yet one that also exists as a physical, legal and cosmological entity. There is thus a range of forms of perception within the occupied forest, which audiovisual works like *Mencer: Ni Pewma* and *Forest Law* help us to understand. The work of protecting the forest must go beyond merely using the faulty instrument of the law to protect it. Instead, we must work to apprehend the laws of the forest to address it not as 'the remainder', but as the sustenance for planetary life.

1   I have written at length about the Mapuche territorial struggle in the face of pine and eucalyptus plantation expansion in the Bío-Bío region of southern Chile, and about the work of Francisco Huichaqueo in representing the forest differently. See Macarena Gómez-Barris, *The Extractive Zone: Social Ecologies and Decolonial Perspectives*, Durham, NC and London: Duke University Press, 2017.

2   See Michel Serres, *The Natural Contract* (trans. Elizabeth MacArthur and William Paulson), Ann Arbor, MI: University of Michigan Press, 1995. Originally published in French as *Le contrat naturel*, Paris: François Bourin, 1990.

3   Dirk Bryant, Daniel Nielsen and Laura Tangley, *The Last Frontier Forest: Ecosystems & Economies on the Edge*, New York: World Resources Institute, 1997, available at https://pdf.wri.org/lastfrontier forests.pdf (last accessed on 1 October 2019).

4   Jonathan Lash, 'Foreword', in *ibid.*, p.5. Emphasis the author's.

5   See M. Gómez-Barris, 'The Colonial Anthropocene: Damage, Remapping, and Resurgent Resources', *Antipode Online*, 19 March 2019, available at https://antipodeonline.org/2019/03/19/the-colonial-anthropocene/ (last accessed on 2 January 2020).

6   World Resources Institute is a global research non-profit organisation that is focussed on climate change and deforestation. For a more recent discussion see WRI Forest Experts, 'Ten Big Changes for Forests Over the Last Decade', *World Resources Institute* [blog], 10 January 2020, available at https://www.wri.org/blog/2020/01/10-big-changes-forests-over-last-decade (last accessed on 24 January 2020).

7   Anna Lowenhaupt Tsing, 'Natural Resources and Capitalist Frontiers', *Economic and Political Weekly*, vol.38, no.48, November 2003, pp.5100–06.

8   See Eduardo Galeano, *The Open Veins of Latin America*, New York: Monthly Review Press, 1973.

9   See M. Gómez-Barris, *The Extractive Zone*. See also Alberto Acosta, 'Extractivism and neoextractism: two sides of the same curse', in Permanent Working Group on Alternatives to Development, *Beyond Development. Alternative Visions from Latin America* (ed. Miriam Lang and Dunia Mokrani), Quito and Amsterdam: Rosa Luxemburg Foundation and Transnational Institute, 2013, available at https://www.tni.org/files/download/beyonddevelopment_extractivism.pdf (last accessed on 24 January 2020).

10 Kyle White, 'Indigenous Climate Change Studies: Indigenizing Futures, Decolonizing the Anthropocene', *English Language Notes*, vol.55, no.1–2, Fall, available at https://papers.ssrn.com/sol3/papers.cfm?abstract_id=2925514 (last accessed on 17 January 2020).

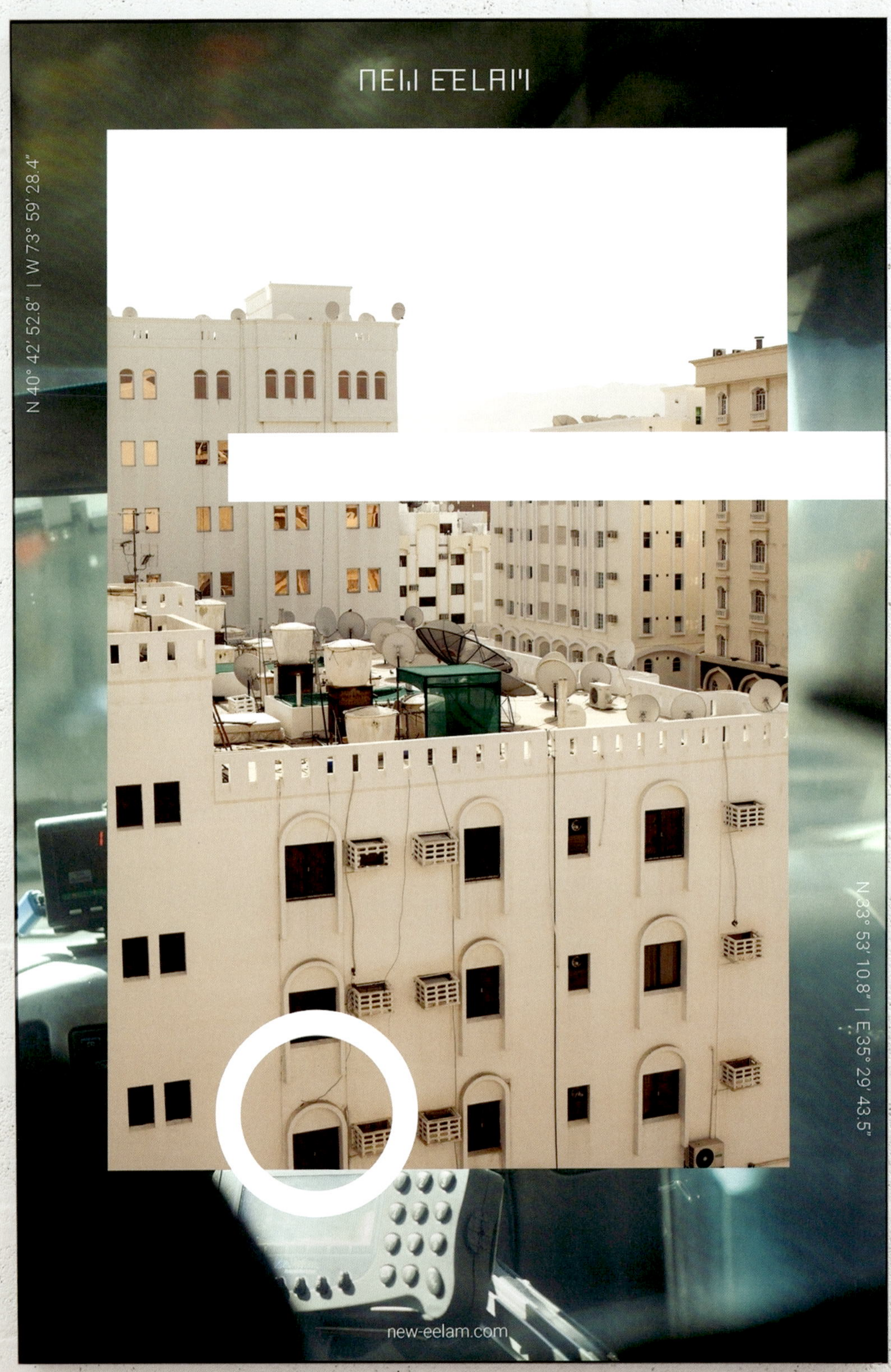

NEW EELAM
N 40° 42' 52.8" | W 73° 59' 28.4"
N 33° 53' 10.8" | E 35° 29' 43.5"
new-eelam.com

Christopher
Kulendran Thomas in
collaboration with
Annika Kuhlmann,
NE_LB_13, 2019.
Courtesy Max
McClure

Artistic Economies: Shelter, Food and Clothing

— Danielle Child

On viewing Christopher Kulendran Thomas' film *60 Million Americans Can't Be Wrong* (2016), one could easily mistake the work for another ironic critical take on the contemporary obsession with the virtual; one in which people's lives are experienced through smart technologies and social media.[1] However, this film is not a tongue-in-cheek spoof but rather a real-world proposal for a 'democratised off-shore economic system' that allows people to become or remain transitory citizens – 'citizens of the cloud for whom the whole world could be home.'[2] The film is part of a project by Kulendran Thomas and Annika Kuhlmann titled *New Eelam* (2016–ongoing), a start-up company billed as a 'subscription housing' service. The project ambitiously proposes to cross legal and nation-state boundaries in offering a fluid form of citizenship in which what we call 'home' could be anywhere. It plans to reorganise housing to 'function more like informational goods'.[3]

A work like *New Eelam* begs the question, what makes artists suitable figures to propose new or alternative economic models? In recent years a number of artists have engaged in proposing and also effectively employing alternative economies. What is meant here by alternative economies are practices that, by extending artistic strategies into the wider economic sphere, articulate non-standard models of economy as well as of artistry. Operating beyond the institutional space of the gallery, the goods and services produced here go beyond the artistic. Of course, such strategies have themselves been subsumed within dominant models to an extent. It is perhaps worth reiterating the now-well-rehearsed story of the co-optation of the artist as model worker in the contemporary period. In *The New Spirit of Capitalism*, originally published in 1999, Luc Boltanski and Eve Chiapello observe the way in which management discourse from

Danielle Child examines the extent to which artists' proposals for alternative contemporary economies successfully revive the historical avant-garde project of returning art to the praxis of life.

the 1990s began to absorb the 'artist critique' of capitalism.[4] As a result, a Romantic model of the artist became a validated model of productive worker. Traits such as creativity, thinking 'outside of the box' and flexibility became desirable qualities for the new worker. However, as Maurizio Lazzarato has argued, this conception of the artist was already out-of-date by the time of its capitalist co-option post-1968.[5] It is a conception based on the problematic nineteenth-century bourgeois conception of the bohemian artist as freed of capitalist production. The stereotype that results from this is still commonly found in creative industry discourse[6]; moreover, it is well understood that the idea of the artist as un-alienated worker makes the role particularly conducive to the neoliberal work environment.

The neoliberal ideology has been crucial to fostering values of individualism and selfhood and, in the UK, the birth of the 'Creative Industries', cementing the inclusion of 'creative' values within dominant economic models. New working models associated with immaterial, flexible and service-based work thus become aligned with a certain assumption of what an artist is or does. When labour begins to adapt to skills aligned with a certain conception of the artist, it is unsurprising that the artist becomes comfortable in crossing the line between art and the economic to propose their own economies.[7]

In the documentary *60 Million Americans…*, *New Eelam* is framed as a project for the displaced. Its title is based on a lost Tamil state in Sri Lanka – Eelam – that following the neo-Marxist revolution was governed for three decades (until 2009) as an autonomous state, and was also the home of Kulendran Thomas' family. The film tells of how, after the state fell, the people of Eelam travelled to the West to look for a better life. This forms the inspiration for *New Eelam*'s proposal of a model of housing for the displaced and transient, categories that today resurface in the form of the flexible worker. From this proposition, it appears that Kulendran Thomas and Kuhlmann might be developing a housing model for the precariat.

In his book *The Precariat: The New Dangerous Class* (2011), Guy Standing observes that the precariat do not yet constitute a social class. It is not, he argues, a homogenous group but rather one that ranges from cleaners, care workers, refugees and migrants to creative workers.[8] Although the practical application of *New Eelam*'s economic model is not yet fully realised, the viewer is told that there would be a flat rate subscription to the proposed housing cloud 'at a level equivalent to the cost of rent', reduced over time to a 'trivial rate'.[9] From the outset, then, *New Eelam* is presumably initially available only to the employed, or to those who can afford rent in cities across the globe. Although the film and title suggest that the self-governed housing model is for the politically displaced, such as those who left Eelam to look for a better life, the literature that accompanies the project at Bristol's Spike Island pitches the housing model to people who 'work freelance or change their job frequently'.[10] This proposition seems to appeal to one group within Standing's understanding of the precariat – the creative, flexible worker – while potentially excluding those whose mobility or transience is more a result of, say, immigration status than career path.[11]

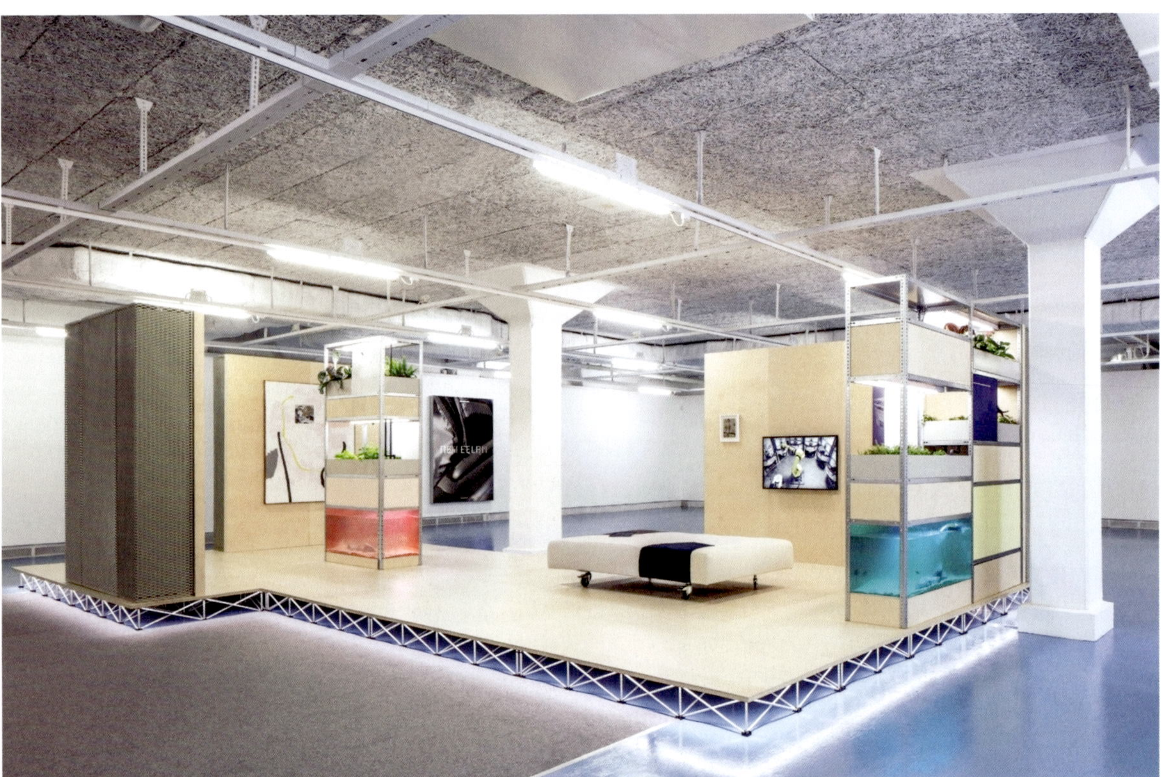

Christopher Kulendran Thomas in collaboration with Annika Kuhlmann, *New Eelam*, 2017. Installation view, 'New Eelam: Tensta', Tensta konsthall, Stockholm. Photograph: Jean-Baptiste Beranger. Courtesy the artist

Other contemporary artistic economic practices return to questions of material production, thinking in particular about co-operative production. Company Drinks (2015–ongoing), based in East London is an example of one such project, which, in stark contrast to the 'real estate technology company' of *New Eelam*,[12] returns to material production in the field of soft drinks. Company Drinks is a Community Interest Company (CIC) that began as an art project titled *Company: Movements, Deals, and Drinks* in 2014 (subsequently registered as a Company Drinks CIC in June 2015), initiated by the artist Kathrin Böhm in Dagenham and Barking, East London. Böhm's practice, as part of the Myvillages collective, puts forward a new understanding of the rural as a site of cultural production. Company Drinks builds on Böhm's interest in the rural through exploring its relationship to urban working-class history. Like *New Eelam*, it revisits for its inspiration a lost historical practice associated with a specific place: that of hop picking in Kent. In the early twentieth century, locals from the East End of London would travel to the nearby countryside in Kent to undertake the seasonal labour of hop picking. It was largely women and children (those not in permanent employment) who made the journey, escaping the congestion of the city. This practice ended in the 1950s, but has been revived as part of Company Drinks' production

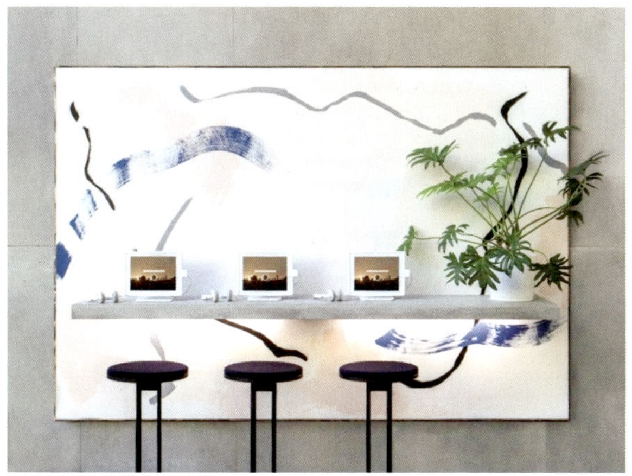

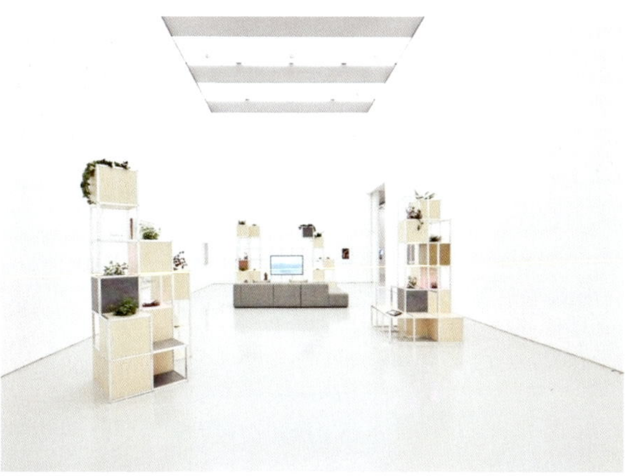

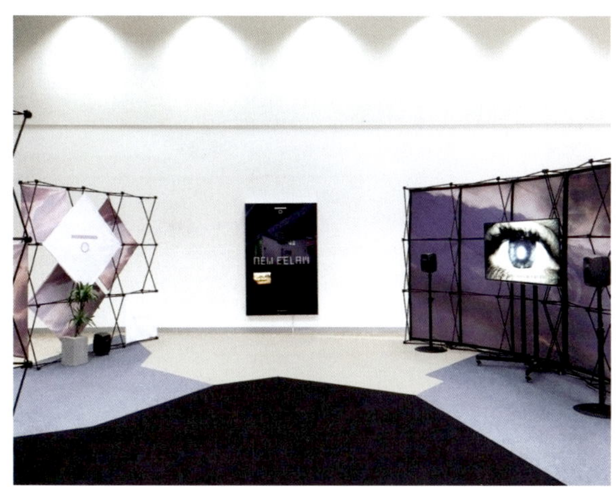

process, in addition to foraging for botanicals in local urban parks. For some this is a nostalgic return to a lost time in which leisure and labour were demarcated for workers who stayed on the farms for around four to six weeks per year.[13] But while looking to the past, the project also makes visible the new workers who undertake the labour of fruit picking for commercial farmers in Kent today. In the Company Drinks and Myvillages film *Foreign Pickers* (2016), we meet a small group of Eastern European workers who come to Kent to work on the farms during the picking season. By making these contemporary workers visible, the project exposes some of the economic conditions of global labour. Although the location of origin of the workers has changed, the idea of a temporary relocation of people to undertake low-cost seasonal work has not.

Böhm stresses that Company Drinks is 'run in a way that is clearly not a neoliberal model'.[14] It is important that the company offers an alternative economy to that posed by contemporary capitalism. Its production process is based around the company's five 'C's – culture, collective, community, collaborating, commerce'.[15] It started from the idea of returning to a historic community practice and, as Böhm explains: 'It is trying to merge a cultural idea with an economic concept.'[16] Rather than prioritising the economic in this relationship, the company reverses a typical commodification of the 'local' or 'artisan' under neoliberalism by employing a practice in which the 'commercial supports the communal and cultural'.[17] This is perhaps where art has a role to play in a project that is also a functioning business.

Böhm insists that what she terms the 'privilege' of the art world should be 'shared and interconnected with other efforts.'[18] She uses art as a way to think about economic practices that take place outside of the art institution (including the art market), developing a practice that attempts to avoid neoliberal economic methods. Her position and skills as an artist help her facilitate a project that might otherwise be 'just another company'. She maintains that the company is part of her art practice, while simultaneously being viewed as a place for employment.

Böhm is not alone in initiating a community project that resulted in the establishment of a CIC. In 2014, artist Jeanne Van Heeswijk worked with the local community in Anfield, Liverpool on *Homebaked* (2010– ongoing) initiated as part of the Liverpool Biennial. Like Böhm the artist did not approach the community with an idea for a business model, but began to talk to those interested in working with her in meetings held in an empty, closed-down bakery. The idea of resurrecting the bakery – once part of the community – came from the participants. Today *Homebaked* is run as a cooperative business in Anfield selling pies to football supporters on match days, and bread to the locals. As with Company Drinks, the artist made use of distance to allow for the projects to develop from the work of participants rather than top-down. This artistic distance (beyond economic thinking) allows for the development of long-term collaborative projects, such as the Centre for Plausible Economies (which Böhm works on alongside curator Kuba Szreder and economist Katherine Gibson) that focus on the representation of local economic practices within communities. Böhm does not avoid politics in her practice:

Company Drinks is a cultural project but also a practical one in terms of how we reorganise resources, trade differently, have different ethics and ultimately take back the economy as a richer cultural realm, different from this machine that destroys us.[19]

Böhm's intentions are to create an economy as an alternative to that of the destructive neoliberal capitalist machine.

In a final example of alternative economies in art, another historical model of labour is invoked to develop an economic practice. Unlike *New Eelam* and Company Drinks, this project is less engaged in aspiration than with the preservation of history.[20] Irena Haiduk's *Nine Hour Delay* (2012–58) returns to material production, this time through shoe manufacturing:

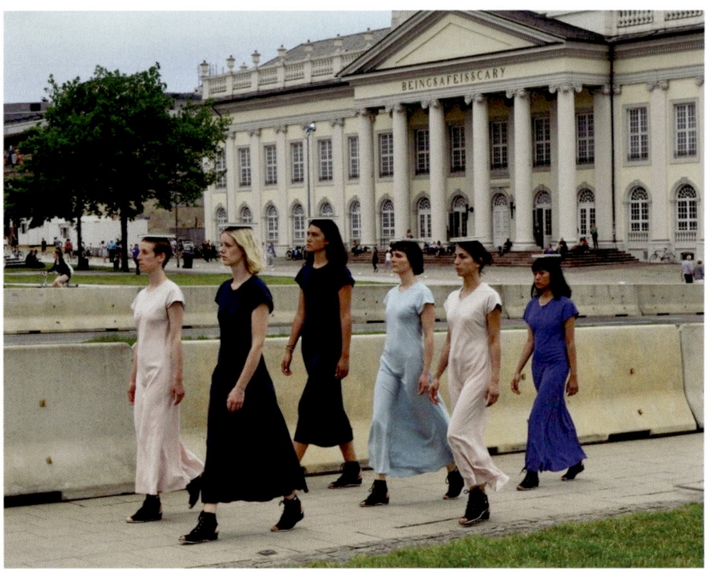

Irena Haiduk, *Spinal Discipline: Julia Allnoch, Isabella Artadi, Mustafa Boğa, Annika Katja Boll, Beryl Chepkirui, Mona Eing, Ozgür Genc, Mila Gligorić, Josefine Mundri, Andara Shastika, Wenti Sheng and Alma Weber working,* Kassel, 2017. Photograph: Anna Shteynshleyger. Courtesy the artist

Previous page, top to bottom: Christopher Kulendran Thomas in collaboration with Annika Kuhlmann, *New Eelam,* 2016. Installation view, 9th Berlin Biennale, Akademie Der Künste, Berlin. Photograph: Laura Fiorio. Courtesy the artist

Christopher Kulendran Thomas in collaboration with Annika Kuhlmann, *New Eelam,* 2019. Installation view, 'New Eelam: Bristol', Spike Island, Bristol. Courtesy Max McClure

Christopher Kulendran Thomas in collaboration with Annika Kuhlmann, *New Eelam,* 2016. Installation view, 11th Gwangju Biennale. Courtesy the artist

The Borosana shoe was first developed over a nine-year period (1960–69) at Borovo Rubber Industry Headquarters in Vukovar, Yugoslavia. After being designed and tested by the Borovo female workforce and an orthopedic surgeon, the shoe was mandatory for Yugoslav women working in the public sector. Borosana was launched in 1969, in white and navy colors, featuring an ergonomic platform, calculated as ideal for nine hours of standing without hurting the wearer's spine. In the declining years of Yugoslav communism the model was withdrawn from mass production. Fabrication was abandoned when Vukovar became a war zone in 1991.[21]

Haiduk resurrects the Borosana shoe by putting it back into production. When the work/shoe was exhibited as part of documenta 14 (2017), Haiduk sought out the skilled women who were able to produce the shoe (and other products known as Yugoform) for the exhibition. During the exhibition, female gallery workers were asked to sign a contract in which they agreed to only wear the Borosana shoe during their working hours. As Haiduk explains:

When labour begins to adapt to skills aligned with a certain conception of the artist, it is unsurprising that the artist becomes comfortable in crossing the line between art and the economic to propose their own economies.

Nine Hour Delay (NHD) has made something half alive, and by delineating between labour and leisure (women wearing the shoes wear them only when working), art work imposes an opposition to the endless labor hours that fill 'the new spirit of capitalism'.[22]

The artist refers to this process as the 'continuous zombification of Yugoslavia' that is financed by keeping the historical Yugoslavian factory (now in Croatia) alive after the country itself has ceased to exist. Here, skilled workers are employed to manufacture the shoes for workers, but these are not workers employed to undertake the same kind of work as those for whom the original shoe was designed. With the eradication of the 'clocking-in card' of the factory, the shoes act as a reminder that work and leisure time was once clearly divided, something not so common with the advent of immaterial forms of labour that blur work and life. The skilled manual work of the shoemakers here is juxtaposed with the immaterial labour of the gallery worker.

Nine Hour Delay forms part of a larger project that has been exhibited under the title *Seductive Exacting Realism* (SER) (2015). In the process of producing the shoe, Haiduk

Irena Haiduk,
*Seductive Exacting
Realism*, 2015–
ongoing. Installation
view, Waiting
Room, Neue Neue
Galerie, Kassel,
documenta 14, 2017.
Photograph: Anna
Shteynshleyger.
Courtesy the artist

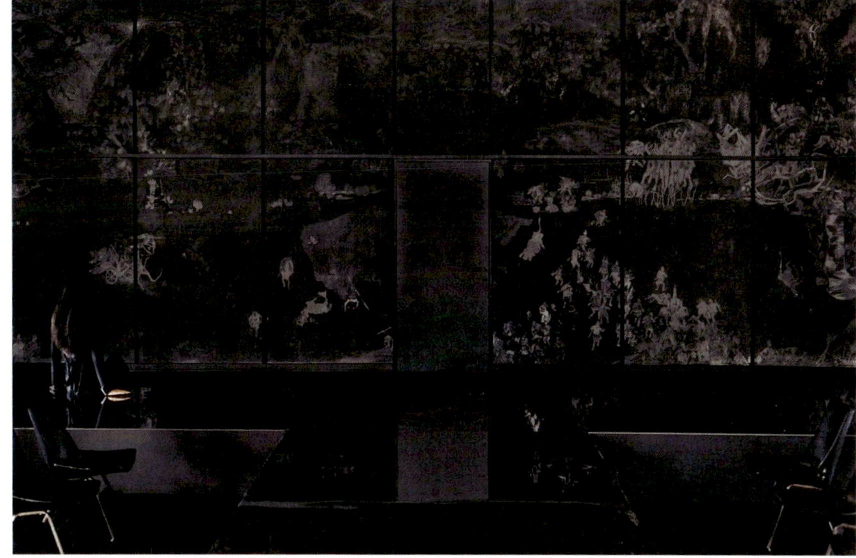

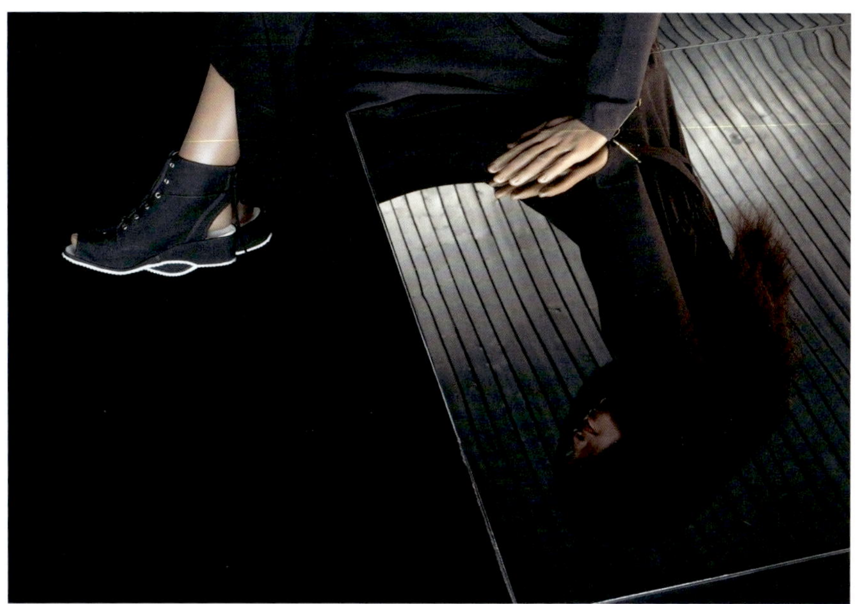

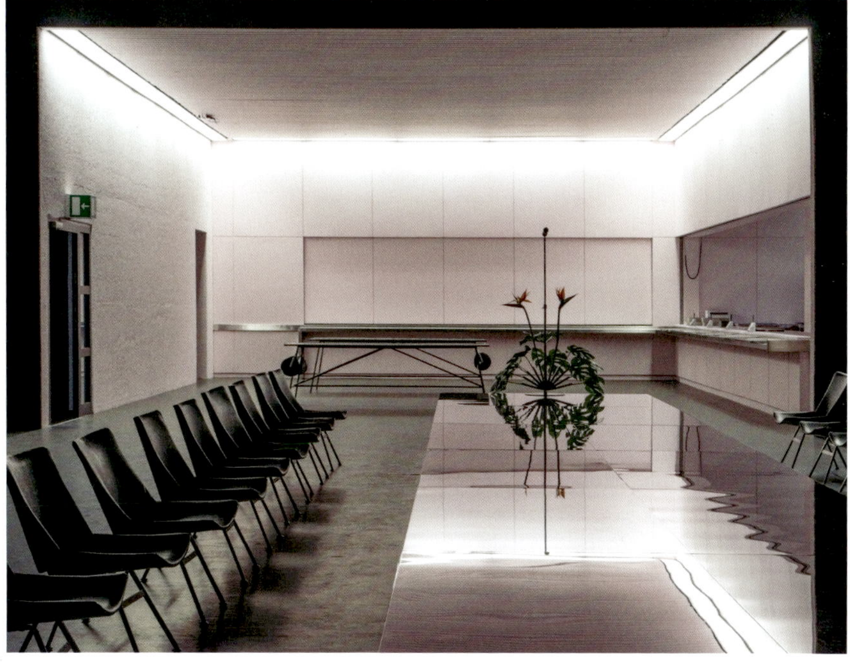

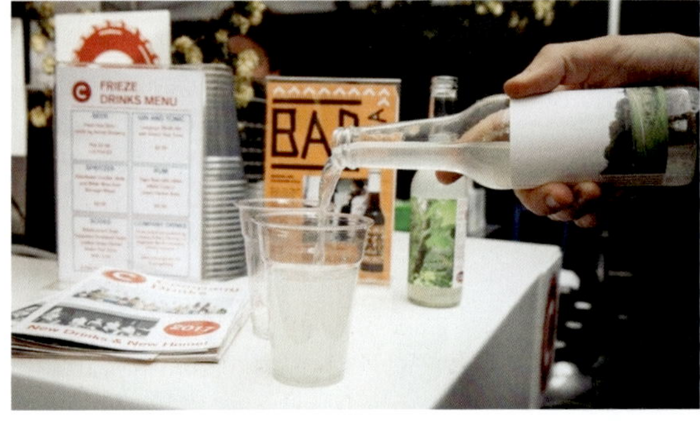

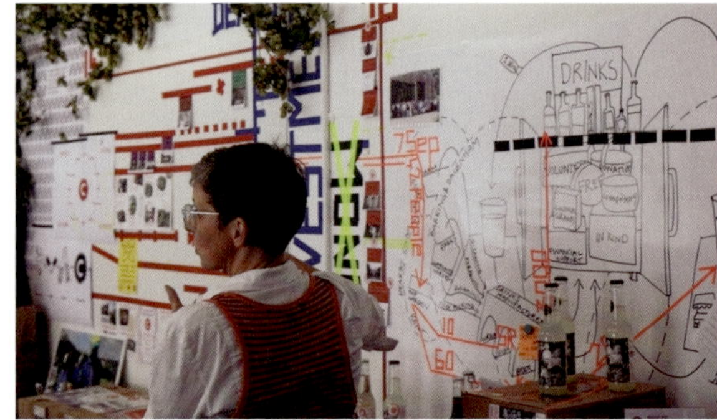

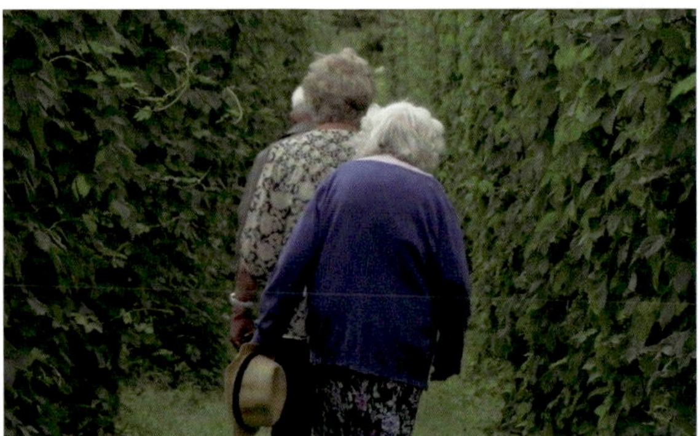

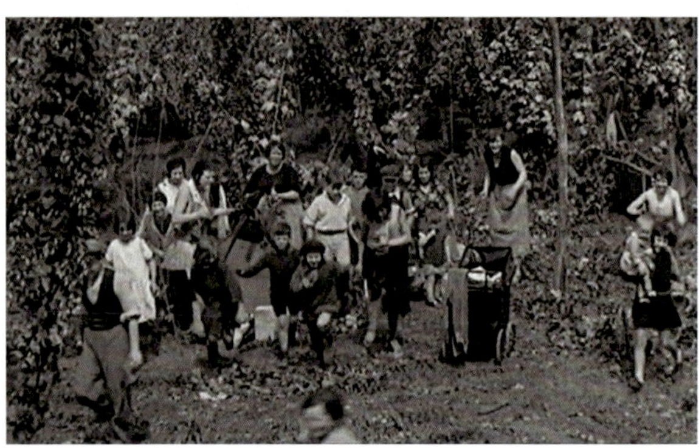

established a new Limited Liability Company (which is referred to as a 'blind non-aligned oral corporation'[23]) called Yugoexport, registered in the US.[24] In SER Haiduk presents a 'transactional area' in which visitors are able to purchase items. But this is a shop with a difference. On entering, visitors are shown neither the items nor a price list. In order to see the items, they have to ask an employee; Haiduk has described this as a way of slowing down the transaction – the visitor has to talk first.[25] The visitor is then asked to define their income level for the price (of the Borosana shoe or another item, such as a functional dress designed in the Mussolini era) to be revealed. Items can also be purchased from the Yugoexport website.[26] This is a fully functioning company – Haiduk draws a salary from Yugoexport, and has stated that the corporation's profits finance the salaries of its workforce as well as the development and production of current and future artworks.[27]

The task of the historical avant-garde was to return art to the praxis of life. In the examples discussed here, artists have initiated new economic practices, each returning in some way to history for their models – be they the historical state of Eelam, previous practices of hop-picking or an ergonomic shoe designed under communist rule – as if to alert us to the fact that contemporary economic practices have in various ways failed. These are also political practices that in different ways refer to the displaced. *New Eelam* appeals to the voluntarily displaced creative worker while imagining a future in which home could be provided for the those displaced due to political circumstances. Company Drinks offers an economic model for a deprived and overlooked area in which Böhm has identified possibilities. And *Nine Hour Delay* keeps alive a factory and form of production that once belonged to a now-lost country.

Of these contemporary working practices, *New Eelam* is the most aligned with 'the artistic', offering immaterial services through a model that embraces the criticised technical determinism of Marx and Engels.[28] The course of history has demonstrated – as Raniero Panzieri warned us via Marx – that capitalist technologies are not neutral.[29] It is difficult to distinguish between the new 'platform capitalism' and the alternative model of housing that Kulendran Thomas and Kuhlmann describe. The financial details of *New Eelam* are still unclear, particularly in terms of the cost of the service.[30] Company Drinks works on an alternative pricing structure. The drinks produced are priced in accordance with the local demographic: in the area in which the bottled drinks are produced, they are sold for £1 and in West London they are priced at £3. This practice is echoed in Haiduk's *Yugoexport*, where each product – be it a rubbing of a contract from a marble engraving, the Borosana shoe or a functional dress – is priced according to the buyer's income.

Clockwise from top left:

Company Drinks Bar, Frieze Art Fair, London, 2018. Photograph: Jennifer Balcombe

Kathrin Böhm explaining the diverse economies of Company Drinks at 'Centre for Plausible Economies' Study Day, Company Drinks, Barking, 2018. Photograph: Kevin Haegele. Courtesy the artist

Sue Giovanni, still from *Foreign Pickers*, 2018, film, colour, sound, 22min 05sec. Commissioned by Delfina Foundation, London

Sue Giovanni, still from *Foreign Pickers*, 2018, film, colour, sound, 22min 05sec. Commissioned by Delfina Foundation London

This 'economic' or 'business' turn in recent artistic practice could mistakenly be understood as an effect of the neoliberal 'new spirit of capitalism'. Mistakenly because the practices discussed here explore (with varying efficacy) the possibility of micro-economies that attempt to escape the economy of contemporary capitalism. This takes form in post-capitalist, cooperative or historical production models (but with revised pricing based on income rather than production of value). Some artists might now be more comfortable crossing the line between art and production. Yet these companies aren't simply the result of out-of-date notions of artists exercising creativity in the service of neoliberalism. The emergence of these kinds of artistic economies could be understood as critical responses to the capitalist co-option of 'unalienated' artistic labour. That is, a response to the return of art to life praxis when the work/life boundary seems less and less visible.

1   I am reminded of Hito Steyerl's *How Not to Be Seen: A Fucking Didactic Educational .MOV File* (2013), which unveils the often hidden relationship between warfare and digital technologies.

2   *60 Million Americans Can't Be Wrong*, dir. Christopher Kulendran Thomas in collaboration with Annika Kuhlmann, 2016, available at https://dis.art/series/60-million-americans-can-t-be-wrong/ (last accessed on 5 December 2019).

3   *Ibid*. On a related project see also Renate van der Zee, 'Fairbnb.coop launches, offering help for social projects', *The Guardian*, 13 November 2019, available at https://www.theguardian.com/travel/2019/nov/13/fairbnbcoop-holiday-rental-website-launches-help-social-projects (last accessed on 29 January 2020).

4   See Luc Boltanski and Eve Chiapello, *The New Spirit of Capitalism*, London: Verso, 2005.

5   See Maurizio Lazzarato, 'The Misfortunes of the "Artistic Critique" and of Cultural Employment', 2007, available at http://eipcp.net/transversal/0207/lazzarato/en (last accessed on 20 January 2020).

6   See my discussion of Lazzarato's critique in relation to a possible contemporary misconception of artist in Danielle Child, *Working Aesthetics: Labour, Art and Capitalism*, London: Bloomsbury/Radical Aesthetics Radical Art, 2019, p.77.

7   There are, of course, prior examples of art crossing into the realm of production, such as early twentieth-century Russian Productivism and the Artists Placement Group in 1960s London.

8   Guy Standing, *The Precariat: The New Dangerous Class*, London: Bloomsbury, 2016, p.3.

9   Christopher Kulendran Thomas, '*New Eelam*: Bristol' (exhibition leaflet), Spike Island, Bristol, 2019. See also *60 Million Americans Can't Be Wrong, op. cit.*

10   *Ibid.*

11   It is perhaps telling that the project was initiated by a conversation between Kulendran Thomas and Kuhlmann about 'ways to streamline how they had both been living'. Louisa Elderton, 'Proto typing the Future: An Interview with Christopher Kulendran Thomas', *Berlin Art Link*, 27 September 2017, available at http://www.berlinartlink.com/2016/09/27/work-prototyping-the-future-an-interview-with-christopher-kulendran-thomas/ (last accessed 14 September 2019).

12   C. K. Thomas, '*New Eelam*: Bristol', *op. cit.*

13   In the short film *Company Drinks*, one participant recalls how, as a child, she would see her cousins at this annual event. The film *Foreign Pickers* further confirms this nostalgia when those who used to go hop picking as children return to the site of work. See *Company Drinks*, 2019, https://player.vimeo.com/video/326901966 (last accessed on 4 December 2019) and *Foreign Pickers*, dir. Company Drinks and Myvillages, 2017, https://vimeo.com/181628877, (last accessed on 4 December 2019).

14   Kathrin Böhm interviewed by Ellen Mara De Wachter, 'Arteconomies', *Art Monthly*, no.429, September 2019, p.3.

15   *Company Drinks, op. cit.*

16   *Ibid.*, p.2.

17   'About', Company Drinks website, http://companydrinks.info/about/ (last accessed on 5 December 2019).

18   K. Böhm interviewed by E. M. De Wachter, 'Arteconomies', *op. cit.*, p.3.

19   *Ibid.*

20   Haiduk uses the Balkan phrase 'hope is the greatest whore' in her work to refer to the idea that by eradicating hope, you eradicate the cruelty of waiting. Nada Endrissat and Ana Alacovska, '"Hope is the Greatest Whore": hope, critique, and management studies in Irena Haiduk's artwork', *M@n@gement*, vol.23, no.3, 2018, pp.1135-53.

21   Irena Haiduk cited in 'Borosana Shoe Issue with Irena Haiduk', documenta 14 website, available at https://www.documenta14.de/en/calendar/15826/borosana-shoe-issue (last accessed on 20 January 2020).

22   See Monika Szewczyk, 'Realismically Speaking, Irena Haiduk', *Mousse*, vol.50, p.243, available at https://renaissancesociety.org/media/files/mm50_haiduk_doppie.pdf (last accessed on 4 December 2019).

23   Expanding on blindness, Haiduk notes that oral history is changeable and can be misunderstood. See I. Haiduk, 'Against Biography', *Seductive Exacting Realism* (ed. Haiduk and Solveig Øvstebø), Berlin: Sternberg Press, 2017, n.p.

24   The name is a play on a Yugoslavian clothing company that went bankruptcy in 2003.

25   See M. Szewczyk and Yugoexport / I. Haiduk, 'Political Futures', talk at Kunsthalle Wien, 2 February 2018, available at https://www.youtube.com/watch?v=xklMfvG5PV0 (last accessed on 4 December 2019).

26   The Yugoexport website also asks the customer to define their income – mid, lower or upper – before prices are revealed.

27   See M. Szewczyk and Yugoexport / I. Haiduk, 'Political Futures', *op. cit.*

28   Marx and Engels have been criticised for the emphasis that they placed in their analyses of industrial capitalism on the role of technology in advancing capitalist production and, subsequently, society, in their analyses of industrial capitalism.

29   See Raniero Panzieri, *The Capitalist Use of Machinery: Marx versus the Objectivists*, 1964, available at http://libcom.org/library/capalist-use-machinery-raniero-panzieri (last accessed on 30 January 2020).

30   See Nick Srnicek, *Platform Capitalism*, Cambridge and Malden, UK: Polity Press, 2016.

Darcy Lange's *Māori Land Project* (1977-80)[1]

— Mercedes Vicente

In a compelling interview in 1975 with *Avalanche* magazine editor Willoughby Sharp, artist Darcy Lange expressed the need to transgress the conventional boundaries of the art world, asking: 'Why should a videographer be confined to galleries and the art world?' He defined his activity as 'being something very close to social activism',[2] reflected in a video practice that had begun to rely primarily on experiential and relational exchanges with his recorded subjects.[3] He saw video as a medium that could effect change within a broader cultural context – a tool to raise social and political consciousness, contributing to a counter-culture defined by left-wing political agendas.[4]

After living in London for nearly a decade, Lange made an extended visit to his homel and Aotearoa New Zealand (hereafter referred to as New Zealand) in 1977 where he imme-diately began the three-year-long *Māori Land Project*.[5] With this work he joined the efforts of fellow documentary film-makers to raise awareness and mobilise support for Māori over their land rights. The 1970s saw the rise of the Māori renaissance, a movement that sought self-determination, standing against colonialism and its enclosures of Māori land, and demanding reforms to land rights. It was fuelled by the formation of Māori activist groups and a string of land occupations and marches including the 1975 Land March to Parliament, Bastion Point (1977-78) and the annual protests started in 1971 by *Ngā Tamatoa* (Young Warriors) on Waitangî Day, commemorating the Treaty of Waitangî, signed in 1840 by representatives of the British Crown and Māori chiefs. The reforms led to the establishment of the Waitangî Tribunal in 1975, a permanent commission for land claims regarding legislation, policies, actions or omissîons of the Crown that are alleged to breach the promises made by the Treaty of Waitangî.[6]

The political backdrop to the Māori protest movement was the emergence of the New Left in New Zealand that was influenced by the civil rights and international liberation movements, and growing Marxism and feminism. The so-called long 1970s (from the late 1960s to early 1980s) was a period characterised by mass dissent in New Zealand, with the demonstrations against the Vietnam War and sporting contacts with Apartheid South Africa, which, gaining mass support in the early 1970s, became the catalyst and lay the groundwork for other protest movements such as the ecology, anti-nuclear, feminist and Māori self-determination movements.[7] Many *Pākehā* (of European descent) shared Māori self-determination as an extensîon of their anti-capitalist and anti-colonialist posîtions, and indeed, as New Zealand historian Toby

Mercedes Vicente discusses Darcy Lange's *Māori Land Project* at the intersection of militant film, collaborative practice and political struggles in New Zealand.

Boraman acknowledges, 'support for Māori sovereignty became the default Pākehā leftist view by the early 1980s onwards'.[8]

The high visîbility of a 'radical urban Māori culture' and its activism created 'a para-digmatic shift in how the nation was conceived'.[9] The term *tangata whenua* (people of the land) became increasîngly sîgnificant for the identity politics of the 1990s. It not only emphasîsed the interconnectedness of Māori to the land (*whenua* also means placenta), but to the increasîng importance of indigeneity to Māori rights, the term became key so as to 'nationalize indigenous political agency'.[10] This political climate was captured in documentaries made by Pākehā and Māori film-makers including Barry Barclay's televisîon series *Tangata Whenua* (1974), Leon Narbey and Geoff Steven's *Te Matakite o Aotearoa/ The Māori Land March* (1975), Chris Strewe's *Waitangî: Die Geschichte eines Vertrages und seiner Erben (The Story of A Treaty and Its Inheritors)* (1977), and Merata Mita, Leon Narbey and Gerd Pohlmann's *Baŝtion Point Day 507* (1980).[11]

The Making of *Māori Land Projeĉt*

Lange's *Māori Land Projeĉt* emerges within this political and cultural context. This complex and vast work documented two cases of land alienation: Takaparawha (at the time referred

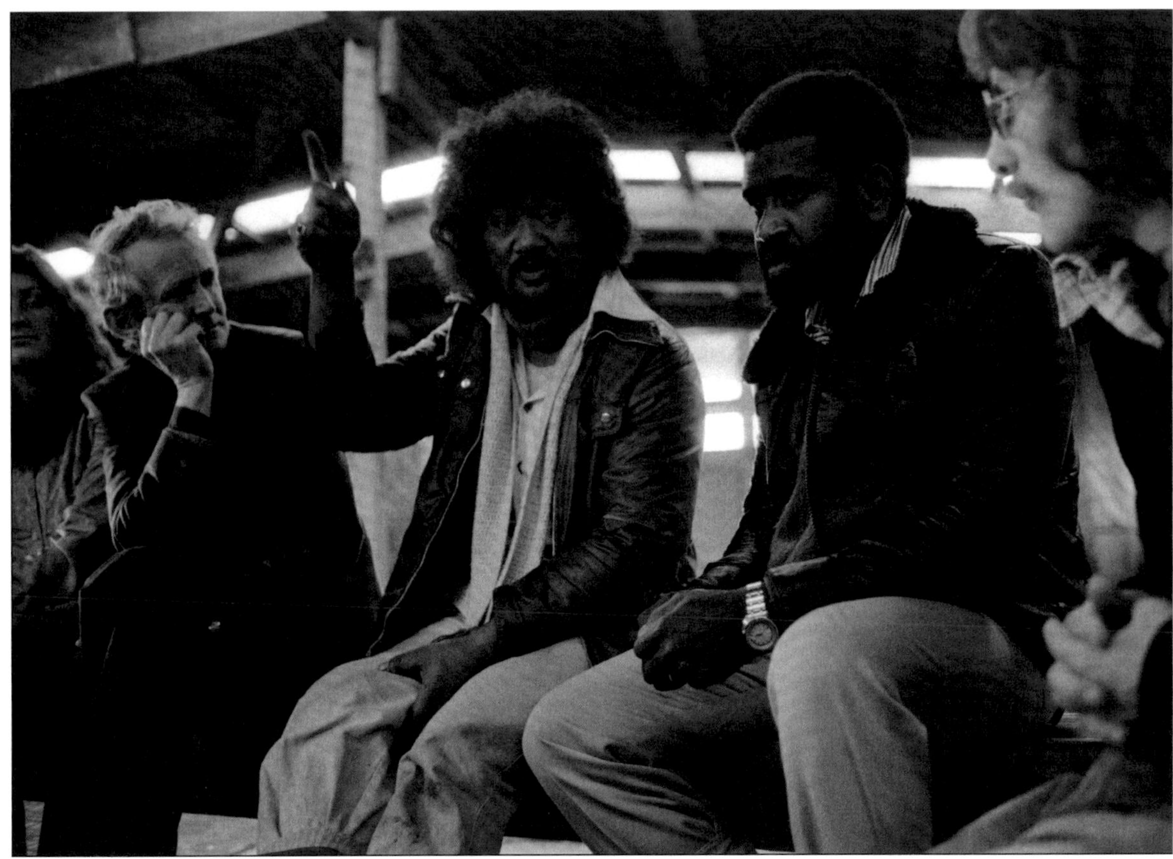

to as Bastion Point) in Auckland and the Ngātihine land block, near Kawakawa, Tai Tokerau, north of Auckland.[12] The former case concerned Māori land confiscated by the government in 1840 and turned into a military post in 1885, and later gifted to the city council, who in 1976 was planning to sell it for real-estate development. The occupation of Bastion Point led by *Ngāti Whātua-o-Ōrākei* lasted over sixteen months, and became one of the most public cases of Māori political action (later the government returned the land to *Ngāti Whātua*, the local tribe, as part of the Treaty of Waitangi settlement process).[13] The Ngātihine case, on the other hand, involved a legal dispute to stop land from being leased by a forestry corporation, under the argument that Māori owners had left their land underdeveloped.[14]

It is unclear what initially brought Lange to become engaged in this project, but he recalls meeting, through a friend who had worked on the film *Te Matakite o Aotearoa*, people who were involved in the Māori struggles. Lange established close relations with key Māori such as Joe Hawke, spokesperson for the Bastion Point occupation, Colin Clark of the Ōrākei Action Committee and most especially, with *Ngāpuhi* land rights activist and photographer John Miller, who introduced him to the Ngātihine case, travelled with him and even shot some of the material.[15] Over the course of three trips to New Zealand during 1977–78, Lange gathered interviews with important Māori activists, politicians and members of parliament that captured contrasting perspectives. In addition to Hawke, Clark and Miller, they included Taura Eruera, anthropologist and founder of *Ngāti Tamatoa*; Duncan MacIntyre, Minister of Māori Affairs of the National Party; Matiu Rata, former Minister of Māori Affairs of the Labour Party; Matiu Tarawa, land rights campaigner; Tim Horopapera, Tasman Mill site pulp and paper worker and unionist; and finally Virginia Shaw, a reporter with New Zealand's TV One who brought some of these contacts with key politicians and media individuals.[16]

Lacking funding in his country for the project, Lange sought support from the Netherlands.[17] He collaborated with René Coelho, former television producer and founding director of MonteVideo, the first video art gallery in Amsterdam, and with sociologist lecturer and film-maker Leonard Henny, at the Sociology Institute in Utrecht University.[18] On account of these collaborations and drawing on Lange's footage, three videos were produced: *The Māoris*, a 30-minute version produced by Coelho for NOS television (the

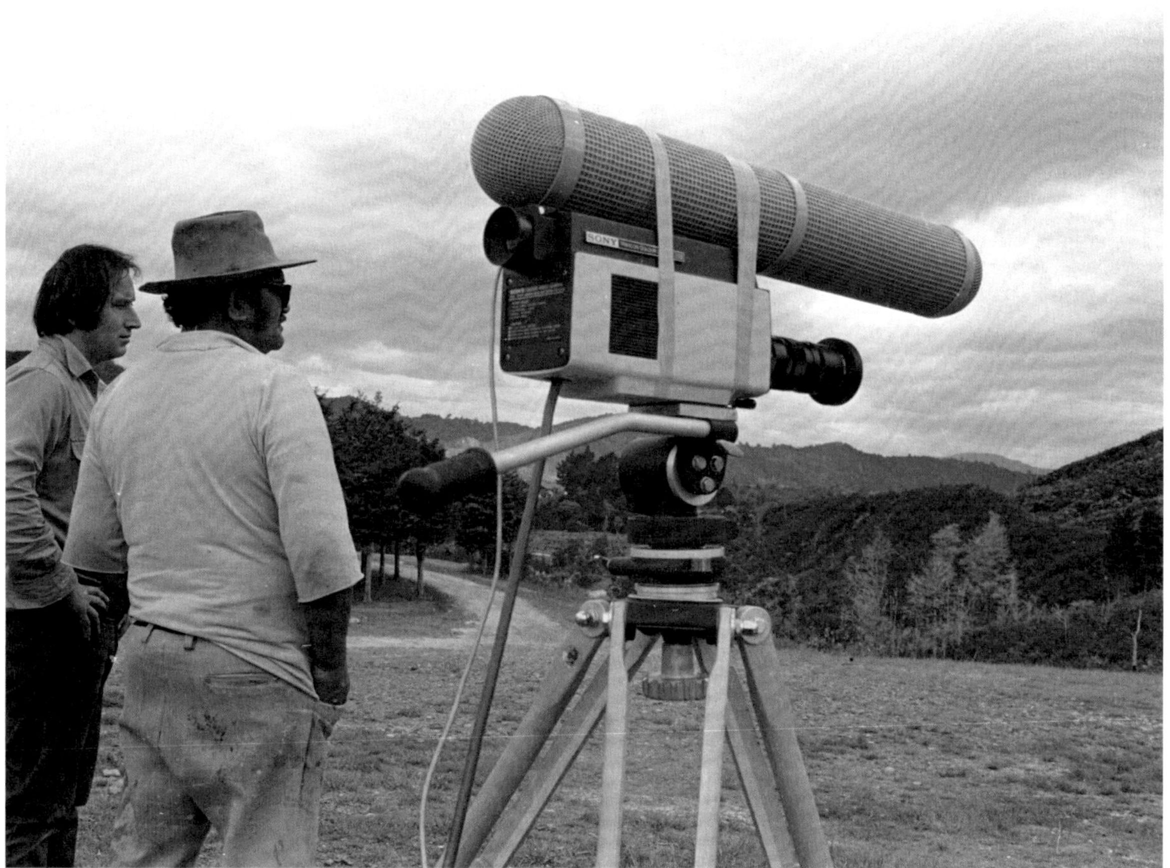

Dutch Broadcasting Foundation); *The Māori Land Struggle*, directed by Henny, made of two different versions of 23 and 26 minutes each that were used as part of his research conducted with secondary-school children to investigate the effect of media in forming their opinions; and *Bastion Point*, a 140-minute more personal study edited by Lange. These were shown as part of the exhibition 'Māori Land Project' at Stedelijk Van Abbemuseum (11 January–10 February 1980) in Eindhoven and at the Internationaal Cultureel Centrum (ICC) (29 March–27 April 1980) in Antwerp.

The notion of media manipulation and the politics exercised by the media became the focus of the exhibition, while it prevailed for Lange and his collaborators the wish to provide international attention to Māori struggles.[19] It established a dialectical, open-ended structure, based on Coehlo's, Henny's and Lange's contrasting versions made from the same material and edited for different purposes: for three different publics (television audiences, secondary-class pupils and museum visitors), by three different agents (a television producer, a sociologist and an artist), and three different institutions (broadcast organisation, university and museum).[20] Jan Debbaut, curator at the Van Abbemuseum, in a 9 April 1980 letter to Peggy Gale, curator at A Space, Toronto, described the contents and the layout of the exhibition as the result of 'an integrated teamwork' and as 'a "multi-purpose" set of information on the Māori issue with which one could do whatever one liked'.[21] In addition to these videos, contextual documentation was on display on a table and pinned to the wall including maps, letters, books, newspaper clippings, and the report and findings of Henny's sociological survey with the secondary schools.

Influenced by the writings of Paulo Freire and Bertolt Brecht's radical notions of radio, Henny's research was engaged with the use of media in political education to help raise awareness about the problems faced by the minorities living in the Netherlands.[22] Key to raising consciousness was for people to reach an understanding of the social forces that might determine their own situations. He was experimenting with the effectiveness of film's partisan and bipartisan formats in generating discussion among pupils and in translating the problems in the film, Māori struggles in New Zealand, to their own situation – what Freire termed a 'generative moment' in his 1970 book *Pedagogy of the Oppressed*.[23]

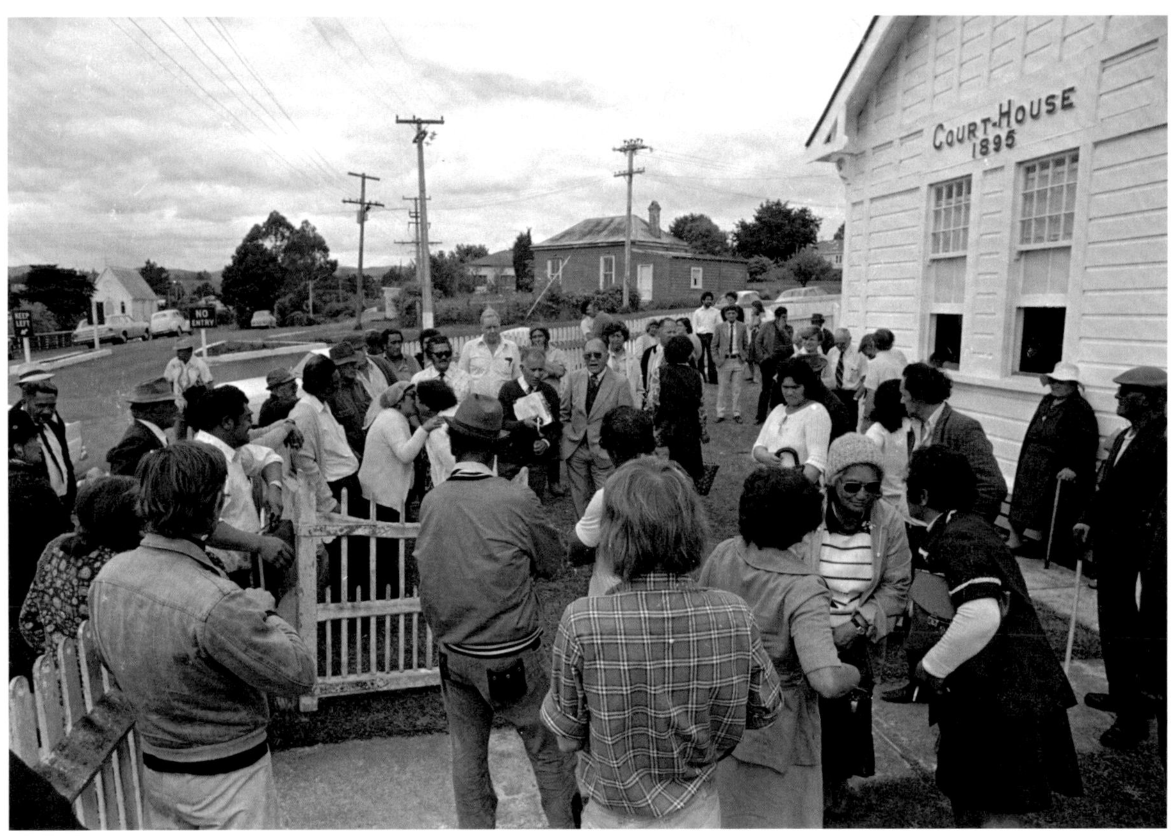

The Māoris, The Māori Land Struggle and Bastion Point

Seen side-by-side, Henny's two versions of *The Māori Land Struggle* and Coelho's *The Māoris* feel rather close in pace, style and length, because all three use practically the same footage and many edited sequences, and their script and editing have the stamp of the Victor Jara Collective. *The Māori Land Struggle* and *The Māoris* were edited by Ray Krill, in the latter with assistance from Lange. Both of their scripts were by Gloria Lowe, in the former together with Cris Kooiman.[24] The selection of shots and sequences are dictated by the respective emphasis of each film, as geared to different audiences and purposes (education and television) and in Henny's films in order to support partisan and bipartisan perspectives. *The Māoris* does not have a distinct broadcast value, as it did not follow the conventional commercial guidelines for television.

> *Lange's long takes have a greater political implication as, with duration, the subjectivity and the singularity of Māori are released. It contributes to the subjectivation rather than objectivation of his subjects, and therefore to establishing a sympathetic relationship with them.*

Lange's lengthier *Bastion Point* stands out from the other films in that it does not rush through a storyline of events nor presents a political argument. His use of long takes (of five to fifteen minutes) with a static camera or very limited movement and unedited or sparsely edited sequences, lends a documentary integrity to the image – in his words, a 'documentary quality of scientific research' in the 'attempt to produce a legal proof' – in that reality unfolds in real time.[25] This also gives this work a sense of immediacy. His non-abbreviated temporality challenges the reified endings and instrumental identifications of his peers' versions. This in turn, I would suggest, gives this work a degree of indecisiveness and irresolution, and perhaps even a failed potentiality. But then again, *Bastion Point* conveys an intimate involvement with Māori not found in the other versions, and appeals to the viewer at the empathetic level that Lange established with Māori and their cause.[26]

Shareholders of the 5514 ha. *Ngatihine* Māori land block gather outside the Kawakawa Court House, for the Māori Land Court session, concerning a proposed 99-year lease to a private forestry company, September, 1977. Photograph: John Miller

Maori land fight— it's all on film!

By ROBERT JONES

AN AVANT garde film which the makers claim will "blow the whistle" on Maori land deals in New Zealand is being offered abroad.

The movie focusses on Maori land rights issues— from the Maori view.

It is being offered to documentary film-makers for distribution in both Europe and the United States.

The make is designed to have both a human and a shock political impact, emphasizes one of the pro-producers, Mr John Miller.

"There's never been anything like it done in New Zealand," he said.

Mr Miller rates it as the New Zealand equivalent to radical documentaries on land issues involving the Red Indians in America, the aborigines in their uranium-rich territory, and even on conflict between black and white in South Africa.

Says Mr Miller:

"What we're doing is blowing the whistle on big forestry companies and the way they operate by leasing Maori land into perpetuity . . . thus alienating the people," says Mr Miller.

"It throws light on a subject which must be looked into. The whole system of control through Maori Affairs and the Maori Land Court is antiquated."

erations as Maori workers see them.

It also contains clips of the Maori land march on Parliament.

Mr Lange has taken the film overseas for what he hopes will become international viewing.

A second copy is being held here for editing and the addition of commentary.

"It's a very serious, honest look at the issues in a way never before attempted in this country," says Mr Miller.

When processed, other copies of the film will be offered to universities, educational institutes, trade unions, the Federation of Labour, and Federated Farmers.

"Any profit will be used to fight Maori land issues."

The Auckland Trades Council has endorsed the green ban placed on the Ngatihine Maori land block in Northland — and has referred the issue to the Federation of Labour.

Whangarei's trades council applied the original green ban.

Fresh legal moves have been launched in the Auckland Supreme Court in an attempt to nullify a controversial leasing of the 5.514 ha. to Carter Holt forestry company.

And Ngatihine representatives have been invited to attend an open field day near Warkworth on the farm forestry property of Mr Michael Malloy, under the auspices of the North Farm Forest Association, on January 14.

Mr Malloy, an Auckland solicitor, has called for a commission of inquiry into the Maori Affairs Act and procedures of the Maori Land Court.

"It will give other ideas to people overseas who think of New Zealand as a truly multi-racial society."

Netherlands-based expatriate New Zealand artist and film-maker Darcy Lange started filming segments of Maori land protest activity some months ago.

He has been assisted chiefly by Mr Miller, liaison and research officer, Te Matakite O Aotearoa; and former junior lecturer in anthropology at Auckland University, Mr Taura Eruera.

The film, which has a running potential of up to three hours, looks at:

● A drawn-out wrangle over Maori owners' refusal to endorse a 75-year lease of 5514ha of Ngatahine land in Northland.

● Bastion Point and the stand made by Joe Hawke and followers.

● The east coast of the North Island, and the actions of major forestry interests in winning control of Maori land there.

● Kaweran pulp mill op-

Note: Darcy left for the USA and Europe on Friday, 16th December 1977 and returned to NZ around Monday, 3rd July, 1978.

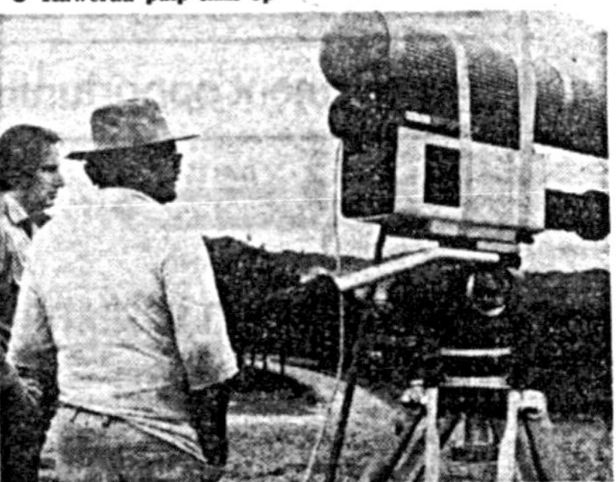

DARCY LANGE and Motatau Shortland (foreground) on Ngatihine land in Northland with the camera used for filming a Maori land issues documentary.

..text follows on to the fourth column then back to the second column.

---

8 o'clock newspaper article by Auckland journalist Robert Jones, 23 December 1977. Courtesy John Miller Archive

Lange's film moves through a series of scenes collecting moments in the daily life of the occupants living in Bastion Point. In one scene inside the *wharenui* (meeting house) at night, with Hawke, family and children all gathered resting down on mattresses on the floor, the camera fluidly moves around the room, in real time, intimately zooming in on each individual as they speak – some in *te reo* Māori – about their personal experiences during the occupation. Lange strives to convey with the camera the sense of *experiencing* – in his words, 'the feeling that you are actually there'[27] – that leaves a vivid impression of Māori, their customs, language and communal living, rather than *narrating* it. Māori film-maker Barry Barclay promoted the notion of the '*hui* (Māori assembly) as filmmaking' – the camera acting 'with dignity at a *hui*' and 'a certain restraint, a feeling of being comfortable with sitting back a little and listening'.[28] He noted: 'the filmmaker is faced with the challenge of how to respect this age-old process of discussion and decision-making while using the technology within a climate which so often demands precision and answers.'[29] Lange understood this temporality and let people speak without editorialising, end-slated scenes in order to allow conversations to begin organically, and valued the talking head over voice-overs.

Lange's long takes have a greater political implication as, with duration, the subjectivity and the singularity of Māori are released. It contributes to the subjectivation rather than objectivation of his subjects, and therefore to establishing a sympathetic relationship with them. This affective and empathic effect of Lange's video is constitutive in the mediation of the political. Further, his account reflects the intimate time spent with the occupants of Bastion Point over the quiet months. Based on the intimacy of these shots, Miller and Peters argue, Lange clearly established with Hawke and his family 'a relationship of trust', at least in this initial stage.[30]

Māori Demands for Self-Determination Through Visual Representation

During the development of the exhibition, Miller remained in close dialogue with Lange and Henny through correspondence, continuing the conversations Lange held back in

New Zealand with Hawke, Eruera and Tarawa. Miller conveyed that while Māori may have willingly chosen to participate in the making, more determinant was their involvement in the editing process. The Māori land issue, he wrote to Henny in April 1979, was 'one that has suffered for far too long from a lack of proper analysis and even in New Zealand at the present time, we are still developing this analysis'.[31] He stated also that there was already film material in New Zealand, 'finance being the main stumbling block', but 'if we could establish our own infrastructure here, we could, I'm sure begin to produce our own documentary material'.[32] With these words, Miller brought to bear Māori desire to retain control over their own image and the imperative to engage in the analysis of their condition on their own terms, as well as to manage the means of production.

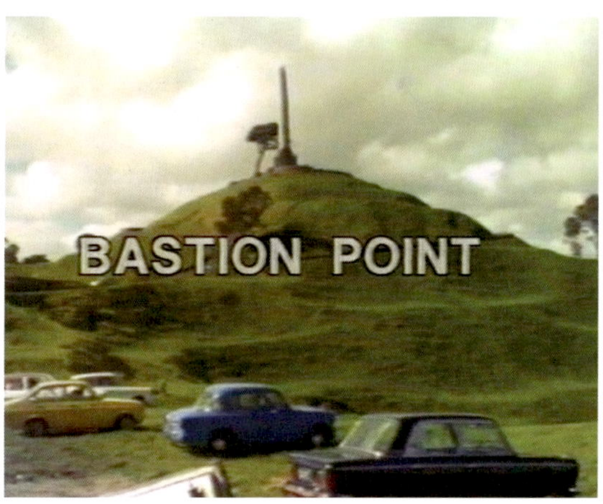

The spokesperson for the Bastion Point occupation, Joe Hawke was invited to the Netherlands to assist with the editing, but the funding fell through at the last minute. As a result of this lack of involvement by Māori in the editing process, the circumstances being beyond Lange's control, it was felt that the trust of Māori was breached with respect to continuing the exhibition without their input. As Miller and Peters state in 2008 reflecting back: 'Although it's clear that Lange tried everything within his power to find the money to bring a Māori consultant to Amsterdam, [...] [f]rom today's standpoint, the lack of informed consultation at the crucial editing stage and the decision to proceed with the films despite this, denied Ngāti Whātua-o-Ōrākei the opportunity for self-determination through visual representation – although unintentional, this was effectively another form of colonisation.'[33] Efforts to involve Māori continued after the exhibition and Henny was successful in raising funding for Colin Clark to attend the Fourth Russell Tribunal in Rotterdam later that year, to represent Māori in this tribunal for the rights of indigenous peoples in the Americas.

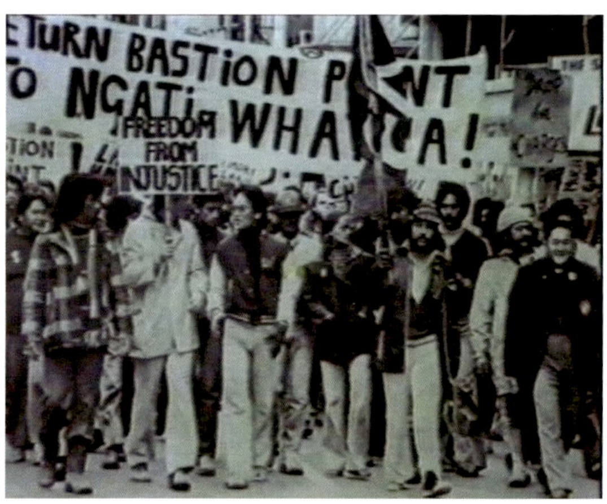

The solidarity and efforts of Lange and his Dutch collaborators to bring Māori struggles to international attention were no doubt in earnest. However, as Miller and Peters state, their failure to recognise the imperative of Māori to articulate their own history in an editorial form, inevitably positioned Māori as being subject to a media gaze, perpetuating the uneven hegemonic power that reinforces the objectivation of the colonised. This situation re-inscribed what Gayatri Chakravorty Spivak described as the subaltern's lack of a speaking position, a condition that is relentlessly constituted in the discourses of power.[34] Henny and the Victor Jara Collective understood that failing to include Māori in the editing process re-inscribed the very power relations that the project aimed to overcome, that is, in Edward Said's terms, their Western '*positional superiority*'.[35 36] Lange had a more compromised position than his Dutch counterparts as he was also a settler.[37]

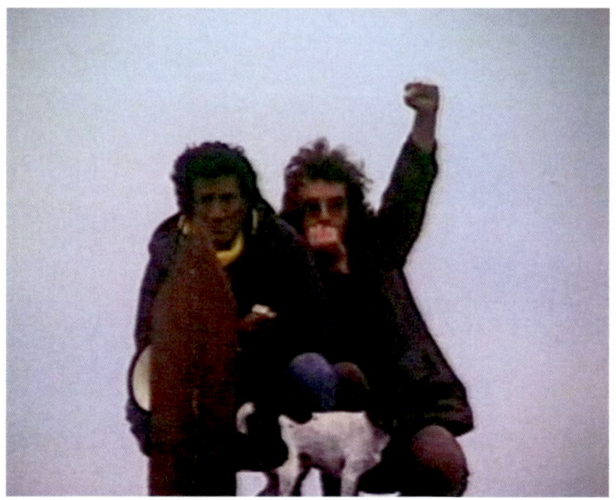

If Māori would have been included in the editorial process, I would argue that *Māori Land Project* would have challenged further the established regimes of representation that the project sought to oppose: not only through Māori's own anti-colonial criticism of the

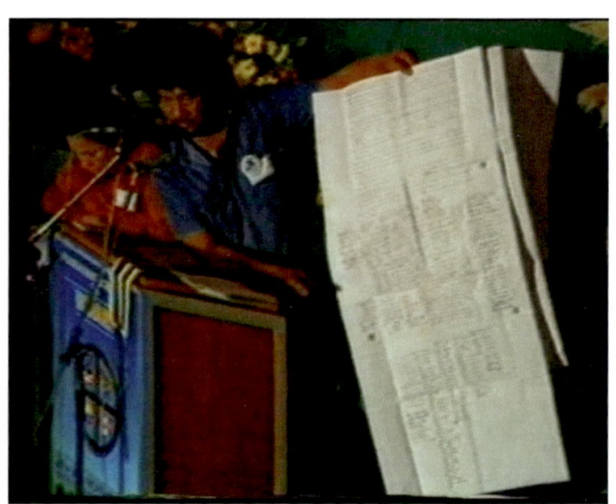

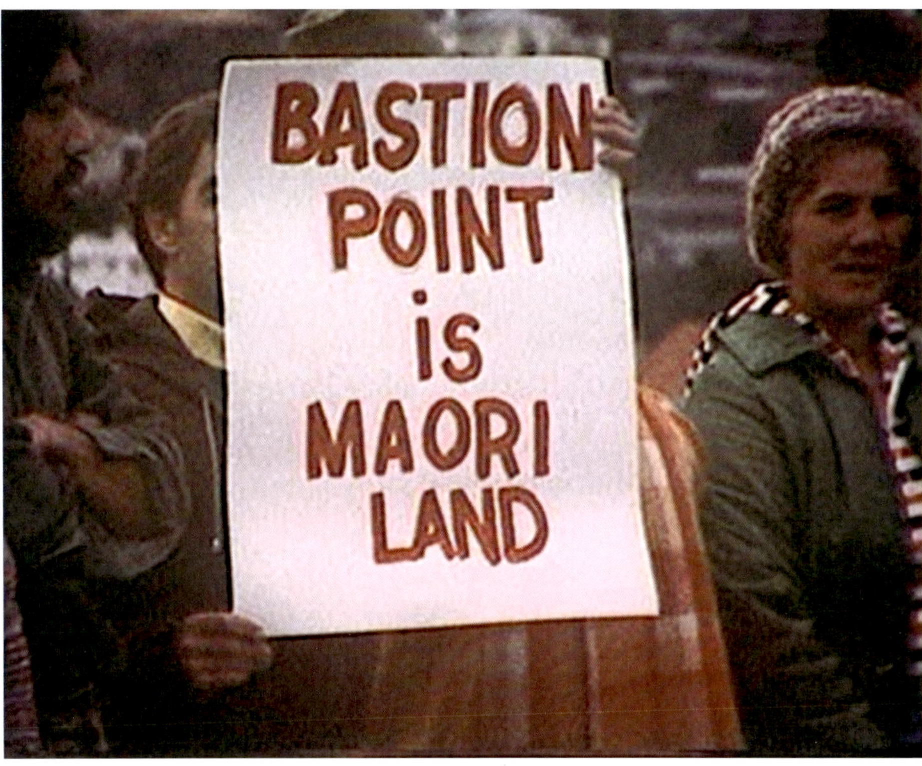

way indigeneity is mediated and constructed under colonial power and their resistance
to it, possibly challenging Lange and his collaborators' own assumptions, but also in
their distinct Māori terms. This would have activated the conditions for a claimed space
of self-realisation by engendering Māori sovereignty, by means of *re*interpretation and
*re*insertion of Māori culture into the project.

After relocating to New Zealand in January 1984, Lange continued to make recordings
from 1985.[38] He revisited some of the sites of the *Māori Land Project* and had ongoing
relations with individuals such as Tarawa and David Goldsmith, both involved in the
project. Miller and Peters claim other later recordings such as *Lack of Hope* (1986) as
continuing and being also part of *Māori Land Project*.[39] In *Lack of Hope*, Lange critically
addresses the drastic neoliberal reforms introduced by the Labour government (1984–90)
that led to unprecedented unemployment, and proposed *Māori* systems of communal work
practices as a way forward to resolve this crisis.[40]

For Lange a sense of inconclusiveness loomed over *Māori Land Project*. In 2001 he
wrote that it had been his 'biggest undertaking so far' and had had 'the most lasting effect
on my thoughts and way of life', but 'it is in fact not resolved and may never be'.[41] He assembled all of the footage for *Māori Land Project* and deposited the tapes at Auckland Art Gallery's library collection. Former librarian Ron Brownson (currently Senior Curator, New
Zealand and Pacific Art, Auckland Art Gallery) referred to these tapes as 'research files',
perhaps reflecting Lange's desire to make the material available to others in the future.[42]
In 1978, there had been attempts of an exhibition at the Auckland Art Gallery, which fell
through when the gallery proposed to move it to their 'outreach' space, to the dissatisfac-
tion of Māori involved in the project. They saw the move as 'an insult to the memory of our
ancestors' and as an indirect way to censor what might have been perceived as politically
polemical material.[43 44] Lange wrote in 2001:

> I have not made these tapes available as yet because they are probably in fact more
> clearly less mine than other material. [...] However, all my recordings could be seen
> as belonging to those who were filmed. [...] [A] great deal of hope and support was
> put into my activities and to this day I feel that I have been unable to fulfil that trust.
> Perhaps the publishing of this book may bring a guiding spirit, which will allow the
> completion of the Aotearoa Land Pains Project.[45]

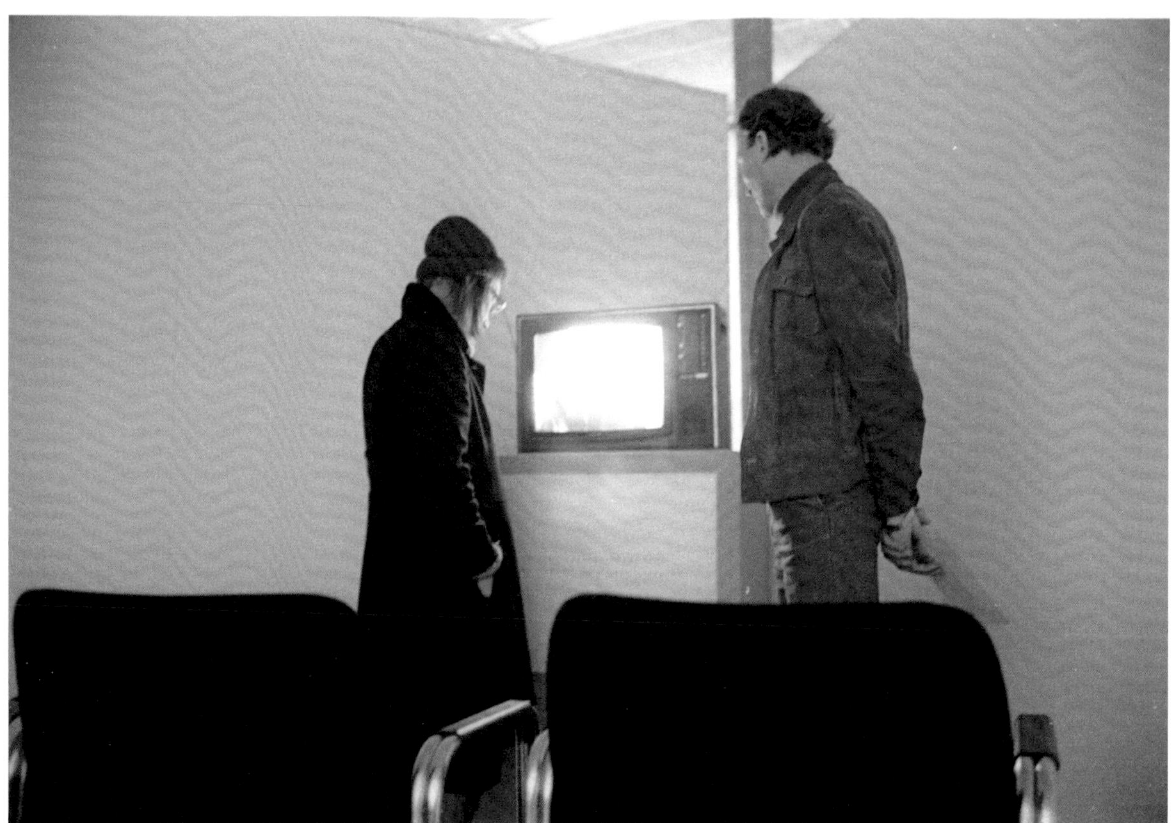

Lange began to recognise the infringement of speaking for others – the 'indignity of speaking for others', denounced by Gilles Deleuze and Michel Foucault in 1972, for whom only 'those involved finally have their say from a practical standpoint' – and to also question being the rights holder of these tapes.[46] In this way, *Māori Land Project* points towards larger questions surrounding indigenous self-determination and the reinforcement of colonial power dynamics through and by means of authorship.

Miller's words to Henny about the Māori land issue being for them 'still under analysis' resonate with even more currency today, implying the process of decoloniality as one becoming and still unfolding. One starts to ponder if these 'research files' are waiting to be edited (or treated however appropriately, if at all) by the *Ngāti Whātua* in order to re-inscribe their history and perspective, underpinning *kaupapa* Māori (that is, working through and from the position of Māori customary practices, principles and ideologies) and adopting *tikanga* Māori (Māori ethical protocols). Going further, perhaps rather than 'exhibiting' it in an art gallery context – even though the project already exited the gallery in being broadcast on television and stepping into the educational system of secondary schools – it needs to de-link itself altogether from these colonial structures and be presented to the communities directly concerned and in their place of assembly or *marae*. Many of the people appearing in the recordings have passed away, but today a new generation of Māori film-makers such as Sharon Hawke (Joe Hawke's daughter) or Hepi Mita (Merata Mita's son) are taking on the legacy of their elders with renewed impetus, recognising that alongside political action there is a need for the revitalisation and reformulation of culture.

Darcy Lange, *Māori Land Project*, 1977–80. Installation shot, Stedelijk Van Abbemuseum, 1980. Courtesy Darcy Lange Archive and Govett-Brewster Art Gallery, New Plymouth, New Zealand

1   This essay draws from the last chapter of my PhD dissertation, 'Images of People at Work: The
        Videomaking of Darcy Lange', London: Royal College of Art, 2017 and my introduction to the book
        I edited titled *Darcy Lange: Study of an Artist at Work*, New Plymouth and Birmingham: Govett-
        Brewster Art Gallery and Ikon Gallery, 2008, pp.15-31. It also draws from John Miller and
        Geraldene Peters, 'Darcy Lange: Māori Land Project - Working in Fragments', *ibid.*, pp.143-55. I am
        indebted to Miller and Peters' painstaking efforts to contrast sources contained in the artist's and
        Miller's own archives and the meticulous recording of Māori affairs done by Miller in seeking
        historical accuracy. Their essay provides further contextual information regarding Māori
        historical events and individuals appearing in Lange's vast project giving it coherency.
2   Darcy Lange in an interview with Willoughby Sharp, 'Darcy Lange Videography: Work', *Avalanche*,
        no.11, Summer 1975, p.13.
3   See his series of work studies in schools, *Study of Three Birmingham Schools* (1976) and *Studies of
        Teaching in Four Oxfordshire Schools* (1977).
4   The potential of video as a tool for social change was embraced by the first video community
        generation of the late 1960s and 1970s formed around Radical Software in New York, and Fantasy
        Factory, Graft-ON and other community activist groups in Britain. The critical discourse around
        this first wave of video was informed by information theory, Conceptual art and film theory as well
        as the political language of the New Left and the 1968 student uprisings.
5   Lange referred to this project by different names such as the 'Māori Land Video', 'Aotearoa Land
        Pains project' and 'Māori Social, Cultural and Land project'. However, 'Māori Land Project' was
        the title more commonly used and the one given to the exhibition at Stedelijk Van Abbemuseum
        [now Van Abbemuseum] in 1980. J. Miller and G. Peters, 'Darcy Lange: Māori Land Project -
        Working in Fragments', *op. cit.*, fn.2, p.143.
6   https://waitangitribunal.govt.nz/about-waitangi-tribunal/ (last accessed on 4 February 2020).
        Further, the establishment of the Waitangi Tribunal in 1975, which led to land claims and
        settlements starting in 1992, continues today. Reforms supporting biculturalism also resulted
        in policy changes such as the revival of *te reo Māori* (Māori language), culminating with the
        passing of the Māori Language Act in 1987, and in the education system with the formation of
        kōhanga reo (Māori-language pre-schools), *kura* (schools) and *wānanga* (universities). See *Te Ara - The
        Encyclopedia of New Zealand*, available at http://www.teara.govt.nz/en/Māori-pakeha-relations/
        page-6 (last accessed on 9 September 2019).
7   Toby Boraman, 'The Independent Left Press and the Rise and Fall of Mass Dissent in Aotearoa
        since the 1970s', *Counterfutures*, no.1, 2016, pp.38 and 40. Further, according to John Miller,
        Vietnam demonstrations abruptly ceased, after July 1972, while anti-Apartheid demonstrations
        continued well into the 1980s. Note made by J. Miller, 4 February 2020.
8   *Ibid.*, p.53.
9   Brendan Hokowhitu and Vijay Devadas, 'Introduction: The Indigenous Mediascape in Aotearoa/New
        Zealand', *The Fourth Eye: Māori Media in Aotearoa New Zealand*, Minneapolis: University of
        Minnesota Press, 2013, p.xxiii.
10   *Ibid.*, p.xx.
11   Regarding Chris Strewe's *Waitangi: Die Geschichte eines Vertrages und seiner Erben (The Story of A
        Treaty and Its Inheritors)* (1977), according to 1977 film crew member, Gerd Pohlmann, the
        primary release was in German, under the German title - a later version was made with Chris's
        English commentary. Note from John Miller, 4 February 2020.
12   *Ngātihine* is the spelling used by the *Ngātihine* Block Action Committee, the tribe is usually known
        at *Ngāti Hine*.
13   In 1991 the Orakei Act finally returns *Takaparawha* Bastion Point to *Ngāti Whātua* with NZ$3
        million compensation.
14   See Andrew Sharp, *Justice and the Māori: Māori Claims in New Zealand Political Argument in the
        1980s*, Auckland: Oxford University Press, 1990.
15   While Lange was *Pākehā*, therefore an outsider to Māori affairs, Miller and Peters argue that
        Lange's farming ancestry meant he was 'not unfamiliar with Māori perspectives during the early
        stages of his lifetime'. Further, 'his family who owned a farm in Urenui, north Taranaki worked
        closely with the local *Ngāti Mutunga* community, and Lange himself had close friendships with
        local people such as "Uncle" Ra Raumati, and later, Te Miringa Hohaia of Parihaka'. J. Miller and G.
        Peters, 'Darcy Lange: Māori Land Project', *op. cit.*, p.143.
16   For a more detailed account see *ibid.*, pp.143-48.
17   Correspondence found in Lange's archive corroborates that he sought funding support from the Queen
        Elizabeth II Arts Council and made failed attempts to have the work broadcast in the country,
        approaching TV One and TV Two with the support of his friend, journalist Virginia Shaw. In the
        United States, Lange also approached unsuccessfully the National Endowment for the Humanities
        and CBS television's producers of the *60 Minutes* programme, through networks established with the
        support of the film producer Wieland Schulz-Keil in New York. Lange sought support
        from Granada Television in Manchester with no success. Miller and Peters argue that Lange's initial
        intention in 1977, as per his statements in his correspondence with Joe Hawke and in the exhibition
        catalogue, was 'to do a series of poetic recordings and that the television programme was an
        afterthought, intended to assist Māori with the international articulation of land alienation
        struggles'. It was only after a documentary with NOS television was secured in 1978 that he thought
        of approaching other televisions. *Ibid.*, pp.147-48.
18   MonteVideo was founded in 1978 in Amsterdam, alongside other organisations emerging in the
        seventies that produced and distributed videos in the Netherlands, such as Meatball (The Hague,
        1972) and De Appel (Amsterdam, 1975). De Appel, a centre for radical art forms with a strong
        commitment to video art, was also instrumental in the foundation of the Association of Video
        Artists that lead to the formation of Time Based Arts in 1983 for the exhibition and promotion of
        video art in the Netherlands.
19   Lange states: 'I was interested in how the people for whom a film or videotape is made influence
        the form and content of the work.[...] I did this [sharing the material] because I believe, on the basis
        of art-historical analysis and my personal political convictions, that artists in the post-Duchamp
        period [...] should work together with representatives of other disciplines. [..] I had political and
        democratic reasons for handing over the material that was originally shot exclusively for the
        purpose of making a long, artistic version of my own for the benefit of the Māoris. I saw it as my
        duty to give the problems of the Māoris international publicity, and to realize a news programme
        about them. I must admit it was difficult for me as an artist, trained to be an individualist, to have
        to work with other people in the project.[...] I believe that art is formed by collective knowledge.'
        'Interview Darcy Lange', *Darcy Lange: Māori Land Project*, Eindhoven and Antwerp: Stedelijk Van
        Abbemuseum and Internationaal Cultureel Centrum, 1980, pp.32-33.
20   In addition to 30 hours of ¾in. Lo-Band U-matic video, 16mm film and slides recorded by Lange over
        the course of three trips to New Zealand during 1977-78, there were also extracts from Leon Narbey

and Geoff Steven's *Te Matakite o Aotearoa/The Māori Land March* (1975) and Chris Strewe's *Waitangi: The Story of A Treaty and Its Inheritors* (1977); newsreel footage depicting the eviction of Bastion Point; sound from Barry Barclay's television series *Tangata Whenua* (1974); and 16mm film footage by Murry Saviden. *Darcy Lange: Māori Land Project*, p.41.

21   Correspondence with Gale, Vancouver Art Gallery curator Jo-Anne Birnie Danzker and Alberta College of Art Gallery curator Brian Dyson, indicates interest in touring the exhibition which never eventuated. Lange was establishing links in Canada. Dan Graham invited him to teach workshops at the Nova Scotia College of Art and Design in Halifax in 1977 and 1978. There, he also met art historian Benjamin H.D. Buchloh, artists David Askevold, Brian MacNevin, Ian Murray, Krzysztof Wodiczko (who coined Lange 'the Engels of videotape') and critic John Bentley Mays among others.

22   See Bertolt Brecht, 'The Radio as an Apparatus of Communication', *Brecht on Theatre* (ed. and trans. John Willett), New York: Hill and Wang, 1964, available at http://www.medienkunstnetz. de/source-text/8/ (last accessed 21 September 2019). Brecht's theory of two-way communication was influenced by Walter Benjamin's essay 'The Author as Producer' (1934). See also Leonard Henny, *Action Research with Film and Video*, Utrecht: Media Studies Program at the Sociological Institute, University of Utrecht, 1978 and Leonard Henny, *Raising Consciousness Through Film: Audio-visual Media and International Development Education*, Utrecht: Media Studies Program at the Sociological Institute, University of Utrecht, 1980.

23   Paulo Freire, *Pedagogy of the Oppressed* (trans. Myra Bergman Ramos), New York and London: Continuum, 1970.

24   Ray Krill and Gloria Lowe were members of the Victor Jara Collective. This collective from Guyana, named after the Chilean musician and dissident Victor Jara, formed out of a Marxist study group at Cornell University. The collective had just finished their documentary *The Terror and the Time* (1978) on British colonial rule over Guyana during the 1950s and the Guyanese people's struggle for independence. They were influenced by the New Latin American and Third Cinema movements, as well as the theories of Soviet montage and the European avant-garde.

25   D. Lange, 'Interview Darcy Lange', p.34. Further, he states: 'In my tape I have tried to stick to the chronology of the events and meetings as these took place in reality. My meeting with Joe Hawke, for instance, and the events that took place after that are shown in the tape in the same order as I experience them.' When asked why, he responds: 'That's a very important question. I have more faith in what I felt then than in what I feel now. I thought it was safer to leave the events in the order in which they happened because I know how I feel when I am filming, how things develop gradually. I got to know the Maoris gradually, too, and the public gets to know them in the same way.' *Ibid.*, p. 34.

26   Lange's observational style can be seen within the traditions of *cinéma vérité* (Jean Rouch) and of direct cinema and their notions of capturing actuality in its essence through observation and lack of or spare editing. These connections are explored in my dissertation 'Images of People at Work: The Videomaking of Darcy Lange', *op cit*. I argue that Lange's choice for an observational style is not driven by his counterparts' somehow idealised notions of truth, but by an affect produced by an expanded temporality that allows for an empathetic connection with the subjects by the audience.

27   D. Lange, 'Interview Darcy Lange', pp.33-34.

28   Barry Barclay, *Our Own Image: A Story of a Māori Filmmaker*, Auckland: Shoal Bay Press, 1990, p.18.

29   *Ibid.*, p.9.

30   J. Miller and G. Peters, 'Darcy Lange: Māori Land Project ', *op. cit.*, p.146.

31   J. Miller, letter to Leonard Henny in reply to Henny's letter to Joe Hawke of 5 April 1979, c.1979. Darcy Lange Archive, courtesy Darcy Lange Estate and the Govett-Brewster Art Gallery, New Plymouth, New Zealand and with permission of Miller.

32   *Ibid.*

33   J. Miller and G. Peters, 'Darcy Lange: Māori Land Project', p.150. Further they write, 'Lange's letters to Miller and Hawke indicated that at some stage the relationship between Lange and Hawke had broken down, ostensibly over the belief that through the documentary project, Lange had sold the Bastion Point footage to Dutch television. Lange denies this and his letters consistently suggest that he was convinced of the beneficial value of bringing the Māori land issues to world attention through the video projects, that his motivation was to 'help' Māori. Certainly, Lange's near-impoverished financial circumstances suggest he never benefited financially from his work. Correspondence also suggests that Hawke consistently voiced his concerns that the documentary be produced with due care for the complexity of the issues, particularly in relation to Takaparawha/ Bastion Point.' *Ibid.*, p.150. Lange acknowledges these tensions offering some form of apology when he writes, 'To the Māori people, I hope that I have not hurt too many hearts or broken too many territories or spiritual sanctities, to bring a gesture of analysis, and my hope that constructive things will arise from this work and not selfish and destructive and ambitious actions. I feel greatly privileged to have been able to participate in such personally humiliating [sic] and profound experience. And thus to you I send my ahoranui [(deep affection)].' 'Note by Lange, Introduction', *Darcy Lange: Māori Land Project*, *op. cit.*, p.41.

34   Gayatri Chakravorty Spivak, 'Can the Subaltern Speak?', in *Colonial Discourse and Post-Colonial Theory: A Reader* (ed. Laura Chrisman and Patrick Williams), New York and Sydney: Harvester Wheatsheaf, 1993, pp.66-111. First published as 'Can the Subaltern Speak? Speculations on Widow Sacrifice', *Wedge*, vol.7-8, Winter/Spring, 1985, pp.120-30.

35   Henny states: 'The only real lack in this project as a whole, I think, has been that we did all this work without any communication with the Māoris themselves. Darcy was the ony one who had had any contact with them, the only one who knew the atmosphere and who had seen it all happen. All this material came here and a whole lot of people who have no affective ties with the Māoris started working on it. On the other hand I do believe that it is a good thing that this project has been realized because the influence of the media and the prevailing norms is so enormous that if you get an opportunity to raise some questions you should grab it.' L. Henny, 'Interview Leonard Henny', *Darcy Lange: Māori Land Project*, p.39.

36   Edward Said, *Orientalism*, New York: Pantheon, 1978, p.7.

37   Lange's family farm stands on what would have been Māori land. Dan Graham argues that Lange 'was ambivalent about his middle class, land-owning New Zealand family' and that 'his identification with the Maori indigenous people and his Marxism were attempts to undo his middle class values'. Dan Graham, 'Darcy Lange: Great Artist and Friend', *Darcy Lange: Study of an Artist at Work*, p.184.

38   Using a much more portable Sony CCD V8 AF Camcorder. Note from J. Miller, 4 February 2020.

39   J. Miller and G. Peters, 'Darcy Lange: Māori Land Project', *op. cit.*, p.143.

40   Deregulation, liberalisation and privatisation associated with neoliberal policies introduced by the Labour government (1984-90) caused rapid significant reforms to the country's economic and

social institutions during the late 1980s and early 1990s. The reform of New Zealand's Keynesian-welfare institutions was faster and more extreme than elsewhere, including other 'liberal welfare states' like Australia or Britain. See Louise Humpage, 'Neo-liberal reform and attitudes towards social citizenship: a review of New Zealand public opinion data 1987–2005', *Social Policy Journal of New Zealand*, vol. 37, June 2011, available at https://www.msd.govt.nz/about-msd-and-our-work/publications-resources/journals-and-magazines/social-policy-journal/spj37/37-neo-liberal-reform-and-attitudes-towards-social-citizenship.html (last accessed on 21 September 2019).

41   D. Lange, *Video Art*, Auckland: The Department of Film, Video and Media Studies, Auckland University, 2001, pp.85–87.

42   Email from Ron Brownson, 24 March 2019.

43   Robert Jones, 'Māori Film Row', *8 O'Clock*, September 1978. See also J. Miller and G. Peters, 'Darcy Lange: Māori Land Project', *op. cit.*, p.149.

44   *Māori Land Project* was, however, shown in Lange's retrospective titled 'Land Work People' held at Govett-Brewster Art Gallery in 1985 on his return to New Zealand. It featured Lange's *Bastion Point* (not Coelho and Henny's films) and the footage of Russell Tribunal, press clippings and other printed matter, and potted native plants. The Auckland War Memorial Museum in 2000 also presented some of these tapes in a rather modest way, on monitors spread around different spaces outside the galleries. Posthumously, with the advice of J. Miller (who also provided press clippings), *Māori Land Project* was also shown in the 2006 retrospective 'Darcy Lange: Study of an Artist at Work' at Govett-Brewster Art Gallery and Adam Art Gallery in Wellington, and in the monographic exhibitions at Camera Austria in 2010 and at Espai d'art contemporari de Castelló in 2012.

45   D. Lange, *Video Art*, *op. cit.*, pp.85–86.

46   Gilles Deleuze, 'Intellectuals and Power: A Conversation between Michel Foucault and Gilles Deleuze', *Desert Islands and Other Texts 1953–1974* (ed. David Lapoujade and trans. Michael Taormina), Los Angeles and New York: Semiotext(e)/Foreign Agents, 2004, p.208.

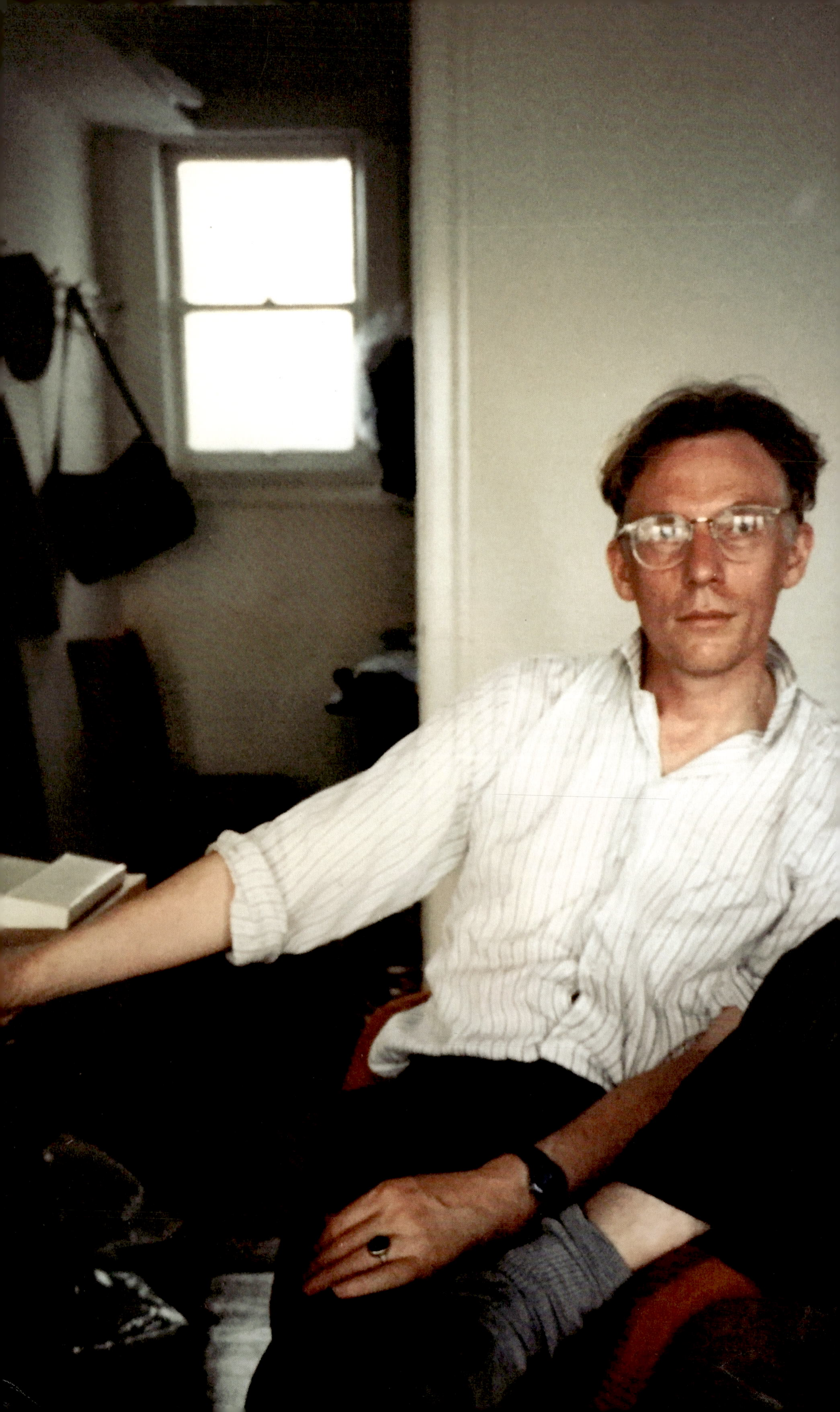

In Memoriam: Peter Wollen

– D.N. Rodowick

Peter Wollen died on 17 December 2019 after having Alzheimer's Disease for many years.
        With seminal publications such as *Signs and Meaning in the Cinema* (1969), Wollen
will be justly remembered as a central figure in the establishment of academic studies in
film and visual culture. However, the fact that *Signs and Meaning* was revised many times
and took on many forms gives evidence of Wollen's restless and uncategorisable intellect.
He was a cinephile, of course, with an enormous range of interests, from experimental film
to classical Hollywood cinema, European art cinema and beyond, and an important critic,
whether writing under his own name or a pseudonym, Lee Russell, for the *New Left Review*.
He was also an important art critic and curator, a political theorist, a militant and an artist
and film-maker, working both alone and in collaboration with Laura Mulvey.

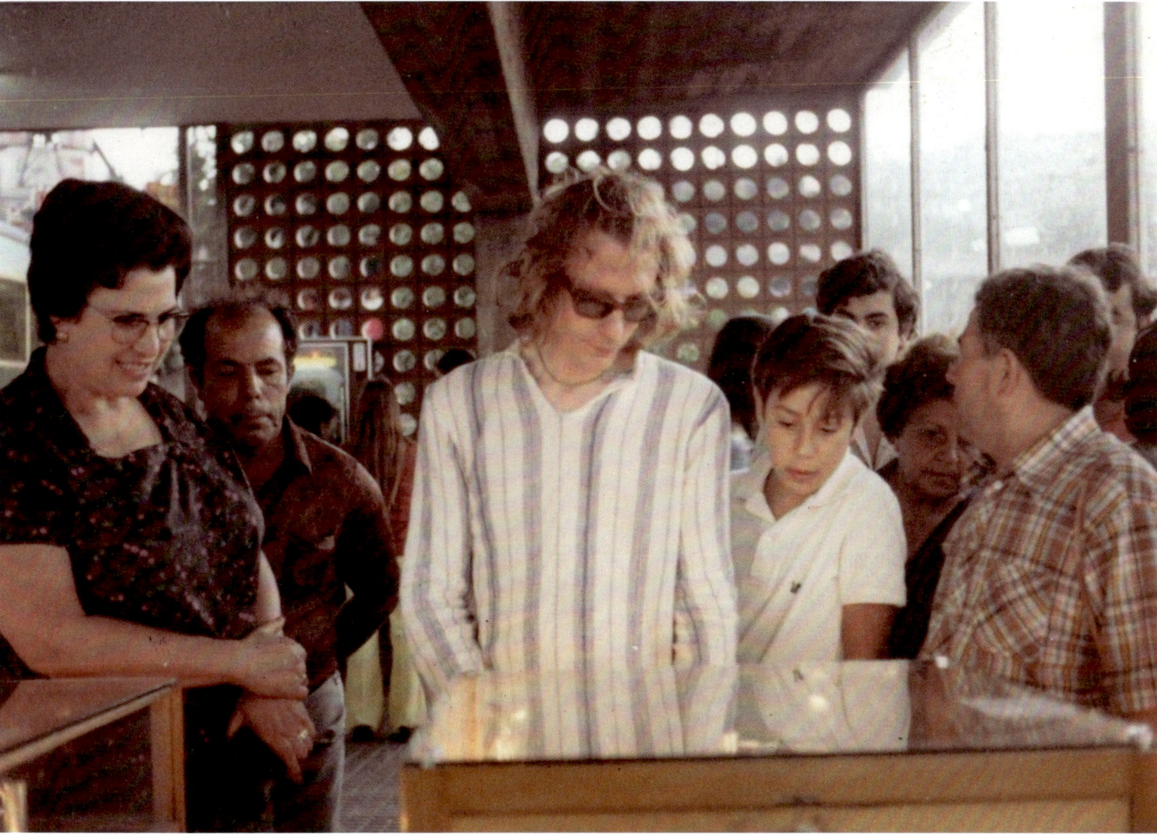

Peter Wollen in
Barcelona playing
pinball while
researching locations
for *The Passenger*,
c.1969-70. Courtesy
Leslie Dick

I suspect that Wollen would not like to be remembered only as a central figure in
film studies. Indeed, *Signs and Meaning* can be read as a work of philosophical aesthetics
as much as a founding text of film theory. When read closely, Wollen is making the case
for two quite astonishing points for the time. The first argument is that the general field of
aesthetics needs to make a full account of film if it is to assure its relevance for the twentieth
century. The second argument arises within Wollen's insistence on the heterogeneity of film's
signifying materials, which pose complex problems for aesthetics and linguistics. Wollen's
perspective was close to that of Christian Metz, who often insisted that his aim was not to
establish a semiology of film, but rather to demonstrate that a general science of signs could
not be accomplished without fully accounting for film's semiotic density and complexity. For
both Wollen and Metz, understanding film meant mastering a broad range of disciplines –

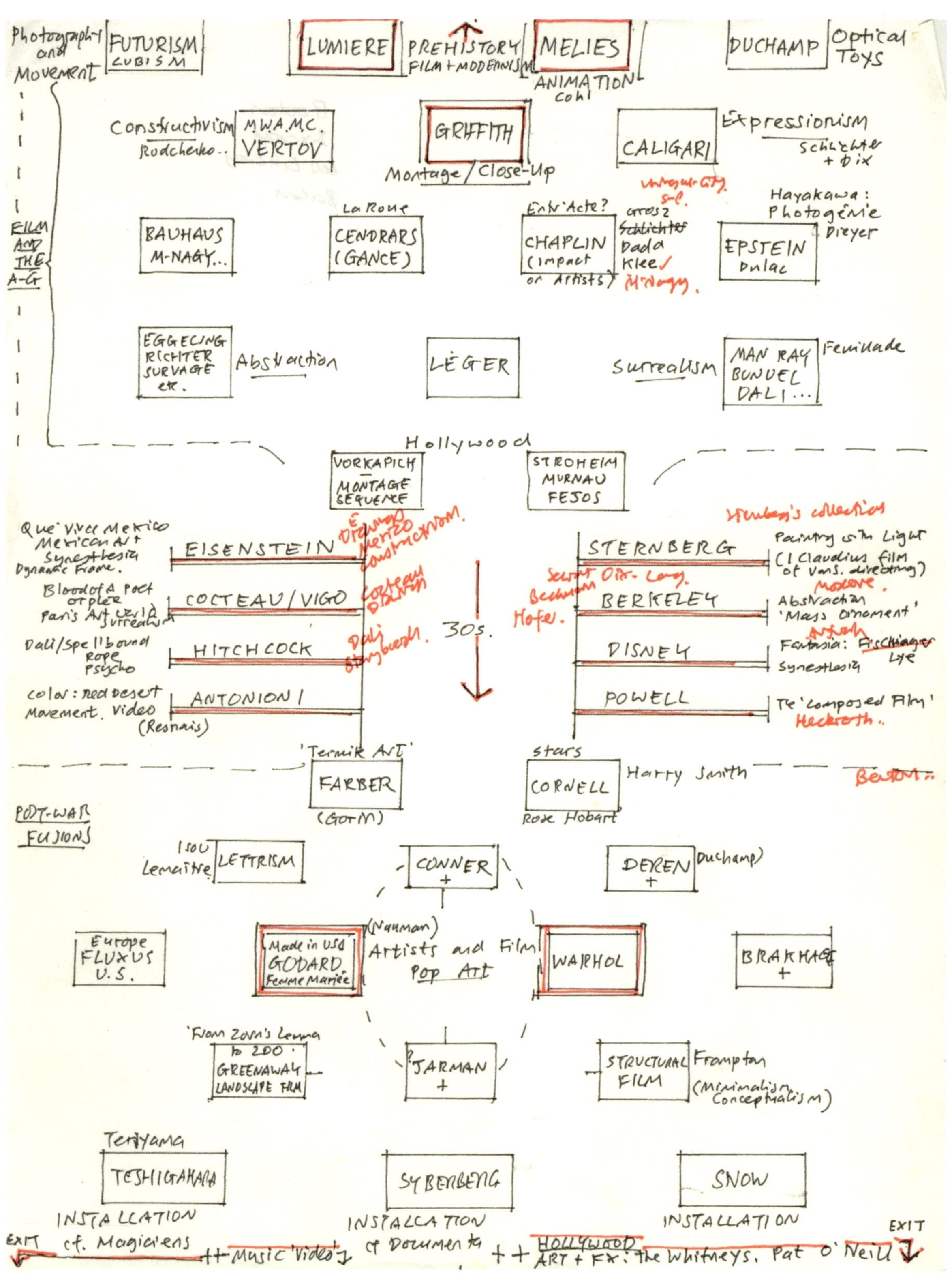

Peter Wollen's diagram for an art installation project, provisionally titled *The Art of Film: A Tearful Autopsy*, 1999-2000. Courtesy Leslie Dick

structural linguistics and anthropology, philosophy of language, philosophical aesthetics, political theory and psychoanalysis – and the study of film was intended as much to expand and enrich these domains as to draw the perimeters for a new discipline.

Wollen's first films, co-directed with Mulvey, are indebted to this huge range of interests, which Mulvey shared, as well as a new and deeply original conception of what film could be. Early works, such as *Penthesilea: Queen of the Amazons* (1974) and *Riddles of the Sphinx* (1977), were created at the same time as important theoretical statements like 'The Two Avant-Gardes', first published in *Studio International* in 1975 and widely reprinted. Although sometimes called 'theory films', this characterisation does not do justice to the creative experimentation, formal innovation and intellectual passion exhibited in these works. In 'The Two Avant-Gardes' Wollen argues that the most forward-thinking works of twentieth-century modernism were split into two tendencies: a literary or semiotic modernism characterised by experiments in language and representation, and a painterly abstraction descending from Picasso and Braque that fractured and interrogated space, time and perspective. These two tendencies flow together in the experimental work of exemplary figures such as Michael Snow and Hollis Frampton, who produced complex works that are neither completely narrative, nor completely abstract, yet contain elements of both in a context of linguistic and plastic experimentation. Within this historical, aesthetic and theoretical framework, Wollen tested tactics for thinking through film, thus bringing his writerly and creative endeavours into a single project. This experimentation also produced other extraordinary works such as *Crystal Gazing* (1982, with Mulvey) and *Friendship's Death* (1987), which, sadly, are rarely seen though still worthy of serious critical discussion.

Wollen moved fluidly between the international worlds of academia and art, and I believe this geographical and intellectual mobility entirely suited Wollen and his creative and intellectual work. As a curator, his interests in aesthetics and art history were innovative and wide-ranging. One of his first exhibitions (curated with Mulvey), which paired the work of Frida Kahlo and Tina Modotti, opened at the Whitechapel Gallery in 1982, and subsequently travelled to Berlin, Hamburg, Stockholm, New York and, finally, the Museo Nacional de Arte in Mexico City. Wollen was an early supporter of Nan Goldin and presented her 'Ballad of Sexual Dependency' at Edinburgh's Fruitmarket Gallery in 1985. He also organised a path-breaking exhibition on Situationist and Lettrist art, 'On the passage of a few people through a rather brief period of time: the Situationist International, 1957–72', which opened at the Centre Pompidou in 1989. His other important exhibitions include, among others, 'Addressing the Century: 100 Years of Art and Fashion' at Southbank Centre (1998). Wollen's most important essays on art are collected in *Paris Manhattan* (2004) and *Raiding the Icebox* (1993), among other important books and catalogues. Let us remember Peter Wollen, then, as a writer, artist and curator above all else.

Contributors

Ute Meta Bauer is the Founding Director of the NTU Centre for Contemporary Art Singapore, and Professor at School of Art, Design and Media, Nanyang Technological University, Singapore. Previously, she was Associate Professor in the Department of Architecture at Massachusetts Institute of Technology (MIT), Cambridge, where she also served as Founding Director of the MIT Program in Art, Culture, and Technology.

Lisa Blackmore is Senior Lecturer in Art History and Interdisciplinary Studies at the University of Essex. A specialist in Latin American cultural studies, Blackmore works in the confluences of practice and research, combining writing on the arts, ecology and memory with curatorial and audio-visual projects.

Ashley Chang is dramaturg at Playwrights Horizons and a Doctor of Fine Arts Candidate in Dramaturgy and Dramatic Criticism at Yale School of Drama, where her research examines the intersections of theatre, performance, and ecology in scholarly criticism and artistic practice from the 1990s to the present.

Danielle Child is Senior Lecturer in Art History at Manchester School of Art, Manchester Metropolitan University. In her research, she adopts an historical materialist approach to explore the relationship between contemporary art and capitalism through the lens of labour. Her book *Working Aesthetics: Labour, Art and Capitalism* was published in January 2019 with Bloomsbury Academic.

Cooking Sections (Daniel Fernández Pascual and Alon Schwabe) is a duo of spatial practitioners based out of London. It was born to explore the systems that organise the WORLD through FOOD. Using installation, performance, mapping and video, their research-based practice explores the overlapping boundaries between visual arts, architecture, ecology and geopolitics.

Macarena Gómez-Barris is the author of *Beyond the Pink Tide: Art and Political Undercurrents* (2018); *The Extractive Zone: Social Ecologies and Decolonial Perspectives* (2017); and *Where Memory Dwells: Culture and State Violence in Chile* (2009). Her new book project is *At the Sea's Edge: Submerged Perspectives on Oceanic Extinction*. She is Director of the Global South Center, Pratt Institute, New York.

Cayo Honorato is a writer, researcher and lecturer at the University of Brasilia. He studies the intersections between art, education and politics, particularly in relation to the work of education in art museums and exhibitions. From November 2018 to October 2019 he was a visiting researcher at London South Bank University.

Hyunjin Kim is a curator and writer, currently the KADIST Lead Curator for Asia. She was the curator of the Korean Pavilion at the 58th Venice Biennale in 2019, the director of Arko Art Center, Seoul from 2014 to 2015 and a co-curator of the 7th Gwangju Biennale in 2008.

Usha Ramanathan lives in New Delhi, where she works on the jurisprudence of law, poverty, and rights. She researches, writes and speaks on issues that include the Bhopal gas disaster in the state of Madhya Pradesh in 1984, mass displacement, eminent domain, civil liberties, beggary, criminal law, custodial institutions, the environment and judicial process. Her work draws heavily on non-governmental experience and its encounters with the state, a six-year stint for a law journal as reporter from India's supreme court, and engagement with matters of public policy.

D. N. Rodowick is Glen A. Lloyd Distinguished Service Professor at the University of Chicago. His most recent book is *What Philosophy Wants from Images* (2017). Rodowick is also a curator and an award-winning experimental film-maker and video installation artist. He is represented by the gallery Campagne Première, Berlin.

May Rosenthal Sloan is an independent curator, writer and educator based in Glasgow. She co-curated the exhibition 'FOOD: Bigger than the Plate' (2019) at the V&A and was formerly a lecturer in Modern American History at the University of Glasgow. Her research interests are wide ranging and include food and food systems, storytelling and constructions of identity, and the role of design and art in everyday life.

Anca Rujoiu is a curator and editor based in Singapore. As curator of exhibitions and later head of publications (2013–18), she was a member of the founding team of the NTU Centre for Contemporary Art Singapore. She is a PhD candidate in Curatorial Practice at Monash University, Melbourne.

Nizan Shaked is Professor of Contemporary Art History, Museum and Curatorial Studies, at California State University Long Beach and author of *The Synthetic Proposition: Conceptualism and the Political Referent in Contemporary Art* (2017). Her *Museums, the Public, and the Value of Art: The Political Economy of Contemporary Art Collections*, is forthcoming with Bloomsbury Academic.

Mercedes Vicente is a curator, writer and researcher. She has held positions as interim Director of Education and Public Programmes at Whitechapel Gallery, London; Curator of Contemporary Art at Govett-Brewster Art Gallery, New Zealand; and Research Curatorial Assistant at the Whitney Museum of American Art, New York. Her AHRC-funded PhD at the Royal College of Art focussed on the work of Darcy Lange. Her ongoing curatorial and archival efforts since 2005 to advance his legacy has entailed the preservation of his videos, the creation of the artist archive and curating exhibitions at institutions such as Tate Modern, Ikon Gallery, Camera Austria and NTU Centre for Contemporary Art Singapore. She is the editor of *Darcy Lange: Study of an Artist at Work* (2008).

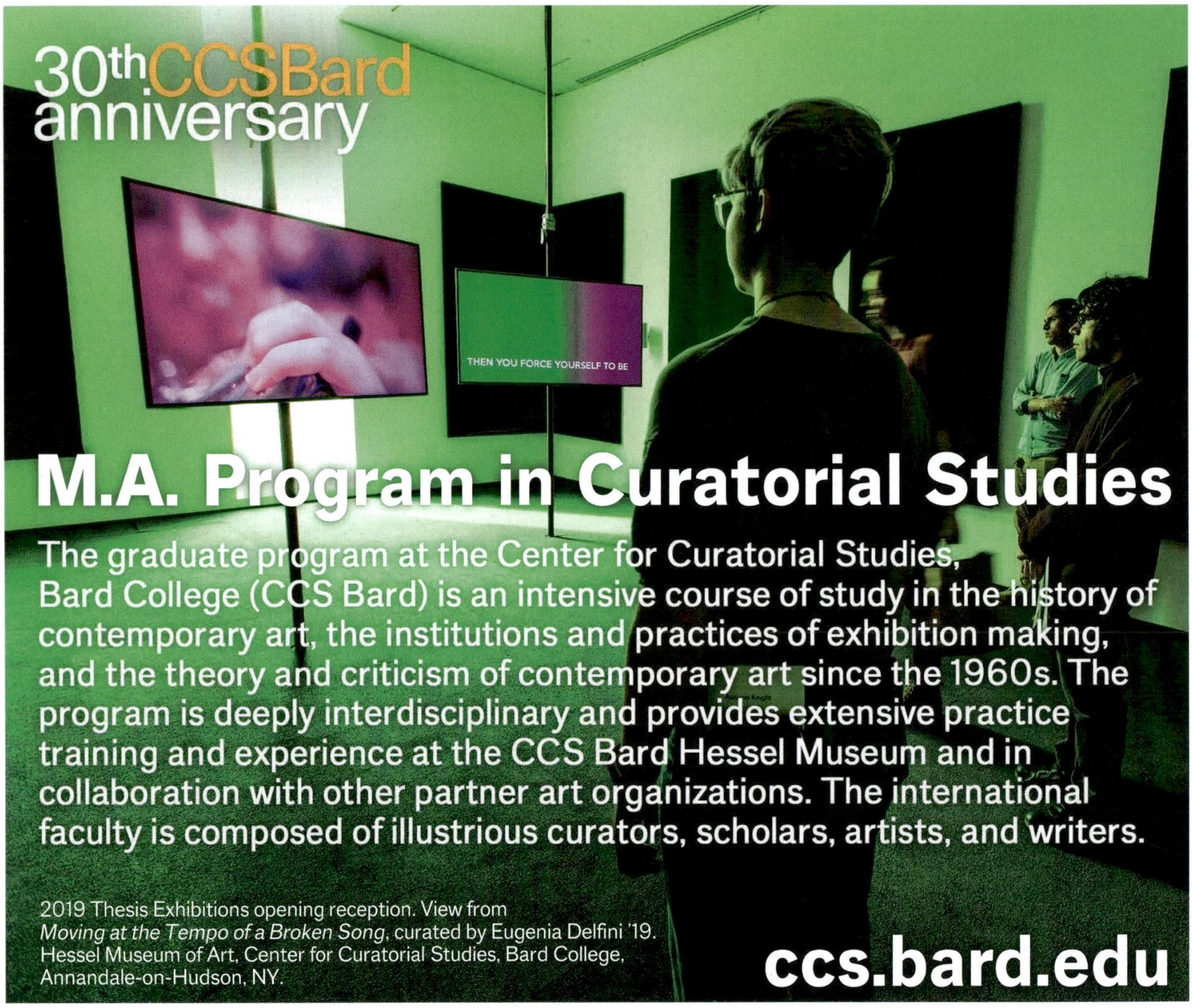

Miss Read: Berlin Art Book Festival
June 5 – 7, 2020
missread.com

Conceptual Poetics Day
June 6, 2020
conceptualpoetics.org

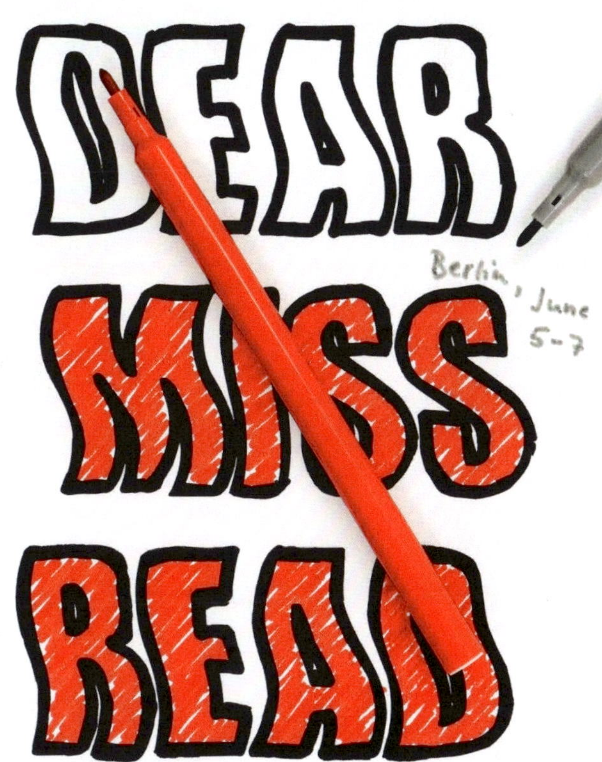

Poster by Nathalie Czech

Haus der Kuturen der Welt
hkw.de · FREE ENTRY

Een recent verhaal   A Recent History   Une histoire récente

Monoculture

25.09.2020–24.01.2021

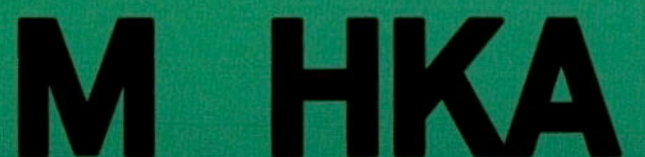

M HKA
MUSEUM VAN HEDENDAAGSE KUNST ANTWERPEN
Leuvenstraat 32, 2000 Antwerpen, www.muhka.be

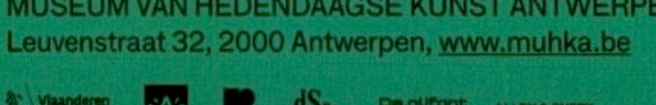

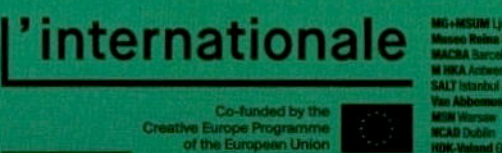

L'internationale
Co-funded by the
Creative Europe Programme
of the European Union
MG+MSUM Ljubljana
Museo Reina Sofía Madrid
MACBA Barcelona
M HKA Antwerp
SALT Istanbul & Ankara
Van Abbemuseum Eindhoven
MSN Warsaw
NCAD Dublin
HDK-Valand Gothenburg

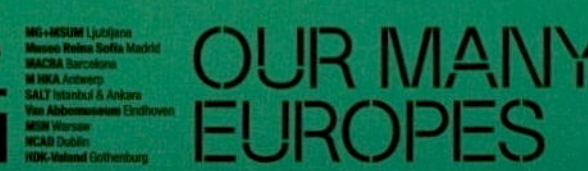

OUR MANY EUROPES

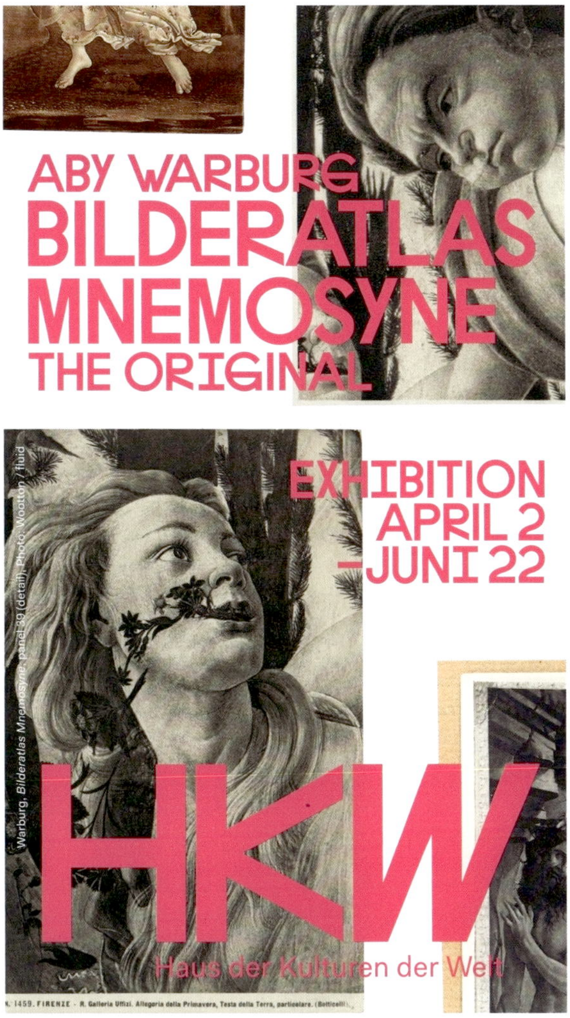

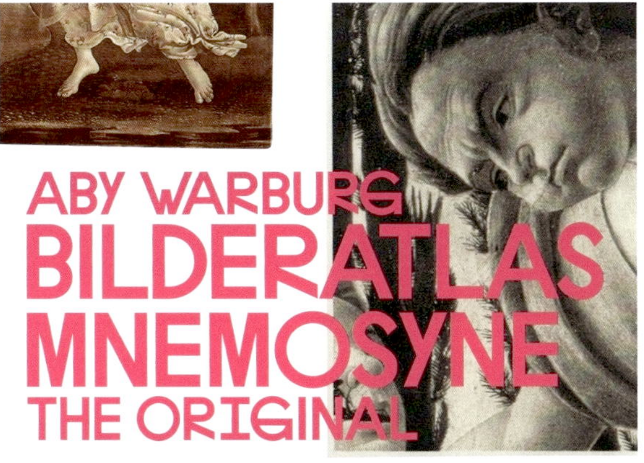

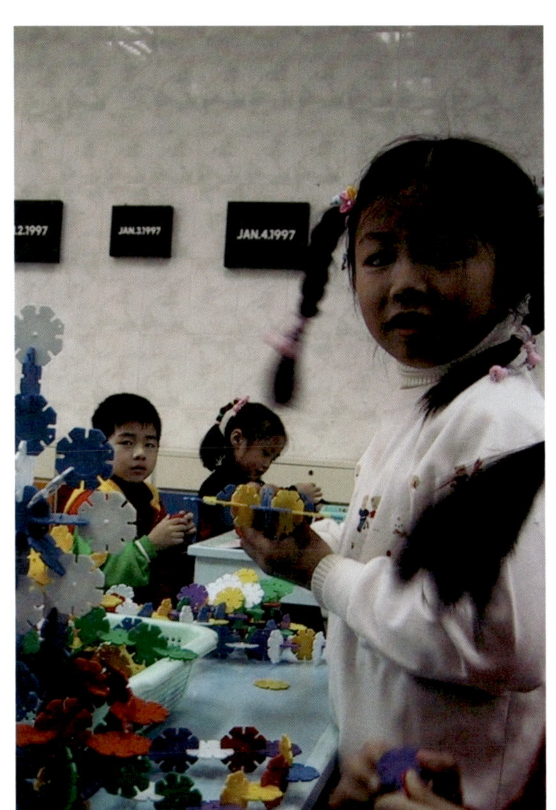

Afterall Books
Exhibition Histories

Coming soon from Afterall Books

Uncooperative Contemporaries: Art Exhibitions in Shanghai c.2000

Jane DeBevoise, Lee Weng Choy, Carol Yinghua Lu and Liu Ding, Mia Yu and others

In 2000, Shanghai was a site for multiple contested understandings of art and exhibition at a transitional moment for 'global' contemporary art. This book will explore what was at stake for modernity, contemporaneity, nationalism, internationalism and globalism in the city at the time, while looking back from diverse perspectives today.

Published in association with Asia Art Archive and the Center for Curatorial Studies, Bard College. Distributed by Koenig Books and ARTBOOK | D.A.P.

Art & Education

Distilled perspectives on scholarship in the arts

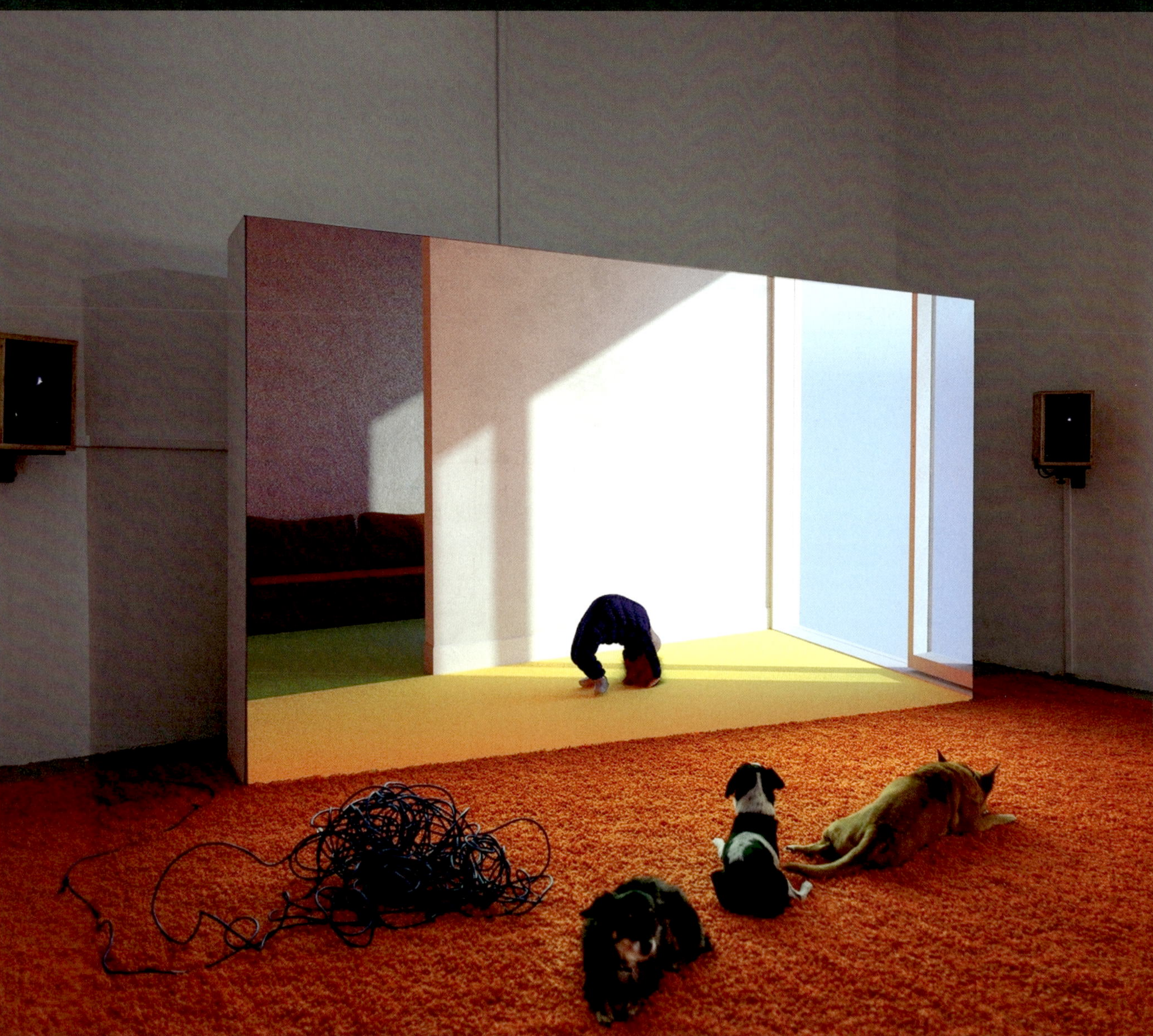

Jessica Wilson. "Smile Driver," 2019. Installation view. Image courtesy the artist.
Featured in the Art & Education New Artists gallery "Say Ever Moves: Bard MFA Class of 2020 Thesis Exhibition."

ANNOUNCEMENTS | SCHOOL WATCH | NEW ARTISTS | CLASSROOM | NEWS | DIRECTORY

Announcements and news from top art and education institutions

Profiles and interviews on art pedagogy

Image galleries of student exhibitions

Curated video series from artists and thinkers

Directory of over 1,000 international arts organizations

artandeducation.net
mail@artandeducation.net

Mårtenstorget 3 • SE–223 51 • Lund • Sweden

lundskonsthall.se

Sammy Baloji

Other Tales

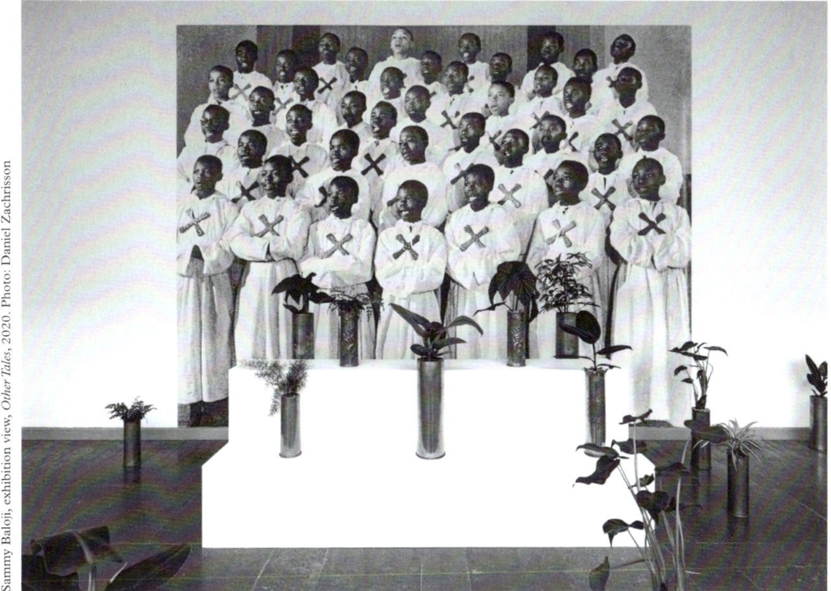

Sammy Baloji, exhibition view, *Other Tales*, 2020. Photo: Daniel Zachrisson

15
– 24

February
May

2020

Lundskonsthall

MRes Art
Exhibition Studies

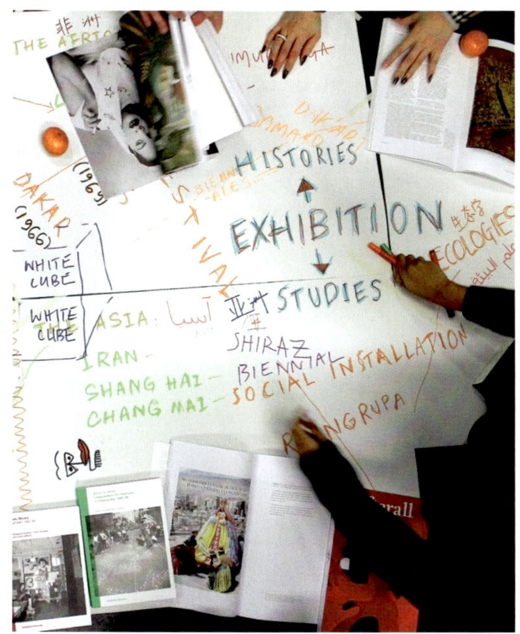

Applications for the MRes Art: Exhibition Studies programme at University of the Arts London are now open for 2020–21 entry.

Delivered in collaboration with Afterall Research Centre, this postgraduate research course based at Central Saint Martins examines the history of contemporary art from the perspective of the exhibition form—analysing how artworks are encountered by publics and shaped by display, discourse and critical reception.

The course is directly tailored to individual interests and strengths, offering rigorous research training and a supportive environment for advanced study. It is led by course co-leaders David Morris and Helena Vilalta, alongside course faculty, and joined by Afterall colleagues such as Charles Esche and Lucy Steeds. Recent visiting lecturers include Maria Tereza Alves, María Berríos, Elena Filipovic, Rebecca Gordon-Nesbitt, Yaiza Hernández, Mary Jane Jacob, Jakob Jakobsen, Pablo Lafuente, Lisette Lagnado, Marysia Lewandowska, Vali Mahlouji, Vera Mey, Paul O'Neill, Farid Rakun (ruangrupa), Laurence Rassel, Filipa Ramos, Grace Samboh, Gayatri Sinha, Kim West and many others.

We recommend you apply by April 1 to avoid disappointment. Applicants wishing to qualify for the UAL UK/EU Postgraduate Scholarships should apply as early as possible.

For more information visit: arts.ac.uk/csm/courses/ postgraduate/mres-art-exhibition-studies/ or email contact@afterall.org.

ual: central saint martins

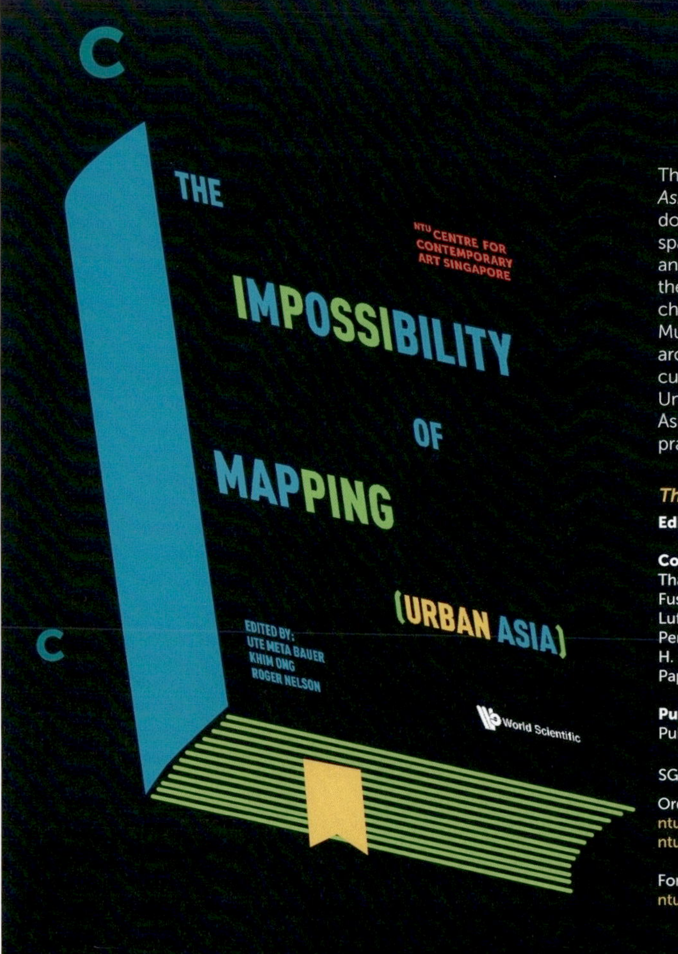

Master of Visual Studies

Studio Art
Curatorial Studies

The Master of Visual Studies (MVS) is a two-year degree at one of the world's top research universities offering two streams of study: Studio Art or Curatorial Studies.

The MVS program operates in the Faculty of Architecture, Landscape and Design, where graduating students complete their research with an exhibition at the Art Museum at the University of Toronto.

Application Deadline: Early December 2020 (for Fall 2021 intake)
Inquiries: graduate@daniels.utoronto.ca

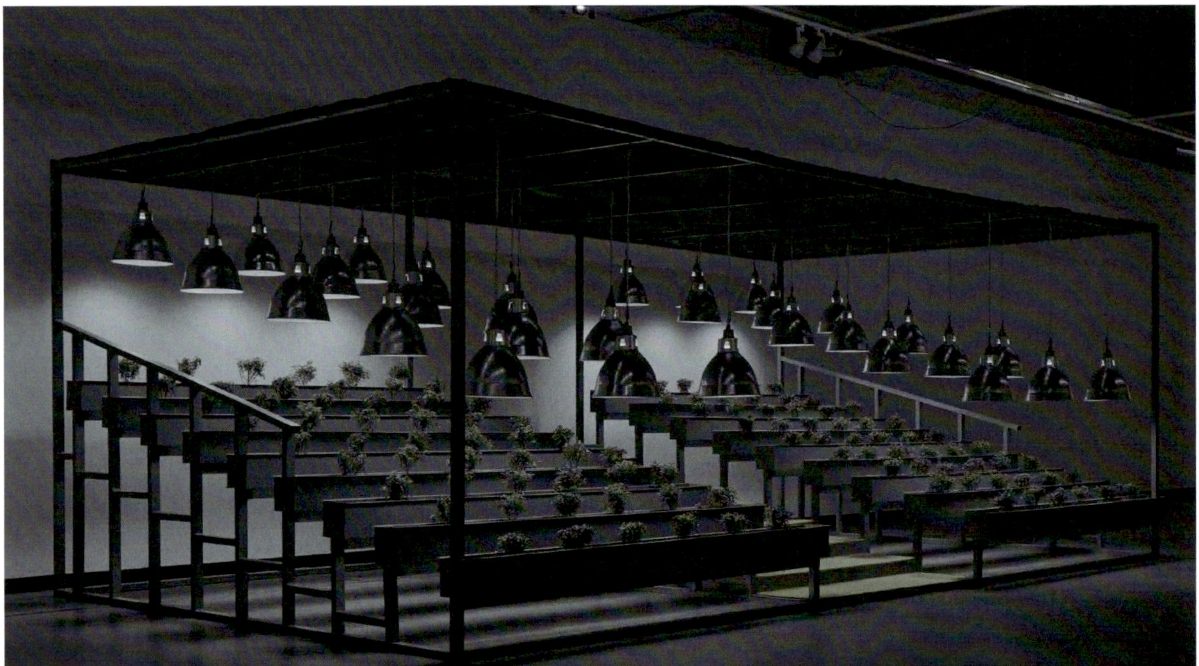

DANIELS

UNIVERSITY OF TORONTO
JOHN H. DANIELS FACULTY OF
ARCHITECTURE, LANDSCAPE, AND DESIGN

Image: *An Audition for Permanence*. Si Shang Museum, Beijing. Rouzbeh Akhbari (MVS2018) in collaboration with Felix Kalmenson & Ash Moniz

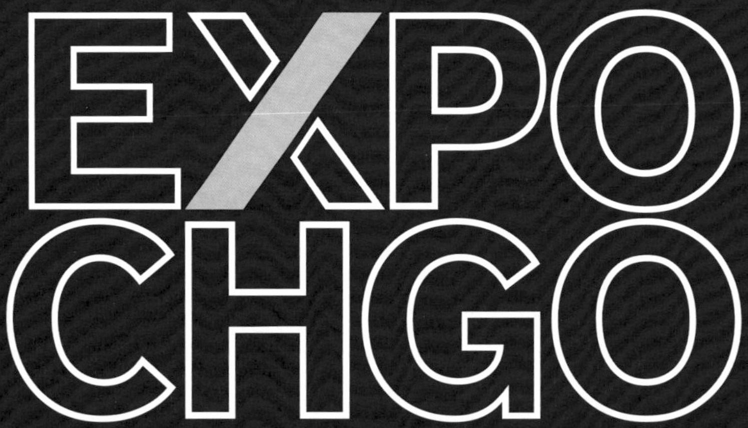

THE INTERNATIONAL EXPOSITION OF
CONTEMPORARY AND MODERN ART
EXPO
CHGO
24–27 SEPTEMBER 2020
OPENING PREVIEW THURSDAY 24 SEPT
CHICAGO | NAVY PIER

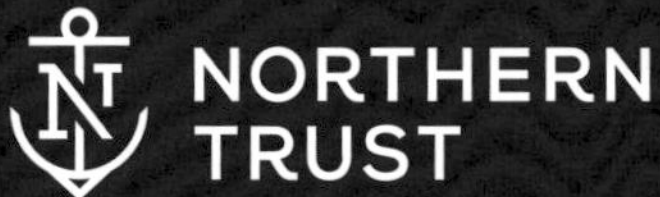

NORTHERN
TRUST
Presenting Sponsor
expochicago.com

Transbordeur photographie

histoire société

Numéro 4   2020   29 €

Worker photography
Transbordeur, no. 4, 2020

<u>Next issue</u>
Photography and design
Transbordeur, no. 5, 2021

All issues are available in bookshops
and at editionsmacula.com

Transbordeur is an annual journal dedicated
to the history of photography. Published
in French by Éditions Macula, its aim is an
appraisal of the full extent and diversity of
photography's impact on history and society.

transbordeur.ch

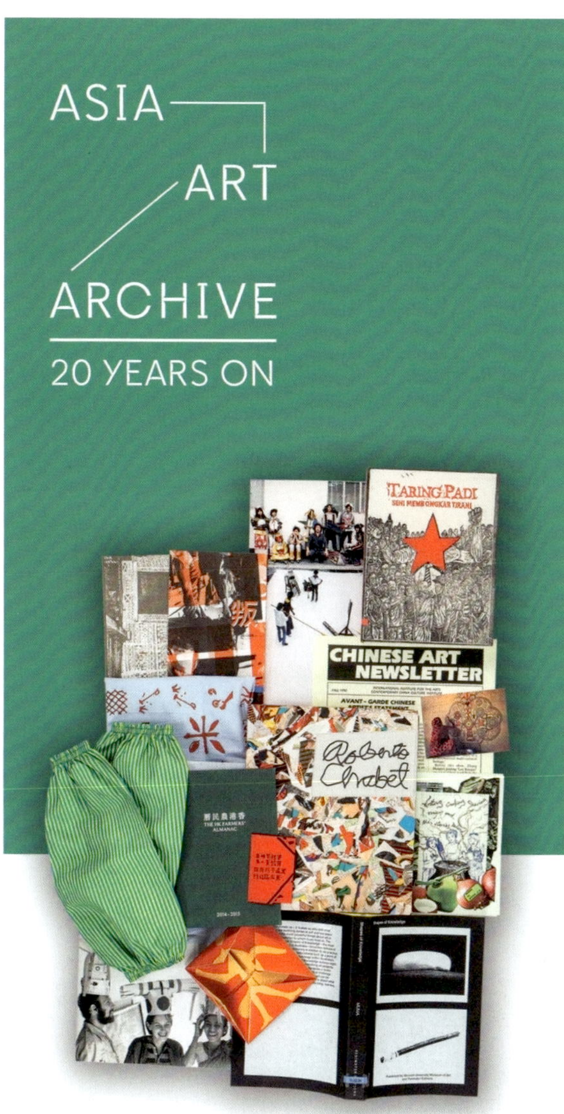

ASIA ART ARCHIVE
20 YEARS ON

AAA celebrates its twentieth anniversary. We are grateful for everyone's continued support in making a more generous art history possible.

Pictured here is a selection from AAA's Collection, with a focus on materials exploring pedagogy —including artist-led and community-based projects.

aaa.org.hk
@AsiaArtArchive
#AAA20YearsOn

Monday to Saturday, 10am–6pm
11/F Hollywood Centre
233 Hollywood Road
Sheung Wan, Hong Kong

Afterall Books
One Work

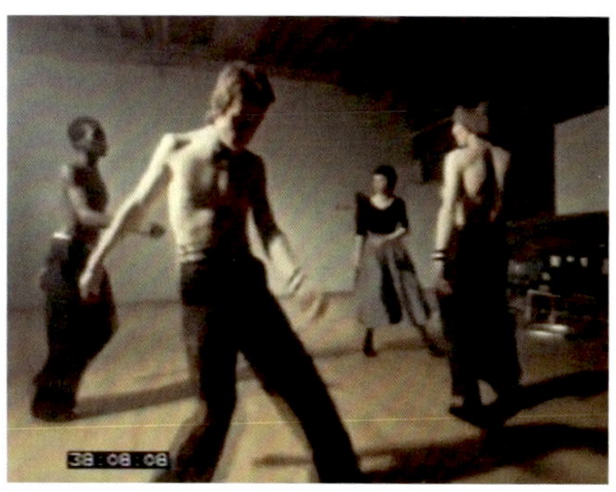

Afterall's *One Work* series focuses on individual works of art that, through radical aesthetic invention, have influenced understandings of art and its history.

Our latest title in the series, *Mark Leckey: Fiorucci Made Me Hardcore* by Mitch Speed, offers the first comprehensive analysis of one of Mark Leckey's best-known works – a video montage that captures fleeting memories from the eve of online file-sharing. *Fiorucci*, argues Speed, a dreamscape both local and expansive in its scope, gives voice to the class and cultural transformations of Britain's Thatcherite era.

We are also pleased to announce two forthcoming titles, *Beverly Buchanan: Marsh Ruins* by Amelia Groom and *Pierre Huyghe: Human Mask* by Mark Lewis.

The *One Work* series is distributed by The MIT Press, and many are available as e-books. All can be purchased at http://mitpress.mit.edu.

Art | Basel
Basel

50 YEARS

Participating Galleries

#
303 Gallery
47 Canal

A
A Gentil Carioca
Miguel Abreu
Acquavella
Air de Paris
Juana de Aizpuru
Andréhn-Schiptjenko
Antenna Space
Applicat-Prazan
The Approach
Art : Concept
Alfonso Artiaco

B
von Bartha
Guido W. Baudach
elba benítez
Bergamin & Gomide
Berinson
Bernier/Eliades
Fondation Beyeler
Daniel Blau
Blum & Poe
Marianne Boesky
Tanya Bonakdar
Bortolami
Isabella Bortolozzi
BQ
Gavin Brown
Buchholz
Buchmann

C
Cabinet
Campoli Presti
Canada
Gisela Capitain
carlier gebauer
Carlos/Ishikawa
Carzaniga
Casas Riegner
Pedro Cera
Cheim & Read
Chemould
    Prescott Road
ChertLüdde
Mehdi Chouakri
Sadie Coles HQ
Contemporary
    Fine Arts
Continua
Paula Cooper
Pilar Corrias
Chantal Crousel

D
Thomas Dane
Massimo De Carlo
dépendance
Di Donna

E
Ecart
Eigen + Art

F
Konrad Fischer
Foksal
Fortes D'Aloia &
    Gabriel
Fraenkel
Peter Freeman
Stephen Friedman
Frith Street

G
Gagosian
Galerie 1900-2000
Galleria dello Scudo
gb agency
Annet Gelink
Gladstone
Elvira González
Goodman Gallery
Marian Goodman
Bärbel Grässlin
Gray
Alexander Gray
Howard Greenberg
Greene Naftali
greengrassi
Karsten Greve
Cristina Guerra

H
Michael Haas
Hamiltons
Hauser & Wirth
Hazlitt Holland-Hibbert
Herald St
Max Hetzler
Hollybush Gardens
Hopkins
Edwynn Houk
Xavier Hufkens

I
Invernizzi
Taka Ishii

J
Bernard Jacobson
Alison Jacques
Martin Janda

Catriona Jeffries
Annely Juda

K
Kadel Willborn
Casey Kaplan
Karma International
kaufmann repetto
Sean Kelly
Kerlin
Anton Kern
Kewenig
Peter Kilchmann
König Galerie
David Kordansky
KOW
Kraupa-Tuskany
    Zeidler
Andrew Kreps
Krinzinger
Nicolas Krupp
Kukje / Tina Kim
kurimanzutto

L
Lahumière
Landau
Emanuel Layr
Simon Lee
Lehmann Maupin
Tanya Leighton
Lelong
Lévy Gorvy
Gisèle Linder
Lisson
Luhring Augustine
Luxembourg & Dayan

M
Jörg Maass
Kate MacGarry
Magazzino
Mai 36
Gió Marconi
Matthew Marks
Marlborough
Mayor
Fergus McCaffrey
Greta Meert
Anthony Meier
Urs Meile
Mendes Wood DM
kamel mennour
Metro Pictures
Meyer Riegger
Massimo Minini
Victoria Miro
Mitchell-Innes & Nash

Mnuchin
Modern Art
The Modern Institute
Jan Mot
mother's tankstation
Vera Munro

N
nächst St. Stephan
    Rosemarie
    Schwarzwälder
Nagel Draxler
Richard Nagy
Edward Tyler Nahem
Helly Nahmad
Neu
neugerriemschneider
Franco Noero
David Nolan
Nordenhake
Georg Nothelfer

O
Nathalie Obadia
OMR

P
P.P.O.W
Pace
Maureen Paley
Alice Pauli
Peres Projects
Perrotin
Petzel
Francesca Pia
Plan B
Gregor Podnar
Eva Presenhuber
ProjecteSD

R
Almine Rech
Reena Spaulings
Regen Projects
Rodeo
Thaddaeus Ropac
Lia Rumma

S
Salon 94
Esther Schipper
Rüdiger Schöttle
Thomas Schulte
Natalie Seroussi
Sfeir-Semler
Jack Shainman
ShanghART
Sies + Höke
Sikkema Jenkins

Bruce Silverstein
Skarstedt
Skopia / P.-H. Jaccaud
Société
Pietro Spartà
Sperone Westwater
Sprovieri
Sprüth Magers
Nils Stærk
Stampa
Standard (Oslo)
Starmach
Christian Stein
Stevenson
Luisa Strina

T
Take Ninagawa
Tega
Templon
Thomas
Tokyo Gallery + BTAP
Tornabuoni
Travesía Cuatro
Tschudi
Tucci Russo

V
Georges-Philippe &
    Nathalie Vallois
Van de Weghe
Annemarie Verna
Vielmetter
Vitamin

W
Nicolai Wallner
Barbara Weiss
Wentrup
Michael Werner
White Cube
Barbara Wien
Jocelyn Wolff

Z
Thomas Zander
Zeno X
ZERO…
David Zwirner

Feature
1 Mira Madrid
Ben Brown
Ellen de Bruijne
Experimenter
James Fuentes
Christophe Gaillard
Garth Greenan
Hosfelt

Jhaveri
Kasmin
Levy
David Lewis
Loevenbruck
Max Mayer
Lorcan O'Neill
Parker
Project Native
    Informant
Yancey Richardson
Barbara Thumm
Upstream
Vedovi
Venus Over
    Manhattan
waldengallery
Zlotowski

Statements
Bank
Bodega
Bureau
Commonwealth
    and Council
Company
Bridget Donahue
Emalin
Lars Friedrich
Grey Noise
High Art
Isla Flotante
JTT
LambdaLambda-
    Lambda
Magician Space
Queer Thoughts
Simone Subal
Temnikova & Kasela
Union Pacific

Edition
Niels Borch Jensen
Cristea Roberts
mfc-michèle didier
Fanal
Gemini G.E.L.
Sabine Knust
Lelong Editions
Carolina Nitsch
Paragon
Polígrafa
René Schmitt
Susan Sheehan
STPI
Two Palms

September 17–20, 2020

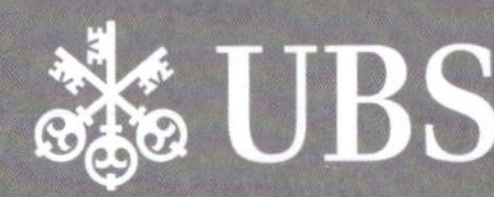

Colophon

Editors
Ute Meta Bauer
Nav Haq
Mark Lewis
Adeena Mey

Contributing Editors
Amanda Carneiro
Amber Husain
Charles Stankievech

Founding Editors
Charles Esche
Mark Lewis

Issue Conceived by
Ute Meta Bauer, Bart de Baere,
Ana Bilbao, Charles Esche,
David Morris, Charles Stankievech
and Rose Thompson

Project Manager
Lauren Houlton

Programme Coordinator
Beth Bramich

Copy Editor
Janine Armin

Design and Typography
Designed by Andrew Brash
with inside pages based on an
original design by A2/ SW/HK

Typefaces by A2/SW/HK + A2-Type

Printed and bound by die Keure, Bruges

Advertising Director
Berit Fischer
T +44 (0)20 7514 8173
E adverts@afterall.org

Contact
T +44 (0)20 7514 7212
E contact@afterall.org

Editorial Board
Elvira Dyangani Ose, Ntone Edjabe,
Barbara Fisher, Vasif Kortun,
Anders Kreuger, Ana Longoni,
André Mesquita, Wanda Nanibush,
Emily Pethick, David Teh,
Christine Tohmé

Subscriptions
Individual and institutional subscriptions are available worldwide in both print and electronic formats. Please direct all subscription enquiries, back-issue requests and address changes to:
University of Chicago Press Journals Division
1427 E. 60th Street Chicago, IL 60637-2902, USA
T +1 877 705 1878 (USA & Canada only)
T +1 773 753 3347 (International)
F +1 877 705 1879 (USA & Canada only)
F +1 773 753 0811 (International)
E subscriptions@press.uchicago.edu
www.journals.uchicago.edu

M HKA manages subscriptions in Belgium, the Netherlands and Luxembourg. Please direct all enquiries for these countries to Sabine Herrygers:
M HKA
Leuvenstraat 32
B-2000 Antwerp, Belgium
T +32 (0) 260 80 98
E info@muhka.be

Distribution
North America: Disticor Magazine Distribution Services
1000 Thornton Road South, Unit B
Oshawa, Ontario L1J 7E2, Canada
T +1 905 619 6565
F +1 905 619 2903
E dkasza@disticor.com

Europe: Central Books Ltd
50 Freshwater Road, Chadwell Heath
London RM8 1RX, UK
T+ 44(0)20 8525 8825
F+ 44(0)20 8599 2694
E magazines@centralbooks.com
www.centralbooks.com/afterall

Postmaster: send address changes to University of Chicago Press
1427 E. 60th Street Chicago, IL 60637-2902, USA. Postage paid in Chicago and additional mailing offices.

All text protected under Creative Commons Attribution-NonCommercial-NoDerivs 3.0 Unported licence. Please inform the editors if you intend to transmit or reproduce any of the articles.

The views expressed by the writers are not necessarily those of the editors. Unsolicited material is welcome but will not be returned.

ISBN 978-184638-217-8
ISSN 1465-4253

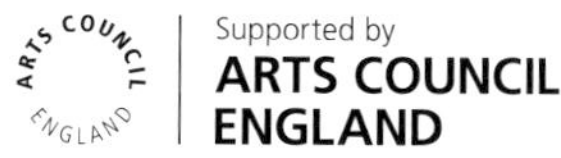
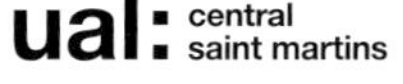
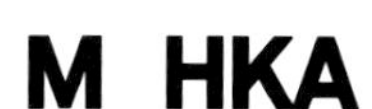
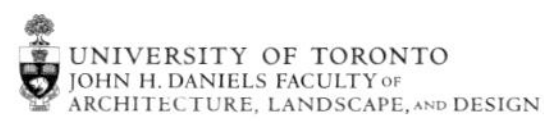
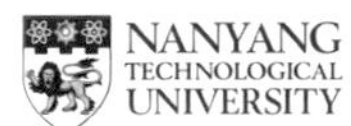

Afterall would like to thank the following individuals for their generous support:

The M.T. Abraham Foundation, Tomma Abts, Laylah Ali, Paweł Althamer, Hurvin Anderson, Ibon Aranberri, Edgar Arceneaux, Lara Asole, Jean-Michel Attal & Charlotte Gounant-Attal, Aud and Paolo, Bart De Baere, Monika Baer, Mirosław Bałka, Fiona Banner, Barry Barker Marie-Claude Beaud, Julie Becker, James Benning, Walead Beshty, Pierre Bismuth, Jennifer Bornstein, Gavin Brown, Will Bradley, Alex Branczik, Pablo Bronstein, Glenn Brown, Pavel Büchler, Craig Burnett, Renate Buschmann, David Bussel, Gerard Byrne, Alistair Carr, Nigel Carrington, John Carson, Marc Camille Chaimowicz, Marvin Gaye Chetwynd, Adam Chodzko, Michael Clark, Sadie Coles, Phil Collins, Aileen Corkery, Tommaso Corvi-Mora, Martin Creed, Joyce Cronin, Glen Davis, Dexter Dalwood, Thomas Dane, Enrico David, Sian Davies, Tacita Dean, Clémentine Deliss, Jeremy Deller, Thomas Demand, Dexter Sinister, Thea Djordjadze, Peter Doig, Trisha Donnelly, Mark Dunhill, Sam Durant, Benoit Duverger, Maria Eichhorn, Tim Eitel, Olafur Eliasson, Nuria Enguita Mayo, Kodwo Eshun, Elena Filipovic, Nicoletta Fiorucci, Ceal Floyer, Barbara Fosco, the Fosco Family Foundation, Mark Francis, Bill Furlong, Charles Gaines, Ryan Gander, Andreas Gegner, Isa Genzken, Candida Gertler, Liam Gillick, Douglas Gordon, Antony Gormley, Rodney Graham, Cornelia Grassi, Melissa Gronlund, Boris Groys, Graham Gussin, Rachel Harrison, Mona Hatoum, Drs. Lynn Hauser & Neil Ross, Hauser & Wirth, Richard Hawkins, Mary Heilmann, Flora Hesketh, Matthew Higgs, Roger Hiorns, Thomas Hirschhorn, Maja Hoffmann, Inge and Philip van den Hurk, Pierre Huyghe, IRWIN, Sanja Iveković, Alfredo Jaar, Joan Jonas, Eungie Joo, Lisa Junghanss, Ilya Kabakov, Stefan Kalmár, Alan Kane, Emma Kay, Mike Kelley, Janice Kerbel, Rebecca King Lassman, Jutta Koether, Joseph Kosuth, the Kroll Family Trust, Surasi Kusolwong, Marta Kuzma, Pablo Lafuente, Jim Lambie, David Lamelas, Louise Lawler, Serge Le Borgne, Malcom Le Grice, Sara Le Turq, Mark Leckey, Dieter Lesage, James Lingwood, Judy Linn, Sharon Lockhart, Richard Long, Anne Lydiat, Christina Mackie, Goshka Macuga, David Maljkovic, Tim Marlow, Kerry James Marshall, Daria Martin, Paul McCarthy, Julie Mehretu, Alan Michael, Jeremy Millar, Victoria Miro, Shabin Mohamed, Jonathan Monk, Sarah Morris, Amaury & Sandra Mulliez, Laura Mulvey, Rosalind Nashashibi, Michael Newman, Olaf Nicolai, Cristina Noghes-Menio, Nils Norman, Elisa Nuyten, Bruno Pacheco, Patrick Painter, Maureen Paley, Lisa Panting, Seb Patane, Toby Paterson, Dan Perjovschi, Manfred Pernice, Pilar Corrias, Marjetica Potrč, Richard Prince, Florian Pumhösl, Walid Raad, Alessandro Raho, Cristiano Raimondi, Yvonne Rainer, Michael Rakowitz, Tobias Rehberger, Bob Rennie & Carey Fouks, Rennie Collection, Olivier Richon, Daniel Richter, David Roberts, Dieter Roelstraete, Ellen Roland, Martha Rosler, Allen Ruppersberg, Ed Ruscha, Alex Sainsbury and Elinor Jansz, Anri Sala, Wilhelm Sasnal, Thomas Scheibitz, David Schnell, Maaike Schoorel, Nicholas Serota, Indre Serpytyte, Joe Shlesinger & Samara Walbohm, Yinka Shonibare MBE, Andreas Slominski, Pete Smithson, Sean Snyder, Nedko Solakov, Andreas Spiegl, Malin Stahl, Polly Staple, Frances Stark, Bernhard Starkmann, Simon Starling, Jemima Stehli, Joanna Stella-Sawicka, Lily van der Stokker, Do Ho Suh, SUPERFLEX, Ingrid Swenson, Anne Tallentire, Silke Taprogge, Jeremy Till, Jan Verwoert, Helena Vilalta, Wolfgang Tillmans, Hayley Tompkins, Sue Tompkins, Rosemarie Trockel, Luc Tuymans, Chris Wainwright, Jeff Wall, Rebecca Warren, Lawrence Weiner, Matthias Weischer, Jack Wendler, Neil Wenman, Richard Wentworth, TBA21, TJ Wilcox, Christopher Williams, Jane and Louise Wilson, Chad Wollen, Catherine Wood, Richard Woods, Richard Wright, Cerith Wyn Evans, Helen Zell and Andrea Zittel.